Cushing of Boston

✠

Cushing of Boston

✠

A CANDID PORTRAIT

BY

JOSEPH DEVER

"Sir, I don't care though I sit all night with you!"
—Johnson to Boswell

BOSTON

BRUCE HUMPHRIES

PUBLISHERS

ACKNOWLEDGMENTS

Firstly, to Richard Cardinal Cushing, gracious patron, noble Patriarch, for conversations, manuscripts, previously printed material, and the original impetus of this book on both the practical and inspirational levels; on him be its virtues, on me its failings.

To the book's original editor, and my good friend, the able ecumenical journalist and novelist, Michael Novak.

To Rt. Rev. Msgr. George Casey of Lexington, Mass., South Boston schoolmate of the Cardinal, for invaluable insights on the Cushing boyhood; to Rt. Rev. Msgr. Paul Hanly Furfey, distinguished sociologist and a Boston College classmate of the Cardinal, for a helpful and gracious letter; to Alma Mater, Boston College, and to college librarian, Rev. Fr. Brendan Connolly, S.J., for stack privileges and whole-hearted suggestions; to the Boston Public Library and its superb Patent and Documents Room, where extensive use of *Boston Pilot* microfilms and those of other Boston newspapers was made; to my old friend, *The Pilot* itself, to Msgr. Francis Lally, editor, and more specifically to his lay staff members, George Ryan and Connie Buckley, for personal courtesies; to another old friend, the Jesuit weekly, *America*, for citations from Cardinal Cushing's book review of *The Cardinal Spellman Story;* Herb Kenney of the *Boston Globe,* for their friendly cooperation; to Father Francis Moran, former editor of *The Pilot,* and Attorney Peter Kerr of Boston for some anecdotes; to Guy Livingston, New England editor of *Variety,* for many courtesies; to Robert F. Muse, William J. Devine, Paul J. Burns, and Edward T. Sullivan for just being friends; and to Robert L. Bell, my publisher, for that little extra enthusiasm and interest.

And, last, but by no means least, to my wife, Margaret, for her patience and enduring belief.

DEDICATION

Come back to us, the dust has claimed our idols,
Boyle O'Reilly moulders, Pearse will speak no more,
The shining knight you buried from St. Matthew's
Now haunts the mist of ancient Celtic lore.

Come back to us, the dogs of March have wearied,
Soon April cues the robin to the sun-stirred loam;
Soon, soon the lilacs riot in your dooryard,
The theologian dozes o'er the musty tome.

Come back to us, gaunt Prince, brave stentor,
Berate the beads on radio, or castigate the Russ;
Last of our heroes, return, beloved chieftain;
Come back to us, come back to us!

—J.D.

Contents

BOOK FOUR: GOOD POPE JOHN—THE BIG
BREAK-THROUGH

BOOK FIVE: THE CARDINAL TODAY

Introduction

By MICHAEL NOVAK

Author of: A *New Generation* and *The Open Church*

Ecclesiastical biography is one of the most underdeveloped areas in Catholic life today. Too often, fifty or seventy-five years seem to be required after a prelate's death before biographers begin to treat him as a man among men. Until that time a special lens is used in looking at his life, a lens which distorts both the meaning of the Church and the special word which God was trying to say through that prelate's life.

Joseph Dever's informal profile of Richard James Cushing of Boston is an attempt to sound a new note in ecclesiastical biography. Candid, witty, lively, his record of the life and personality of a man he deeply loves and respects stands as a tribute to that man, the candid and almost legendary Cardinal of Boston. And yet, as often as not between the lines, and even openly, it criticizes where to the author criticism seems due. We can only hope that future ecclesiastical biographies continue further in the direction Mr. Dever opens.

One of the astonishing things about the Cardinal of Boston, moreover, which makes him beloved by people throughout the world, is his own honesty and directness. When Pope John XXIII and Cardinal Cushing first met, it is said they recognized each other. Neither was "an ecclesiastical type." Both, often violating the cautions adopted by men of responsibility, say what they mean and mean what they say. Neither values bureaucracy, nor hierarchical authority, as more than a means to an end: and the end is living human persons. Persons first, system afterwards, seems to be the law of their lives.

It is not surprising, then, that one of the most candid books about a living prelate should concern Cardinal Cushing. "Take your priesthood seriously, but never yourself," was a program the young Cushing took as his own. Mr. Dever's "candid portrait" takes the Cardinal's priesthood seriously at all times, but he doesn't hesitate to record or to criticize those aspects of the Cardinal's long life which are quite human, though these would usually be neglected in ecclesiastical biographies of the living.

It is, in fact, one of the great vices of the Catholic people that they insist in public upon glorifying their prelates (however they may broil them in private). For this compulsion blinds those swayed by it to one of the most central meanings of the Church, *viz.*, that God has given his graces into the hands of human beings, who remain in all respects human. To become a pope, a bishop, a priest, or a nun, is not to lose the self-love, rationalizations, quest for power and security and love common to all poor human beings. On the contrary, it is to receive the condescension of God, who even through leaking vessels of clay from generation to generation transmits the waters of His life. To neglect to notice the clay of these vessels, to pretend that they are made of bronze or silver or gold, is to overlook this greatest of mysteries. It is to falsify the nature of the Church and the goodness of God. Wherever there is falsification or pretense, cruel injustice is done the Church, and God's astonishing goodness is minimized.

For the beauty of Catholicism lies not in illusions but in realities: in the reality of poor and weak men doing the best they can, and sometimes less than the best, to witness the gospels and to live from the sacraments. The Church is not blasphemous. It does not pretend to be composed of angels or of gods. It is made up of laymen p and q, mon-

10

signor X at the parish, bishop Y at the local See, pope Z presently reigning in Rome.

The Church is concrete, human, living in actual history. All the ambiguities of history attend her every move, every election of a new pope, every consecration of a new bishop, every baptism of a new member, Christ has entered into history. He manifests Himself in inconsistent, complex, stubborn, erratic men. That is the great mystery which the Church continues to live.

To write of prelates as they are is to write as a Catholic who keeps this mystery before his eyes. To put a good light on things, to make prelates appear as they are not, is to sin against the truth and hence against the faith.

Mr. Dever is, then, to be praised for his candor. His is not a learned nor a pompous book. It cannot claim to have exhausted all that is to be known about Cardinal Cushing's life and activities. It is probably not yet quite as frank as it would be if it were about a mayor or a senator instead of a Cardinal. But it is as good a short ecclesiastical biography as we are likely to have for some time.

Moreover, by its sly humor and frank perceptions it seems to have caught the very flavor of the Cardinal of Boston. Perhaps only a Boston Irishman could have written such a book: the sadness, the nostalgia, the imagination of a higher and better culture elsewhere, the humor, the energy, the relentless self-punishment of Boston's older generation of Irishmen have an echo in the tonal qualities of Dever's prose, and in the story he tells.

Cushing the rich and idiosyncratic human being is here; the moody, surprising, contradictory, devoted, energetic, generous Cardinal Archbishop walks through every page. This is not the Cushing of hagiography, nor the Cushing of newspaper objectivity. It is a frank, unpretentious portrait, by a Boston writer who has lived near Cushing all his life, who has often been helped by Cushing and has often been in contact with him. It includes material from

11

interviews not granted anyone else. And yet it remains free, ironic, whimsical, and critical, as befits good biography.

Let us have more such, for the good of all of us.

November, 1964
Cambridge, Mass.

Author's Note

In October of 1963 I was privileged to be asked by Richard Cardinal Cushing to help him with research and editorial work on his biography of Pope John XXIII, published eventually as *Call Me John* by the Daughters of St. Paul Press, Boston.

Between October of 1963 and March of 1964 I performed this and a few other minor editorial and research chores for this overwhelmingly busy man. I did the work in libraries and at home, and visited his residence when summoned.

In the process of these interviews and work sessions, the Cardinal reminisced at considerable length. When he was in a good mood—which means when he wasn't suffering from a night-long siege of asthma or migraine headache— he would ruminate about the past, and indeed the present, in his lovely, trusting, open-hearted way which no personal affliction can ever quite subdue in him.

We thus engaged, to my great delight and inspiration, in some long, pungent, and quite intimate conversations about his life, his times, his career.

At one time he seemed quite seriously interested in having me help him with the research and editing on an autobiography which might be published in connection with his 20th anniversary as an Archbishop in November, 1964.

In November and December of 1963, after the devastating ordeal of the President's assassination and funeral, the Cardinal became less interested in an autobiography, indicating to me, as he sometimes does to other journalists, that he has kept no personal memoirs, letters, records, and that an autobiography couldn't be made adequate. He still, however, expressed serious interest in having me do an informal biography. I had been taking notes and he had given me other material, with an eye to the autobiographical form which he was now rejecting.

The Cardinal had also given me some informal stories about his childhood and about later key events and accomplishments in his long and distinguished career. I took more notes, availed myself of certain papers he allowed me to photostat, and went ahead with what is substantially this work.

As recently as April 24, 1964, he seemed quite jaundiced about journalism concerning him, writing to me: "I am all through with any articles or books or biographies. Please believe me, I would do anything in the world for you but I am overwhelmed with all kinds of amateurs, professionals, and great, outstanding writers like yourself, for the story of my life. The point of the matter is, there is no story and there are no records and I decided to have nothing to do with anyone . . . I don't care what they write about me or what they don't write about me."

I found all this somewhat bewildering until I thought about the material I had accumulated. I decided I would, and should, continue with the work I had begun with the Cardinal. In form, it would now have to be a personal profile rather than an autobiography or even a straight biography. It would no longer have the Cardinal's guiding hand; I would have to make judgments and decisions myself. The story would have some material no other has, and a flavor close to the Cardinal and the Boston he loves. But the work and responsibility are now competely my own.

This book, then, cannot be called "official" or "authorized," even though it was originally started under the auspices of the Cardinal.

I have lived almost all of my life in Boston and loved its buildings, streets, people, politics, and events. I don't want to exaggerate the aims or scope of this book on Boston's Cardinal, but I am hopeful that it catches some of his own enthusiasms, experience, and outlook.

14

BOOK ONE

The Hidden Years

CHAPTER I

44-"O" Street

"I will follow Thee, Lord, but let me first take leave of them that are at my house."—Luke IX:1-6

"You're using outdoor paint in here! You've ruined the rectory."

It was the voice of righteous, almost Calvinistic wrath which roared every Sunday from the pulpit of St. Eulalia's Church in City Point, South Boston, the voice of Father Mortimer E. Twomey, pastor.

The object of his Irish fury stood in front of him. He was a City Point boy named Jimmy Cushing. There was little he could say.

"You had several gallons of paint in the cellar! Why'd you pick the wrong ones?"

Father Twomey's wrath cooled steadily. He had been trying to keep husky Jimmy Cushing supplied with odd jobs around the church and rectory for two big reasons. He wanted him to earn some money to help with his education. He wanted Jimmy to see the workings of the Church from the inside.

On this occasion, Father Twomey repented his own hot temper. He let the embarrassed boy complete his work. And he continued to keep him busy about the parish as much as possible.

Boys and girls were leaving Gate of Heaven Parish and St. Eulalia's to become priests and nuns. Jimmy noticed this steady exodus while he was painting and fixing and cleaning. He could not help but wonder about himself.

Jimmy Cushing's full name was Richard James Cushing.

He could not have foreseen that he would become one of the great Princes of the Holy Roman Church, a world-renowned philanthropist, and a distinguished spokesman for important causes, as well. He could not have known that he would become Archbishop of his own city.

Richard Cardinal Cushing's life is no Horatio Alger story, as many might think. "Rags to Riches," or "Bound to Win" do not describe his life or character. The Cardinal has no personal wealth; he took a secret, informal vow of poverty the day he was ordained. He did not have to steel himself in a race to success in the spirit of "Bound to Win." He came from a normal Irish Catholic family which, while poor, was never frustrated or destitute in any serious way. He sprang from working people, as did most of his Irish schoolmates whose fathers, like Patrick Cushing, had steady jobs, and whose mothers, like Mary Cushing, maintained clean, decent tenement homes. It is only in hindsight, and by comparison with plush, modern high-rise apartments, and the rambling urban ranch houses of our day, that we look on his environment as humble. Patrick Cushing, Jimmy's father, had come to this country from Glenworth, County Cork. He was a quiet man of average height and great strength of body. He sojourned to a Boston whose Irish-Catholic population was making steady inroads on Yankee prejudice and dominance.

By 1902, seven years after Richard James Cushing was born, Patrick and thousands of other descendants of the refugees from the potato famine, former denizens of docks and mudflats, once bracketed with newly liberated Negro slaves, contemptuously referred to as biddies, Micks, greenhorns, dock-wallopers, and clod-hoppers, finally produced enough votes in this American democracy to elect their first Irish Mayor, Patrick A. Collins.

In this era of meteoric Irish political ascendency, Patrick Cushing found little difficulty in obtaining a steady job. He

18

went to work as a blacksmith for the Boston Elevated Railway Company, the "El" as it was known. He worked seven days a week over the open forge, repairing street car wheels. His schedule called for eleven hours a day for the first six days and ten hours on Sunday, the extra hour being conceded him so that he could get to Mass. For seventy-six hours of work, Pat earned the grand total of seventeen dollars a week. That was considered a good week's pay in the 90's—enough to get married on, and start a family.

Meantime, Miss Mary Dahill, a tallish, dark-haired, blue-eyed colleen, had come to the sweet land of liberty in the steerage of the liner *Pavonia*. In Boston, she found a place as cook to a local Yankee judge. She needed tips from her Yankee mistress on some things, but not for the corned beef and cabbage dinners she was later to prepare for Patrick Cushing and their five children.

From Mary Dahill Cushing, Richard James was to get his height. From the B.E.R.Y. blacksmith he inherited the whipcord strength of arms and shoulders which made him a good worker for Father Twomey's parish.

Richard Cushing recalls that his father was "a quiet man." "His silences may have come out of the perpetual weariness, carried like a cross, from his endless hours of labor."

"We were happiest at sundown, during the pleasant seaside evenings of spring and summer and fall," the Cardinal recollects. "We would be sitting on the front steps at O Street. We were relaxed and trying to console one another. We talked about the weather and everything under the sun.

"When the children were born, they were born at home, and the neighbors helped out. If a neighbor was sick, my mother would reciprocate.

"Religion was as much a part of the family as eating or breathing. It was never talked about much. It was a simple fact of life.

"We seemed to know only two roadways in life, the one that led from home to Church and the other that led from the Church back to the home.

"My parents prayed the Rosary every day, a custom they brought from Ireland. We said the beads at night. We all had to kneel down and say the beads and my father recited the prayers before and between the decades.

"I think my parents directed the children more by example than words, although at times more forceful measures were applied. Yes, they used the strap on us—without hesitation when it was needed.

"We were five children in all—my three sisters: Elizabeth, Mary and Anne, brother John, myself—we were all obligated to do the right thing—or else!"

Any Irish-American descendant of a workaday immigrant family knows where the culture and learning were located in such a community. The things of the intellect and the arts were rarely in evidence at home. These were invariably found in the rectory, the convent, the parish school.

The culture of the Poles, Italians, Greeks, Armenians, was also preserved by their churches, their festivals, and their schools. And the children of the lower middle class Jews likewise received much of their traditional culture and learning at synagogue schools.

Except for the giant family Bible, there were few books in the Cushing home. But the children, more and more, brought books home from school, and from the public library. The parents of this American Cardinal were deprived of adequate education by British punitive law, which did not permit the teaching of Catholics in Ireland. Mary and Patrick Cushing averaged about three years of primary school education between them.

"What schooling they received," the Cardinal testifies, "was hit-or-miss from 'hedge school masters' who hid with them in the bushes." He says their real schooling in Ireland

20

was in "hardship," and such schooling was necessary for the rough road the immigrants faced in the New World.

"We seemed to do everything the hard way. My parents seemed to take no recreation at all. Life was simply a daily grind. There was no piano, no musical instrument of any kind in the house. No conveniences. If there was any toilet at all, it was in the cellar. For a bath, you went to a public bath house. For a swim, to the beach right down the street."

In retrospect, the Cardinal believes it was inevitable that he inherited his great capacity for daily, long hours of work from a father and mother who knew ceaseless toil as a permanent way of life.

Even as a small boy at the Perry Public Grammar School, he was never afraid of work. He roamed City Point Beach to get salt water for his grandmother's rheumatism. He gathered driftwood near Castle Island for his mother's stove. He went "junking" for iron and brass dumped from industrial plants, which he later bulked and sold. He hawked newspapers through the streets of South Boston and around South Station—perhaps developing that great lung power for which he was to become famous in later days.

To earn money for secondary school and college, he was to do hard labor as a rodman for the Boston "El."

This future Archdiocesan fund-raiser who is world-renowned for his "Midas touch," this very same man who would one day raise and donate a total of four million dollars toward the expansion of his alma mater, Boston College—not to mention other multi-million dollar activities—recalls that the Cushing children "got no allowances, not a dime."

"Oh, we might get a nickel sometime for a nickelodeon show down at the Point, or for a ride on the El to Franklin Park. But, in general, whatever money we had, we earned. There simply wasn't enough cash at home for luxuries."

21

In the meantime there was lots of the normal fun and good fellowship at City Point's Perry School. Gate of Heaven Parish had a school for girls called St. Agnes, taught by the Sisters of St. Joseph, but no parish school for boys until 1922. Jimmy Cushing went to the public school.

But his parish and St. Eulalia's Mission established close liaison with the Catholic pupils who attended the Perry School. The teachers at the school organized the young parishioners for the long walks to Gate of Heaven for seasonal services like Stations of the Cross, Blessing of the Throat, First Communion Lessons.

Monsignor George Casey, columnist for the Boston *Pilot* and the Boston *Herald*, and pastor of St. Brigid's, Lexington, Massachusetts, was a classmate of Cushing at the Oliver Hazard Perry School.

Monsignor Casey recalls Sunday Masses at St. Eulalia's when the priests "used to come in a hack, drawn by two horses, and always associated by us with funerals or state occasions. When they drew up to the door of the church, well, Queen Victoria could not have impressed us more."

He also relates that the organized trips from the Perry School across City Point to the "Gate" for services or instruction were somewhat precarious. "We kids from the Point felt like the Pilgrims going through Indian territory. And we were not safe when we got into church either. Going down the center aisle for the ashes, or what not, we used to get jostled and tripped and then stood a pretty good chance of getting a cuff in the ear from Father O'Brien or Father Brennan for creating disorder."

Brawny Jimmy Cushing must have been a good stout henchman to have along in church among the "Pilgrims" in this "Indian" country.

Social functions held at the mother parish were also thorny affairs for the boys from the Point, according to Monsignor Casey. "One of my earliest recollections was a St. Patrick's Day entertainment in old St. Michael's Hall. Some fellow who must have been regarded as teacher's pet

22

came on the stage to sing a solo, and old fruit and vegetables flew toward him from every angle. In the uproar, we City Pointers scrambled out of there quick and ran down Fourth Street so fast that we almost landed in Pleasure Bay before pulling up."

For the Catholic Church and its future apostolic work, the Perry School group was to prove a goodly company. Among the pilgrims hiking back and forth to the Gate of Heaven Church, were Jimmy Cushing, George Casey, Dan Golden, Frank Burke, George Fox, John Colbert, John Bowman, John Brophy, and Tom Rogers—all of whom became priests.

But prospects weren't particularly bright for the future education of Master Cushing when he graduated from the Perry School in 1909. If he was worried, he didn't show it in the wry, craggy grin flashed in his group graduation picture, where George Casey can also be seen sporting a shiner, caused by a flying South Boston brick.

But there was a benevolent cousin in New York who wanted to sponsor Jimmy financially at Boston College High School. This benefactor was the Cushing family's most distinguished member at that time. His name: Right Reverend Monsignor Richard B. *Cushion*—and note the fancy spelling. ("How that spelling came about is not known to me!" Cardinal Cushing was to comment with cryptic charity, many years later.) Monsignor Cushion was Patrick Cushing's first cousin and a classmate of Cardinal Hayes.

The tuition to the Jesuit high school in the South End of Boston was $63 annually, a tidy sum in those days. For generously providing that sum for four successive years, the late Monsignor Cushion may rest in peace, assured that his name will be spelled in the history books any way he wanted it. It was his generosity which started a gangly, obscure young Boston Mick on the long, winding road that led all the way to good Pope John and the College of Cardinals in Rome.

CHAPTER II

Moonlight over Southie

"Dear Lord, if it is Thy Hand which has penetrated me with the wound of this piercing design, I have the right to show Thee my tender hurt and to unveil my breast."—Father Joseph of Paris

A kind of "two-jobbing" or "moonlighting" was not unknown to hustling, indefatigable seventeen-year-old Jimmy Cushing in 1911, when he was a Junior at the old Boston College High School on James Street in the South End.

By 1911, Boston's new Archbishop, crusty, intellectual William Henry O'Connell, who was to figure so strongly in Richard Cushing's episcopal future, already had sat in the late Archbishop William's chair for three busy years.

President Taft had ordered American cavalry to the Mexican Border under a dashing young officer named "Black Jack" Pershing. John F. Fitzgerald, grandfather of John F. Kennedy, was Mayor of Boston. And his renowned successor, a young golden-mouth named James Michael Curley, was bewitching potential Hub voters in an urbane accent, broad with the Oxford A and sweet with Corkonian blarney.

Although Jimmy's tuition was being paid by his cousin, the family heritage of hard work and the need for extra cash around the house impelled him toward heavy employment after school hours.

In Father Mortimer Twomey, St. Eulalia's pastor, he was fortunate enough to have an employer who persisted in keeping him busy in and around the environs of the former mission which was now a budding, independent City Point parish.

Reflecting on his religious state of mind in those indecisive years, the Cardinal muses: "I wasn't a pious lad. I was not much for being around the church save to do manual work. I identified myself with the other young lads in South Boston and mixed up in all their joys and actions . . ."

Yet it was Father Twomey who saw something else in him that he perhaps could not see himself.

Along with managing the parish-sponsored bowling alley and pool room—a recreation center established by Father Twomey to keep his young men out of less savory establishments elsewhere in the city—Jimmy also performed the duties of church janitor. The janitor's chores—stoking fires, sweeping and mopping, opening and locking up—demanded his attentions largely in the early morning and late afternoon. The bowling alley and pool room management commanded his time and energies in the later evening hours.

It can correctly be inferred that such a schedule would have a negative effect on his studies. It is not known whether Father Twomey realized this bad effect until too late. It is a matter of record, however, that the Jesuit Fathers at B. C. High were to take drastic action on the matter about mid-year. But regardless of Jimmy's academic difficulties, there was a certain "supernatural" method to Father Twomey's "madness."

Mortimer E. Twomey was born in Chelsea, Massachusetts, in 1859. He went to the seminary in Montreal and was ordained by the famed Archbishop Favre of Canada in 1883. It was in the Canadian Seminary and probably in the "fire and brimstone" tradition of Twomey's French professors that this leather-lunged, visionary Irish priest developed his impassioned, stentorian style of pulpit oratory.

As a former curate, at Immaculate Conception, Malden, at Newburyport, as first pastor of St. Eulalia's, and finally, briefly, as pastor of Gate of Heaven, Father Twomey was renowned for his terrifying voice in the schoolyard and on the street corners. He is remembered vividly for his eloquent, wind-tunnel blasts against sin and sloth from the Olympian heights of his Sunday pulpit.

True, the Cardinal reflects that he wasn't "a pious lad." But it was Father Twomey who saw in him a great potential for piety and leadership. And it was Father Twomey who risked the Jesuit academicians' wrath by keeping Jimmy employed around the church and rectory until the rhythm and the color and the pulse-beat of American Catholic parish life were in his blood and bone forever.

The Cardinal acknowledges that Father Twomey's direct and indirect effect upon his vocation was considerable. His Eminence concedes quite openly that his own great-voiced, sometimes too lengthy eloquence of pulpit and platform was influenced by the tradition, style, and sheer bombast of Father Twomey.

Meanwhile, Jimmy Cushing was getting a taste of Boston politics. There is an apocryphal story of Father Twomey literally dragging teenage Jimmy by the scruff of the neck from a joy-ride on a political band wagon. Surely Jimmy was intrigued, like any Boston bucko, by the torchlight parades of the Boston politicos, by the melodious whine of "Sweet Adeline" at lively rallies, by James Michael's golden-mouthed defiance, on a South Boston corner, of Yankee arrogance and power. But the Cardinal says the story is apocryphal. Perhaps it is, yet the sense and spirit of the story must have some truth in it, both about the spirit of the Boston of the time and about the methods of Father Twomey where the young Cushing was concerned.

Meanwhile the bowling alley and pool hall were a full-time job for Jimmy Cushing; they required mature and watchful management. The alleys were open until eleven P.M. Jimmy hired and supervised the pin boys, collected and counted the income, paid the help and all expenses, extracted his salary of fifteen dollars weekly, and gave what was left to Father Twomey. When bowling ceased at eleven, the alleys were swept, steelwooled, and waxed for the next day's business. Jimmy's working time edged past the midnight hour. He couldn't have arrived home much before eleven almost every evening. His study schedule was bound to be affected.

In Jimmy's junior year, Patrick Cushing, master of 44-O Street, received an ominous letter from the Dean of Studies at B. C. High. It concerned, of course, the plummeting grades of his extrovert, two-jobbing son, Richard James.

Supper was brief and tight-lipped that evening in the Cushing kitchen.

"Comb your hair and get your good suit on," Pat Cushing told his older son. "There'll be no bowling alley tonight. We'll take the streetcar over to B. C. High."

The combined high school and college were clustered around the Immaculate Conception Parish on James Street in the South End of Boston.

Shortly after eight, parent and son were seated in one of the grim rectory parlors, on austere wooden chairs, with a giant, musty philodendron plant in the background and a garish, gold-framed print of the Sacred Heart behind them on the wall.

As he talked with the aloof, polite Jesuit Dean of Studies, Mr. Cushing sat erect, his good black hat—saved for funerals and weddings—held firmly in his lap.

"He's been working too hard, Father. He's burning the candle at both ends—the bowling alley and school."

"No question about it. He can't do both. He's leaving his best energies behind him when he comes to school. It's a question of dropping out of the night job or dropping out of school!"

The Cardinal indicates that the Jesuit was inclined to recommend the latter. There were references to "St. Joseph the Carpenter," and "God will find the proper work for this Richard of yours . . ."

But Mr. Cushing knew the perils of the "drop-out." And,

like Father Twomey, he sensed the potential in this boy. He insisted on "another chance."

It was a long ride back to City Point. Jimmy Cushing was braced for a good tongue-lashing and even a whipping. But neither followed.

In the face of the parental storm which he expected to break, Jimmy tried to sound defiant: "They can have their diploma! I'll get a day job and help out at home."

His father's answer was resolute. "You'll stay in school. Do the best you can; 'tis all God asks."

Pat Cushing then spoke critically of the bowling alley atmosphere. Despite the wholesome atmosphere Father Twomey tried to create, it was still no place for a high school student at night. "They need an older man to run it. There are rough and tough customers that go in there. You know that as well as I. Give up the night work now, and get back to your studies!"

The Cardinal looks upon this climactic incident as the turning point in his life: "If my father had taken a different attitude, I would not be where I am today. I would never have finished high school."

Ruminating upon his high school study habits, His Eminence has some candid things to say, in recollection:

"I was by no means a brilliant student. When I worked hard, when I studied, I was able to hold my own. But when I didn't work hard, I fell far below the average.

"I can't think of any one subject in which I particularly excelled. For the life of me, I could never understand algebra or trig. In order to get a passing mark, well, I practically memorized the various problems."

The Cardinal thinks parents could draw a good lesson from his father and this anxious B. C. High experience.

"Parents have the feeling that unless their children get high marks, their tuition money is being wasted. This isn't necessarily true. Some kids, temporarily or permanently, simply don't have the brain-power for high scholastic honors. If they're high-pressured toward this impractical goal they sometimes get discouraged and quit. If they're told to do the best they can they usually keep plugging and get by."

Jimmy Cushing got by very well in his remaining two years at B. C. High. There was no more night work, but he continued to do chores about St. Eulalia's afternoons and during vacations.

A little-known fact about the Cardinal's early life is that at this time he was seriously interested in becoming a Jesuit. Certainly his black-robed teachers must have detected the potential vocation in the boy; their percipience has seldom been remiss among their students. And many a Jesuit student who later might have gone to the diocesan seminary has been "scooped" by the black robes before high school graduation.

The Cardinal recalls that all arrangements had been made for him to "enter" right after graduation. He would have attended the Jesuit novitiate at St. Andrew-on-Hudson, New York.

"I changed my mind the night before I was to leave," the Cardinal reveals. "I again faced the decision at the end of my Freshman year at Boston College and finally decided not to enter the Society at all. I had been observing young men from the parish going away to the Society, to the Benedictines at St. Anselm's up in New Hampshire, to the Oblates. These seemed to be the more popular vocations which Father Twomey developed in many of us, as the instrument of God.

"Naturally, my Jesuit teachers influenced me toward their particular group at B. C. High and later at the college itself. But twice, at the moments of decision, I think I sensed that I was cut out more for the active life and not the teaching apostolate which is the major concern of American Jesuits. I just didn't think I was the academic type."

Jimmy Cushing, who had almost "flunked out" at mid-term in his junior year, had made quite an academic comeback. His Jesuit mentors thought enough of the reformed night worker to award him the Premium on the Edward J. Campbell Medal for scholastic excellence and to select him as one of the Class Orators at the high school graduation ceremonies in 1913.

The emulator of Father Twomey's brassy eloquence is still remembered for the booming oration he delivered, entitled: "The Press as an Intellectual Force."

CHAPTER III

The Old Maroon and Gold

"What are you dreaming, soldier,
What is it you see?
A tall, grey, Gothic tower
And a linden tree."
—Thomas Heath

Up on a hilltop overlooking a broad, sparkling reservoir in the Chestnut Hill section of Newton, there arose a brand new Boston College in the spring of 1913. It was actually the expansion and relocation of the older Boston College on James Street in the Hub's South End.

In the first freshman class to attend the new college on the "Heights" the following September was Richard James Cushing.

The new B. C. consisted of a single massive granite building, topped by a giant Gothic tower which dominated the skyline for miles around. The structure was to be one of a complex of buildings in English Collegiate Gothic style, to be known as "University Heights." The site was the old Bishop Lawrence estate, a soft, pastoral crest totalling thirty-one acres with an assessed valuation then of $187,-500, but now worth millions. It commanded a superb view across the Chestnut Hill Reservoir, over Brighton and Brookline, to the Capitol City. It had been one of three sites under consideration for the move from the congested James Street location where both the expanding high school and college were crowded into the same area. The new Archbishop, William Henry O'Connell, a distinguished alumnus of the James Street college, was clearly and wisely in favor of the Chestnut Hill site. So was the legendary Father Thomas I. Gasson, S.J., after whom the Tower Building is now named. Father Gasson was still President of B. C. during young Cushing's Freshman year.

In 1920, Archbishop O'Connell followed up his successful choice of a site with a building fund donation of $5,000. That was a large sum in those days. The Archbishop could hardly know that, already in 1913, an obscure and retiring member of the first Freshman class to attend the new B. C. was to be his successor—one who would donate to the college sums exceeding four million dollars.

At B. C. High young Cushing had been known as "Jimmy." On the new college campus—according to the venerable Yearbook, *Sub-Turri*, of 1914, they now called him "Dick."

Dick's fellow Freshmen and the upperclass Sophomores and Juniors were not the first students to set foot on the meadow-like campus, dominated by the sky-thrust of the great Gothic tower. The building was ready in the Spring of 1913, and it was decided to let the senior class graduate from the new campus. But Dick Cushing's class of 1917 was the first "four-year-class" at the new B. C.

Even today, a high percentage of B. C. High graduates go to the mother institution. In those years, there was no other Catholic college which sons of devout, poor, immigrant parents could attend in the Boston area. And if a lad had any serious inclination to the priesthood, he either went directly into a seminary after graduation from high school, or he nurtured his vocation religiously and academically at Boston College. So Dick Cushing had two big things propelling him toward B. C.: his attendance at B. C. High and his interest in becoming a Jesuit. Father Twomey and Dick's Jesuit mentors, moreover, aware of his fertile indecision, undoubtedly encouraged him to go on to B. C. where maturation of mind would encourage maturation of decision.

His parents, devout and understanding, were completely sympathetic. The question of tuition and expenses—the modest sum of $30 per semester, plus fees—was not a great obstacle to a strong, resourceful young man who had worked at gainful employment after school and during summer vacations since his early teens.

Richard Cushing soon found out that trekking back and forth to the Heights in the early time of relocation was not an easy duty, either for students or faculty. The street-car ride from Park Street to Lake Street, near the College, required at least forty-five minutes. From the Cushing home, then on 910 Broadway, to Park Street by trolley and subway was good for another half hour. Then, as now, there was the ten-minute walk up the hill from Lake Street to the portals of the Tower Building. That's roughly an hour-and-a-half, one way, or about three hours, going and coming.

The faculty lived back at James Street, so the Jesuit Fathers had about the same trek to and fro. The science labs were also back at James Street, which meant that the upperclassmen were on "alternating current" to and from the two institutions.

All this trundling back and forth with books and lunches, in an era when automobiles were scarce and for the very rich only, was a daily grind. There was little leisure time for campus life and extracurricular activities.

The Cardinal's present recollection is that he had less scope for such activities as a Freshman than as a Sophomore. A check of the campus publications like the yearbook, *Sub Turri,* and the monthly student magazine, *The Stylus,* for the years 1913-1915 indicates, indeed, an impressive acceleration of social, organizational, and athletic activities at B. C. from the Sophomore year on. The name of Richard James Cushing is hardly mentioned during his freshman year, in the pages of the 1914 year book and in *The Stylus* of that year, which included campus news, editorials, and fledgling literary efforts. In the Freshman class picture, class of '17, prominently displayed in the 1914 Year Book, the big, rugged frame of Richard James Cushing with his familiar, lantern-jawed visage, topped by straight-up, brush-like hair, is very much in evidence. Cushing stands to the extreme right, in the first row of his class picture, and makes one think he would be a good candidate for tackle on the football team.

The editor-in-chief of *The Stylus* in the class of '13 was Eric Francis MacKenzie, later distinguished Auxiliary Bishop of Boston and present pastor of the Sacred Heart Church in Newton. John P. Curley, famed Boston College Athletic Director, was Varsity Football Manager in the graduating class of '13. The late Governor of Massachusetts, Charles Hurley, beams out blandly as Treasurer of the class of 1916.

But it was mostly back and forth between home and college for Dick Cushing during that Freshman year of 1913-14. He had a growing interest in the Marquette Debating Society, for which Frosh and Sophomores were eligible. He still continued to do manual chores around St. Eulalia's parish, without any further involvement in night work at the bowling alley.

At the Heights Dick solidified an old Southie friendship with the present Monsignor George Casey who was then a sophomore in the class of 1916. Among his B. C. High acquaintances continued at the College was one with Msgr. Paul Hanly Furfey, originally of Cambridge, and now an accomplished sociologist and professor at Catholic University. Father Furfey excelled as a writer, and was then a poet and essayist in *The Stylus*. Furfey and Cushing did not travel then in the same groups. Nor, as Father Furfey now recollects, did the future Cardinal stand out in his class. In a recent letter to this author, Father Furfey has written:

I remember him as a rather quiet person whom we respected, but actually he did not make a very strong impression on me of any sort.

34

As far as my college recollections are concerned, he was one of the good, solid trustworthy members of the Class of 1917, and he did not stand out very vividly among the others in that category.

Dick Cushing's Freshman year may, of course, have been further subdued socially by a prolongation of his private wrestling match with a possible vocation to the Jesuits. He now had some experience of the life of the Jesuit priest-teachers on both the high school and college level. The academic life: sedentary, studious, a slow, patient process of mind-moulding; this was not for him. He was big, dynamic, restless; his heart pulsed with aggressive action. For good, for a constructive purpose, yes. In the service of God, yes. But not in the academic life which seemed to him the main activity in the American Jesuit Order. He declined sincerely, respectfully, finally, to enter the Jesuits at the end of his freshman year.

Spring and summer of 1914 was a time of "Canals." On April 21, the waters of Buzzards Bay and Cape Cod merged in the mammoth sluiceway of the Cape Cod Canal, shortening the Boston-New York water route by seventy miles. In August, the Panama Canal was opened to commercial traffic. More ominous, and more significant in the lives of many of his school mates, was President Wilson's proclamation of American neutrality on the outbreak of war in Europe that same long, hot month.

In September school started again. Dick Cushing was more active in Sophomore year as a debater and public speaker. Jack Connolly of his own class had won the Marquette gold medal for debating. A well-known Italo-American of the Bay State, Joe Scolponetti of the class of '16, had topped the college oratorical contest. With these goals in his mind's eye, Dick accepted the invitation of George Casey's brother Dan to stump for him throughout South Boston in Dan's campaign for the State Legislature. And in the fall he began speaking for the Marquette Debating Society. Monsignor George Casey, then one of his fellow students, recalls him at the College and agrees with Fr. Furfey: "He was retiring, undistinguished. Nothing like he is now!"

How retiring and undistinguished was he as a Sophomore?

He was elected Vice-President of the Sophomore class, along with R. B. Fitzgerald, President; R. "Reddo" McKeown, Treasurer; Tom Craven, Secretary; F. Flaherty, *Sub-Turri* Representative. He is listed as: R. "Dick" Cushing, Vice-President.

"Each one of these energetic, world-wise men," the 1915 *Sub-Turri* editor tells us, "is in a class by himself."

Retiring? Undistinguished?

"Retiring" Richard was named a member of the Sophomore Dance Committee in November. The following description of the Committee was later printed in the class history, a far cry from later solemn reports about the activities of Dick Cushing: "This body of crippled toe dancers consisted of Craven, Cushing, Dee, Fihelly, Fitzgerald, Nevins, Nolan, and McKeown." The dance was held at Horticultural Hall in Boston, November 27.

While he won no medals, Dick was finally active in the Marquette Debating Society. On November 20, for example, he took the affirmative side in a Marquette Society Debate, "Resolved: That Japan was justified in its claims on Germany." His team-mates, his opponents, and the moderator, Mr. William F. McFadden, S.J., listened while Fr. Twomey's protégé let his voice boom out his convictions. The laconic, soft-spoken Japanese were defended in a style not their own. And the decision was in their favor, and that of Dick Cushing.

On the other hand, Cushing's academic record for his Freshman and Sophomore years was solid, but hardly hinted of distinction. And he seems to have been rather modest and withdrawn in his personal relationships.

Spring of 1915 would bring the shocking torpedoing of the *Lusitania,* with a loss of 1198 lives. The United States

36

was being drawn closer to war. Meanwhile, Dick Cushing was also being drawn closer to an important decision of his own.

By late spring the dancing partners were gone, the debates were over, the roster of class officers would no longer include R. J. Cushing. Dick was parting from his classmates.

By the end of his Sophomore year, in 1915, Richard James Cushing had firmly decided to take the entrance exams to St. John's Diocesan Seminary, just down the hill from Boston College. He who would probably be the most distinguished alumnus of Boston College in the Twentieth Century would not be around to sing "Hail, Alma Mater!" with his classmates at the first four-year graduation of the new College, two years later.

It is now known that Richard Cushing joined the U. S. Army in the early summer of 1915. Because of his asthma he was medically discharged and returned home after a few weeks.

CHAPTER IV

Almost a Roman!

"I decided that when I became Archbishop I would place the Seminary under the care and instruction of my own priests. My decision in this matter was approved by the Saintly Pius X whom I had consulted regarding the Seminary."

—William Cardinal O'Connell
(*Recollections of Seventy Years*)

When Coadjutor Archbishop William Henry O'Connell succeeded the late Archbishop Williams as head of the Boston Archdiocese, he took steps to end the French-Sulpician influence which had long predominated on the faculty of St. John's Seminary in Brighton. The missionary phase of the Church in New England was over. Enough Boston-bred clergy, trained either in Rome or at St. John's itself, possessed the tradition and learning requisite for Seminary teaching.

When Richard James Cushing took up his studies in philosophy and theology at St. John's which were to last from September of 1915 to May of 1921, he and his fellows were beneficiaries of Cardinal O'Connell's American program. Among the professors who were of especial influence on the young Cushing were the Seminary Rector, Right Rev. John B. Peterson, and the learned teacher of Dogmatic Theology, the Rev. Doctor Louis F. Kelleher. In the Seminary and later, both of these men were to affect Cushing's life. Both were to become Bishops: Peterson as the Ordinary of the Diocese of Manchester, New Hampshire; Kelleher, as Auxiliary of Boston, on the recommendation of the Cushing boy whom he used to teach.

"Everybody led the same kind of life in the Seminary," the Cardinal muses, when asked what things were like at St. John's—the daily round of chapel, classes, meals, study, recreation, early to bed and early to rise. There was some gainful employment as summer-time-counsellors at boys' camps, in manual labor with contractors. For many years, groups of seminarians worked for the State Department of Public Works, mowing median strips of lawn, and shovelling loam in and around state highways. Richard Cushing, no newcomer to earning a dollar, worked, among other summer jobs, as a rodman for the Boston Elevated Railway. His boss there was Maintenance Chief Tom Sullivan, who later became Boston Police Commissioner.

Who around Brighton and Boston proper has not observed the seminarians—in capes, cassocks, play-clothes—then and now—walking, walking, back and forth, in and around the Seminary grounds? They are seen, somewhat shy, modest, soft-spoken, at baseball and football games, at the legitimate theatre, in black suits and topcoats, black felt hats, some wearing black ties, some Roman collars, always together, quiet and dignified, in groups large or small.

But always beneath the "sameness," an individuality. The individuality of Richard James Cushing was soon apparent to his fellow seminarians, to his teachers and spiritual advisers, under the day-to-day camouflage of "the same kind of life."

He was impressed then—he is impressed now—by Monsignor Peterson's constant admonition to all his students: "Take your priesthood seriously, never yourself!" This precept which Peterson may have acquired from St. Philip Neri, gives us one of the keys to Richard Cushing's character: the unpretentious, informal, "always-available" presence of the man; the rigid moral purpose and indefatigable service of the priest and prelate.

An irrevocable decision at the end of his second year, on the part of Monsignor Peterson, was to stamp Cushing's character definitely: he would remain Cushing of Boston, not of Rome. Prior to America's entrance into World War I in 1917, Cardinal O'Connell had decided to send three of his most promising seminarians to complete their studies and be ordained at the North American College in Rome.

Meanwhile, Dick Cushing's active interest in the foreign missions was being vigorously demonstrated in the Academia, a student organization with aims and ideals similar to that of the Propagation of the Faith. He devoted his resourceful energy to this work, coordinated as it was with the national group known as the Students Mission Crusade. He maintained good academic grades and, along with his accomplishments in promoting the ideals and practice of the missions, he was looked upon as a promising choice for final studies in Rome.

In the late summer of 1917, U-boat activity had intensified. All but military vessels were discouraged from attempting the ominous waters of the Atlantic. Young Cushing had already been designated for further study in Rome by Cardinal O'Connell. He was looking forward eagerly to the trip, and was very much disappointed when Monsignor Peterson cancelled it, rather than risk the lives of the three future priests.

Cardinal Cushing now recalls that he remonstrated with Monsignor Peterson: "But the boats are still going back and forth, Monsignor!" And he recalls that his superior snapped back: "Yes, and they're still going up and down!"

The answer was: "No."

Cushing was never sent to Rome as a seminarian. Had he gone, his future might have been seriously altered. Even at that time, he wanted very much to go to the foreign missions; in Rome, he might have found a way of attaching himself to a Bishop of South America, Africa or Asia. Or again, as a Roman, he would presumably have returned to Boston possessed of much of the culture, urbanity, sophisticated administrative influence and know-how of an O'Connell, a Spellman, a Stritch. But if a "Roman," Cushing would hardly be the man we now know: the earthy, open man-of-action; the blunt, salty, sometimes unpredictable public commentator on church and state; the munificent, self-deprecating doer and giver; the intellectual "outsider" who can strike the pose of the stubborn plain man at one time, and at another pay homage and respect to the scholars and savants he admires.

He remained at St. John's Seminary, remained in Boston after ordination, acquiring layer upon layer of a folksy Boston-Irish style, eventually to grow rich with liberality of spirit.

Cushing never even visited Rome until he was an Archbishop. Yet being a Roman manqué in no way led him to bitterness or frustration . . . nor did it blunt his passionate and dedicated interest in the missions. He steadily pursued his goals and became, ultimately, one of the greatest patrons of the foreign missions in the history of the Church.

Toward Monsignor Peterson he continued to feel nothing but affection and respect. Later, as Bishop Peterson, the former superior stood beside his former student when Cardinal O'Connell consecrated Cushing as his Auxiliary. And years later, at the funeral mass of Bishop Peterson in St. Joseph's Cathedral, Manchester, March 2, 1944, the young Auxiliary Bishop of Boston was chosen to deliver the eulogy.

In the final, intensive two years of theology at St. John's, as the disappointment about not going to Rome blurred and mellowed into memory, Dick was exhilarated and deepened by the influence of his thoughtful, scholarly Professor of Theology, Louis F. Kelleher. A Boston College debating star, and later an outstanding student at the North American College in Rome, Kelleher was a close friend of New York's future Cardinal Spellman. Kelleher and Spellman met at Fordham, and later broadened their friendship as seminarians in Rome. A year ahead of Spellman at the Roman college, Kelleher was an intellectual prodigy and is credited by the present Cardinal of New York with helping him prepare the famous Latin recitation

41

which so impressed the renowned priest-professor, and later Cardinal, Borgogini-Duca. Kelleher had been himself a prize pupil of Borgogini.

As a philosophy professor at St. John's, Doctor Kelleher was to perform a similar function for Richard Cushing. Under his guidance, Cushing was to compete for and win a major essay prize in the English language.

No Latinist, Cushing was to grow steadily as a distinctively American priest, whose rambling eloquence combines a clean-cut seminary rhetoric, touched here and there with the haunting melody of St. Paul in the Psalms, and an earthy Irish humor—used with stunning unpredictability. It is easy to see where the formal side of Cushing's rhetoric arose. As a seminarian, for example, he was "lector" in Doctor Kelleher's Dogmatic Theology class. He read from the Epistles of St. Paul, and the professor would then comment. But the informal side does not get much documentation from the early years.

When Cardinal O'Connell delivered a series of lectures on the distinguished, socially conscious career of Pope Leo XIII, an essay contest was opened to the seminarians, and a prize was offered for the formal English essay which best summarized and evaluated the lectures.

Dick Cushing entered the contest. He had climbed arduously and long up the academic summit, since the grim hour of his scholastic chastisement at B. C. High. As a student he was a "plugger." Dogged persistence and a natural gift of oral and written eloquence gradually lifted him above academic mediocrity. The persistence was in this case crowned when he carried off first prize in the Leo XIII essay contest.

The Cardinal today looks back on that academic triumph as due largely to the encouragement of his "favorite prof," Doctor Kelleher.

Meanwhile the hard-won scholastic honor did not go unnoticed by the observant William Cardinal O'Connell. This august Senator of the Church had an eye for academic prizes, having swept the boards clean of medals at both B. C. High and Boston College. "Big Bill" had also won several of the major honors at the American College in Rome. Cardinal O'Connell stood aloof from the people; he perhaps lacked the "common touch." He had nonetheless stream-lined, reorganized, and financially solidified the Archdiocese. He no doubt noticed, with his shrewd eye, the organizational ability this young prize-winner also displayed in local and national missionary affairs.

For in his final year at the seminary, Dick Cushing was rewarded by his classmates with the Presidency of the Academia. In this capacity he attended the national conference of the Students Mission Crusade in St. Louis. Once there, he was selected to deliver what might be called the address of the convention. While a transcript of the speech is not available, it is known that the content focused on the ideals and techniques of "missiology" which Cushing consistently advocated at St. John's.

Cushing was then only a seminarian, speaking before scores of priests, brothers, nuns, college students, and other seminarians. But it is recalled that his theme echoed the verse from the Book of Ecclesiasticus which he was one day to adopt as his Archepiscopal motto. This verse, the motto of Boston College High School, the heart of the epistle of the Mass for the Propagation of the Faith, has haunted Cushing's life: *They may know Thee, as we also have known Thee, that there is no God beside Thee, O Lord!*" Recalling the address, one observer wrote: "Although only a seminarian at the time, he made a memorable impression for eloquence and sincerity upon all present."

On May 26, 1921, Deacon Cushing became Father Cushing. He and twenty-seven fellow Deacons prostrated themselves in self-abnegation on the high altar of the Holy Cross Cathedral and were ordained Priests of God by Cardinal O'Connell. Assisting at the ceremony were the Rector, Msgr. Peterson, and Rev. George V. Leahy.

Ruminating about the twenty-seven who were ordained with him in 1921, Cardinal Cushing remarked:

"Twenty-five years ago when I became a Bishop, it was my resolve to build up and nurture vocations to the priesthood to the point where I could ordain at least 100 priests in an annual class at St. John's. I regret to admit that this resolution has not been fulfilled. In June, 1964, my twenty-fifth year as a Bishop, I ordained twenty-seven splendid young men to Holy Orders. Sadly enough, this is approximately the same number ordained in my own class at St. John's over forty years ago."

The Cardinal ascribes this deficiency to "the sensuality, materialism, and abundant, easy living of our American civilization." He continues: "We are losing vocations that should be coming to the seminary and aren't. And frankly, it is a serious problem to keep seminarians in the Seminary itself!" The Cardinal also worries, in this connection, about "the breakdown of family piety and parental discipline over children." But he adds: "I must further be blunt in ascribing vocational decline to the widespread worldliness of the clergy, which I would characterize as the great weakness of the Catholic church in modern times."

Asked about a more positive and optimistic view of religious vocations, he replied: "I can only reiterate what I once said to our beloved Gate of Heaven Parish, South Boston, on the occasion of its Centennial Celebration in May of 1962:

"If Almighty God saw fit to call me to His service, He could call any one of the boys and girls of today, and, indeed, He could permit any of the former to become the leaders of the Church in the future. They have the same and, indeed, probably greater opportunities than I had.

"But to reach the priesthood or the fullness thereof in the episcopacy, they must follow the gospel of hard, persevering work and total dedication to their vocation. Yes, they must resolve to be 'living tools' or 'slaves of Christ' and make every effort to work as though everything depended upon themselves and pray as though everything depended upon God."

We may, perhaps, take these words as the maxims which guided the young Cushing's conscious thoughts through the long years in the Seminary.

There was, as those years came to an end, great joy and fulfillment at his ordination, and again at his First Mass, celebrated in the presence of his mother and father, his brother and sisters, his relatives and friends, at St. Eulalia's Church, May 29, 1921. He went up to the altar of God before their eyes, read them the Gospel, brought them the Eucharist, and gave them his first priestly blessing. He was as close to them as he ever would be in his life—the mother who had worked for a Yankee judge, the father who had kept him in school. And upon the altar beside him was the pastor of St. Eulalia's Church, Mortimer Twomey.

After the gospel, the new priest sat pensively while the old priest spoke from the pulpit. Fr. Twomey spoke about the life behind Father Richard, at B. C. High, B. C., the Seminary; and the life ahead of him as a Priest. He spoke of homage . . . homage to the devout, indefatigable mother, the retiring, vigilant father—homage to the husky young priest whom he had loved and nourished and encouraged in his vocation.

Young Father Cushing sat silently in his cloth-of-gold vestments. His mother was misty-eyed, telling her beads, as the Pastor rolled the great, nostalgic organ-tones of his eloquence up through the arches of St. Eulalia's. Old Patrick Cushing would be dead in less than a year; but he lived to see his son at the altar. This day there was only joy.

After that Mass, what would come no one could have foreseen out of these insignificant beginnings, these long years of hard work and silence.

45

BOOK TWO

The Unparalleled Auxiliary

CHAPTER V

The Old Tiger and the Young Lion:
O'Connell and Spellman

". . . any man exalted above his fellowmen, most of all in ecclesiastical life, can have few intimates. In an extraordinary degree,
Cardinal O'Connell succeeded in combining a genuine love of his
priests and people with a detachment which kept him from the
softening consolation of their friendships; but he paid the price for
this magnificent service to God and Country with a lonely life and
a no less lonely death."—Auxiliary Bishop Richard J. Cushing in his
Eulogy to the late Cardinal O'Connell, Cathedral of the Holy Cross,
Boston, April, 1944.

Newly-ordained Father Richard James Cushing had no
glamorous, scholarly, and influential Cardinal Merry Del
Val brooding richly, from Rome to America, over his
priestly life and career. Del Val, Secretary of State to Pope
Pius X, was the charming, scholarly priest and prelate to
whom William Henry O'Connell grew close as student,
friend, and fellow administrator, in and around the Vatican
and the North American College, and who was to the
hierarchical burgeoning of O'Connell what Eugenio Pacelli, Pius XII, later became to Francis Spellman.

Yet over the life of young, non-Roman Father Cushing
—a markedly provincial, Boston-rooted priest—was cast
the fulsome, golden shadow of Merry Del Val's protégé
now come to his own greatness, the lordly and astute Cardinal Archbishop of Boston. It was Cardinal O'Connell who
had wished to send Cushing and two other seminary mates
to the American College in Rome.

The Rome-trained Prince of the Church had a profound

49

and comprehensive grasp of Catholicism as an international organization. He had been student, scholar, and finally Rector of the American Seminary in the Eternal City. This richly cosmopolitan background was also enhanced by his intimate understanding of French-Canadian language and customs, for he had served as Bishop of Portland in the vast diocese of Maine. He had been a successful papal emissary to Imperial Japan, and had missed a bishopric in the Philippines only because of a prudent last-minute decision at the Vatican. This cosmopolitan understanding of the Universal Church, this bent for universal charity as expressed in his steady patronage of the foreign missions, was to turn his outwardly jaundiced but inwardly keen and sympathetic eye to Cushing. For Cushing had an arresting talent for organization and fund-raising in the work of the foreign missions.

Both Cushing and O'Connell made universal charity, concern for the missions, central to their lives. In later years, Cushing was to pronounce: "Universal charity is, therefore, the key to the life of William Cardinal O'Connell." But Cardinal Cushing himself constantly talks, acts, gives, and lives in terms of the Universal Church and universal charity. Much of this noble impetus came from his apprenticeship under O'Connell—or rather, perhaps, drew the two of them together from the beginning.

Through the attrition of time and event, however, Cushing as a young priest was to learn the wisdom of not being "close to the throne." O'Connell, as Cardinal, was a loner, not given to warm intimacy with his household or Chancery aides. In the old Cardinal's entourage were gifted priests of high quality, iron loyalty, selfless dedication—men like the widely popular, self-effacing Auxiliary Bishop Jeremiah Minihan who served faithfully as O'Connell's companion and secretary; men like the late brilliant Monsignor Walter Furlong, who later was Archbishop Cushing's Chancellor. Perhaps because of their proximity to the episcopal chair, extraordinary favor or displeasure did not seem to be their

50

lot. It was the eventual Archbishop Cushing, in fact, who elevated Monsignor Minihan to the purple. He did the same for Auxiliary Bishops like John Wright and Eric McKenzie who were in and around O'Connell's entourage.

O'Connell was his own man. He seemed to have the whole Archdiocese in the sweep of his periscope, as it were. Whatever human resilience he may have had in regard to favorites was minimized in his character by a fiercely possessive spirit. His priests, religious and faithful, were his.

Thus he became aware and appreciative of Cushing, whom he did not seek for his personal staff. Thus he reformed and refurbished the entire financial and administrative structure of the Archdiocese which had understandably fallen into decay before the kindly and feeble ministrations of the ageing and sickly Archbishop Williams.

O'Connell had seen the incredible surge to Roman power and influence of one of his priests, Father Francis Spellman. It was an almost Spenglerian dynamism which, even as a stern, uncompromising patriarch of his flock, O'Connell simply could not control. With the passing of Pope Pius X and Papal Secretary Merry Del Val and the coming into power of Pius XI and Pius XII—the latter a close friend and intimate of Father Spellman—O'Connell's influence at the Vatican tended to decline. Ironically enough, it was to the rising young Bishop Spellman that he was now forced to turn as a mediator in matters of vital Papal business. That he did so with pragmatic good temper is a tribute to O'Connell's objectivity and balance of mind.

On the other hand, it is to the everlasting credit of the distinguished Cardinal Spellman of New York that he never reacted with insubordination or ill-will toward the sometimes petulant fiats of his former great superior. It would seem that Cardinal O'Connell was almost goaded into the assertion of his local authority over Spellman by the latter's meteoric rise to favor in the Vatican. Outward obedience and sweet temper were the hallmark of Spellman's conduct in all things concerning the will of O'Connell. The higher power of the Vatican made certain circumventions reasonable and possible for him, however.

The late and scholarly Father Francis Beauchesne Thornton, who was a gifted journalist, tells us in *Our American Princes:* "The Pope (Pius XI) prompted by Borgogini-Duca [Papal Secretary of State and Spellman's former professor at the American College in Rome] requested Cardinal O'Connell to release the young priest for the charitable work. Such a request was in the nature of a command and Spellman's Roman friends found it hard to understand his wise decision to return home for the purpose of securing the Cardinal's consent.

"In the course of the interview, Cardinal O'Connell asked Father Spellman what he wanted to do about the offer from Rome."

Spellman had been offered a post as director of the American Knights of Columbus playground charities for the children of Rome. Obviously Pius XI, Borgogini-Duca, and Eugenio Pacelli had plans for the brilliant young American cleric and wanted him close by.

"Whatever my Ordinary wishes me to do," was the quick answer.

"You have answered correctly," the Cardinal said, with a glacial twinkle in his eye.

Needless to say, Cardinal O'Connell honored the Vatican request.

Some mention of this mutual yet passing strain between O'Connell and Spellman—as more comprehensively delineated in Father Robert Gannon's biography of the New York Cardinal—is given here because this situation yielded rich impetus to the destiny of Richard James Cushing. For with Spellman favored abroad, there was a certain vacuum in O'Connell's hopes for Boston. O'Connell's lack of a chosen heir, or protégé, seems then to have been satisfied, however deviously, in the person of brash, unsophisticated and unscholarly Father Cushing.

The fierce, unwavering loyalty of Cardinal O'Connell

toward a native, Boston-Irish clergy, born and bred of immigrant parents, nurtured in local schools and churches, molded and ordained in Boston's own St. John's Seminary, ordained by O'Connell, assigned by him to work in greater Boston parishes—all these hopes needed a glorious focus in a "compleat Boston priest" as Archbishop.

It is not difficult to visualize the proud and portly old Cardinal, in the late, wintry evening of his life, musing in lonely, mellow detachment at the organ which, along with the piano, he had early mastered. Perhaps he sat there playing pieces of his own composition like the well-known "Hymn to the Holy Name," a rousing battle-cry type of outmoded church music familiar to all who attended Boston Catholic churches and schools in the twenties and thirties.

(Remarkably enough, this piece was solemnly played in the presence of Cardinal Cushing—who may have suggested it—by the U. S. Marine Band outside St. Matthew's Cathedral at the funeral of President John F. Kennedy.)

Relaxing at the organ, Cardinal O'Connell must surely have given conscientious thought to that special one who would carry on his work, who would continue to build on the doggedly cleared land of Archdiocesan administration and finance, who would add cubit upon cubit to the stout and symmetrical foundations he had established in education, social welfare, journalism, and the foreign missions. Francis Spellman, who might have been his proud and towering protégé, was practically beyond his control. Indeed, although his own Auxiliary Bishop, the favor of Rome made Spellman rather like a peer than a subordinate. Cardinal O'Connell, as the years passed, knew he needed a successor who would realize his dreams. He needed someone of his own whom he could mold and influence.

In the quiet winter evenings, in the consolation of his gifts and the loneliness of his personality, this changelessly high-minded man, the star of Boston College and the American Seminary in Rome, the favored son of Pius X and

Merry Del Val, the cordial acquaintance of Franklin Roosevelt and the Emperor of Japan—possessed now of a world-
wide reputation for piety and administrative skill—pon-
dered who would come after him, chording lightly on the
organ, gradually releasing the mellow solemnity of his own
composition.

CHAPTER VI

Two Controversialists: O'Connell and Cushing

"The happiest days of my life!"—Richard Cardinal Cushing

A couple of old Irish pastors at St. Patrick's, Roxbury, and St. Benedict's, Somerville, could not use the expression "my new curate" for very long in reference to lanky Father Dick Cushing; he was in parish work with them for less than a year: two months at St. Patrick's, Roxbury, and most of the rest of the year at St. Benedict's. His reputation as a leader in fund-raising work for the missions now intervened and set him abruptly on the high road of his administrative and episcopal career. In 1922, with Cardinal O'Connell's undoubted interest and approval, Father Cushing was named assistant to Monsignor Joseph F. McGlinchey, Archdiocesan Director of the Propagation of the Faith.

Cardinal Cushing tells us he went right to the old Cardinal and bluntly told him he wanted to serve in the foreign missions. Cardinal O'Connell ordered him back to his parish post—but perhaps with a twinkle in his eye. It was not long after this incident that he called him into duty with the Propagation of the Faith.

For seven jam-packed years this rangy young cleric with "the clear, blue, luminous eyes and the large munificent hands," as he is recalled by one observer, labored mightily, begging money in churches, organizing auxiliary groups of laymen to help Monsignor McGlinchey meet the goals of the Propagation office. Cushing had an office and living quarters at the old Chancery building on Granby Street, the present location of the Archdiocesan television facility known as WIHS. At Granby Street he came in frequent, rather brusque and droll contact with Cardinal O'Connell. There, also, he lived near Francis Spellman who, contrary to popular legend and backstairs parish gossip, willingly left Cushing more than a little room at the top.

Through those years as assistant, and later as successor to Monsignor McGlinchey, who became a Lynn pastor in 1928, it was well-known that Father Cushing spent six days a week, fifty-two weeks a year, from nine to five, sitting at his desk. We have heard Cardinal Cushing toss off a complaint from a pastor or a priest about lack of support with the rasping comment: "I never took a vacation." His own work schedule has always been punishing, in his early administrative career at the Propagation office, as before and since.

Father Francis Moran, urbane and witty former Editor of *The Pilot,* tells us that Cushing the missionary leader "constantly pored over mission appeals and devised methods by which the worries of the missioner on the far-flung posts might be lightened. His formula for success has been the only tried and true method; work and more work." Reflecting on his career in the Propagation of the Faith office, Cardinal Cushing recently mused: "I have always been a kind of missionary." He referred to this phase of his career as "the happiest days of my life!"

Anyone who attended Boston Catholic churches in the late twenties and early thirties remembers hearing Father Cushing—later, Monsignor Cushing—give a sonorous sermon begging for funds for the foreign missions. We still recall his tall, rugged figure preaching with blatant power and infectious feeling at the 11:30 Mass in St. Joseph's, Somerville. Even in our poor, workingmen's parish, his stirring appeals on behalf of the girls and boys of our own neighborhoods, then laboring for the Faith in China, the Philippines, and Latin America, commandeered the soft, sweet wafting of folding money into the long-handled wicker basket which he himself angled into the pew-rows, along with other collectors.

As a pleader for financial aid to the missions Cushing was shameless and irrepressible. Anyone moving in Boston Catholic circles during this period easily recalls him popping up to plead for the missions at all sorts of social affairs —play intermissions, parish reunions and bazaars, testimonial banquets, organizational conventions—"That they may know Thee," he boomed out unceasingly, then as now, if he had a chance to preach, "as we also have known Thee, that there is no God beside Thee, O Lord."

His intimate knowledge and understanding of the priests and people, of the churches and schools and institutions, of the financial structure, the assets and liabilities of the entire Archdiocese, flows naturally from the incessant rounds he made during these prodigiously laborious years. He asserts that in seeking money for the missions he visited each parish in the Archdiocese at least three times.

As a consequence, it was his opinion even then, however discreetly expressed to his trusted colleagues, that the successor to Cardinal O'Connell would have to build at least eighty-five new parishes and raise millions of dollars a year.

"I told them: 'I don't know where he is going to get it.' "

His colleagues laughed at him.

"I know what I'm talking about," was his answer. "I have been around this place . . ."

Apparently Cushing did know what he was talking about. To date, as Boston's Cardinal, he has built at least eighty new parishes and twenty new high schools. He confesses to handling over eight million dollars a year to expedite all phases of Archdiocesan business.

Cardinal O'Connell was quite aware of the energy and labor of young Cushing. He didn't show his favor, indeed he tried to disguise it. He seemed, for example, to have something of a mental block about Father Richard's name. "Who's Cushing?" O'Connell used to ask with an abruptness that might well have indicated more interest than pique. His nickname for Father Cushing was "Tunney." "I was very husky in those days," Cardinal Cushing explains. "I looked like Gene Tunney. The Cardinal, who could never remember my name, called me 'Tunney.'"

O'Connell's refusal to remember Cushing's name is in character, as a story about O'Connell and James Michael Curley reveals. Because of his powerful influence in city and state politics, Cardinal O'Connell was known as "Number One." A haughty aristocrat who enjoyed the company of Boston Brahmins, the Cardinal did not approve of Mayor Curley's droll, and at times ruthless, political style. Once when the two were coincidentally traveling on the same ocean liner, the legendary Mayor of Boston told the press that it was an "honor" to be on the same boat with the Cardinal. When informed of the Mayor's compliment, Cardinal O'Connell—perfectly in character, undemonstrative and cool—is reported to have said: "I seem to have heard of him."

Former Boston College All-American guard, Monsignor George Kerr, now of St. Vincent De Paul's Parish in Boston's South End, and often the stout-shouldered companion of Cardinal Cushing, remembers a story about Cushing on Granby Street. Cardinal O'Connell kept a succession of large, strikingly handsome thoroughbred dogs throughout his career. At one time at the old Chancery, he had a giant black poodle named Moro. Despite the dog's size and weight, he was considered delicate of health and the Cardinal kept him on a very strict diet. The dog, of course, was almost always ravenously hungry. He used to wander into the dining room at Granby Street, and Father Cushing felt sorry for him. This surge of compassion led to the surreptitious handing of very solid meat delicacies under the table. Not long after this steady extra diet began, the dog upped and died.

When the Cardinal moved himself and his entourage out to his palatial new residence and Chancery at 2101

Commonwealth Avenue, he left Father Cushing behind. Cardinal Cushing now frankly admits that he wasn't a member of O'Connell's Chancery group and humorously concedes that his celebrated former superior thought him "too loud." Cushing was told to get himself an office "in town." "It didn't bother me," is the Cardinal's raspy comment when recalling the matter.

After Cushing moved into an office at the Catholic Center on Franklin Street there were more cardinalatial complaints about the grating bombast of his voice. Cardinal O'Connell told Richard James that he sounded like Father Coughlin and that he could hear him way up on Commonwealth Ave.

Cushing was also upbraided by O'Connell, a few years later, for preaching loudly into the public address system during a sermon at Holy Cross Cathedral. Cushing now admits he must have threatened the eardrums of everyone in the Cathedral and confesses: "I didn't know there *was* a sound system."

O'Connell's seeming pique with Cushing's gravel-grinding voice and outgoing personality does not seem like a manifestation of interest in Richard James as a possible successor. But, obliquely, it probably was. That was Cardinal O'Connell's way. To have been ignored by him would have been like being cast into exterior darkness.

Cardinal Cushing likes to reminisce about the late Cardinal. "He was the best boss I ever had," he says. "I found him a great man to work for, because when he assigned you to a job, he let you do it. He wouldn't be looking over your shoulders all the time—not even on a job involving millions of dollars a year."

As with the scholarly Louis Kelleher and Francis Spellman, Cushing was deeply impressed by O'Connell's intellectual prowess and attainments.

"I feel that if he could have stayed in the background and stayed out of controversial subjects, he could have been the greatest churchman of his time," he continues. "But his eminence was aging. There was much that needed to be done among the immigrants and the poor; so many churches to be built, so many schools to be erected . . ."

It is not clear, of course, what Cushing is thinking of when he speaks of O'Connell entering into "controversial subjects." Could he have meant that the old Cardinal was guilty of too much political interference—his active disapproval of Curley, his militant fight against birth control legislation, his all but public espousal of Al Smith and Franklin Roosevelt, his alleged interest in the political destruction of a prominent Catholic District Attorney named Pelletier, from Boston's Suffolk County.

"Controversial subjects . . ." Who could ever be more controversial than Cardinal Cushing has been at certain times? As a national and international actionist and spokesman on the issues and events of the times, since 1944, he has made O'Connell's glowering pronunciamentos seem like conversation over tea and crumpets.

While ever the munificent, compassionate liberal of the spirit in matters of personal kindliness and charitable activities, Cushing has been a checkered liberal in politics and government. His relentless crusade against Communism, in all its forms, national and international, sometimes ran him afoul of legitimate, progressive persons, groups and aims. His immense admiration and loyalty for J. Edgar Hoover, chief of the FBI, a rather stuffy conservative-reactionary, sometimes identifies Cushing with the turgid political conservatism of most American Catholic prelates in the thirties and forties. But if Hoover was a crusader against Communism, he was all right with Cushing. To a large extent, Cushing seemed to show the same support for Senator Joe McCarthy also—although there was more of a spirit of toleration than enthusiasm, on Archbishop Cushing's part, with regard to the late Wisconsin Senator.

Cushing's blast at Tito for the persecution of Archbishop Stepinac won international headlines, not long after he became Archbishop.

In the field of the liturgy, the present great champion of liturgical reform was known in the forties to be a conservative. He looked on those early zealots for reform, those who wished to bring worship closer to the people, as "crackpots."

Controversial subjects?

In the early fifties, there was the *cause celebre* of Father Feeney in which Cushing became painfully, reluctantly involved. Did this schismatic hoopla, strictly in the family but for all to see, delay his Red Hat? Some said yes. Some said that Spellman had an insidious hand in the delay. Cardinal Cushing today says: "Ridiculous. Nothing could be further from the truth."

More controversial subjects?

Free bus rides for Catholic school children. He, along with Spellman, was against the Barden Bill. Stevenson's divorce as an issue in the campaign of 1952? Cushing permitted an article in *The Pilot* pointing out that a Catholic would be morally sound in voting for a divorced candidate, under certain circumstances. Stevenson's case fitted those circumstances. A good Democrat had found a way. A reprint of this article was used by Stevenson back in his Democratic presidential campaign in 1956.

The word was out that Cardinal Spellman, in the election of 1952, was for Eisenhower. The New York Cardinal had been Ike's former Military Vicar and occasional social companion to the President of Columbia University. Ike was a liberal and yet the darling of some of the same powerful financial tycoons on Wall Street who helped Spellman with his great philanthropic work. But Archbishop Cushing's friend, the late Gov. Paul A. Dever, gave the keynote speech at the Democratic convention in Chicago in 1956, nominating Adlai E. Stevenson. Stevenson supporters also included other great and good Democratic friends: a young Congressman named John F. Kennedy; an older, battle-scarred veteran of the Congressional wars, John W. McCormack. Cushing was probably for their candidate.

How could Cushing be with a political candidate? O'Connell? Spellman? Any member of the Catholic hierarchy? Bishops are voting citizens, of course. But only on a political issue involving faith or morals would a Catholic prelate make a public statement during a red-hot political campaign. O'Connell must have been sorely tempted to speak out stronger than inferentially for Al Smith in 1928. Al was being murdered on the religious issue. The Catholic prelates might have reasoned they had nothing to lose by speaking out and perhaps might have been able to gain a platform, a national sounding board, for tolerance toward Catholics, yet bishops and priests showed admirable restraint.

It is to the everlasting credit of Cardinal Cushing and the entire American Catholic hierarchy that they again conducted themselves with restraint and dignity when in 1960 John F. Kennedy was in danger of political defeat because of religious bigotry.

Cardinal Cushing, of course, personally was for John F. Kennedy for President, but restrained himself in the area of public statement. He canceled an article in a national magazine of mass circulation, because he didn't want to put the candidate on the spot.

During the Kennedy regime Cushing involved himself in raising ransom for the Bay of Pigs prisoners, a sum of at least one million dollars.

On another controversial issue, the Cardinal has been for, against, and for the John Birch Society.

Because Cushing "hates the sin and loves the sinner," he was bound to be the "checkered liberal" on public issues when those issues were directly connected with people who for certain reasons he liked or admired.

He called Birch Society leader Robert Welch "a good Baptist" and a "crusader" against Communism. Then all the other Birchers, many of the lunatic fringe, jumped on that wagon.

In early 1962, he defended his friend and loyal supporter,

Boston Police Commissioner Leo Sullivan and his beloved Boston policemen in the face of the embarrassing television evidence of the Key Shop Bookie operation which showed Boston policemen entering the shop during book-making hours.

He took a public stand against civil rights boycotts of Boston Schools. These boycotts were agitated by the NAACP and CORE which alleged that certain slum-area schools were suffering from *de facto* segregation. Cardinal Cushing said Negro children were suffering more from economic and social underprivilege at home and in their neighborhoods than from school segregation. In this position he was at odds with the Negro organizations and at least two outstanding Boston priests—one the Jesuit Dean of the Boston College Law School, Fr. Robert F. Drinan, the other, Cushing's old South Boston friend, *Pilot* columnist Monsignor George Casey.

If we now return to Cardinal Cushing's original warning about Cardinal O'Connell and his "controversial subjects," we can see that Cushing is sincere, whole-hearted, and often fearless in his involvement in the "controversial subjects" of the day.

In eulogizing Cardinal O'Connell, the then Auxiliary Bishop Cushing spoke volumes about his own attitude toward such issues: "He attacked evils and wrongs, not persons; he hated the sin but always helped the sinner. And his charity to those who erred knew no bounds." Cushing himself thinks first of persons, then of ideologies or causes. To some committed people, Cushing therefore seems inconsistent.

In his eulogy for Cardinal O'Connell, Cushing went on: "To one to whom nature had given a rock-like resoluteness and a certain stubborn inflexibility of character, and who was by temperament strong, vehement, commanding, this is no small tribute."

This, of course, was a very charitable estimate of O'Connell's stormy temperament, of which the young Cushing was occasionally a victim. O'Connell's volcanic truculence came to the surface when he was seriously crossed. He apparently would not tolerate any serious difference of opinion, especially on the part of his clerical subordinates.

Cardinal Cushing described in conversation, swiftly and without intending to, how cruel O'Connell could be at such times. Cushing has a way of slumping forward while being interviewed, with his head in his hands and his great, craggy face played over like a cinematic screen, with both animation and fatigue. At other times, he can angle himself back and back in his great, red leather chair, until he seems to be resting on his spine at the edge of the seat, his fingers clasped together, with two index fingers touching the point of his chin. In this utterly relaxed position while talking glowingly of Cardinal O'Connell, whom he truly admired and loved, he suddenly broke into a grim, contrasting remark in a laryngeal fury of disdain:

"Then he could turn around and crush with one blow some miserable, defenceless little priest, who may have stepped out of line . . ."

One grim remark like this about the old Cardinal gives more credence to the highly complimentary things Cushing continually voices about him.

O'Connell often repeated an admonition, which Cushing still voices. It concerns the work of the missions: "Remember, this is God's work, keep it in God's Hands." From his unpretentious office on the third floor at Franklin Street, Father Cushing tried to keep his superior's words in mind. He was indefatigable, kindly, and always approachable. Monsignor McGlinchey often received highly complimentary mail about him. The president of a lay organization to which Father Cushing spoke, for example, once wrote: "The young priest from the office of the Society of the Propagation of the Faith addressed us tonight. He will go far and no one will ever hurt him for he cares only for the spiritual aspects of his mighty vocation."

As Director of the Society, succeeding Msgr. McGlinchey, Father Cushing expanded its work with almost mathematical progression. Meanwhile, both Fascist and Communist dictators, to the east and west, made the lot of the priests, nuns, and brothers in the mission fields increasingly difficult.

One of Cushing's major organizational achievements in the thirties was the Sen Fu Club, a missionary organization consisting of 3,000 women members whose primary object was the instruction of people on the home front. Sen Fu is the Chinese equivalent of "Father." According to layman George Ryan, assistant editor of *The Pilot:* "The members were taught missiology and then they carried their knowledge and their enthusiasm into their own homes and into those organizations to which they belonged. It was a very forward-looking movement, heralding a career-long dedication to the missionary Church." Cushing also organized a men's mission auxiliary called the Father Jim Hennessey Club. Father Hennessey was a Boston priest killed in the South Pacific in World War II and a close friend of Cushing. They lived together and socialized frequently at the Cathedral Rectory.

The present editor of *The Pilot*, Monsignor Francis Lally, now widely famed as an author and lecturer in the ecumenical movement, reminds us that Father Cushing developed a mission column in the diocesan weekly. Each week Cushing put together a huge international mail box of news and comment about foreign mission affairs. The feature ran three or four columns weekly and was similar in scope and tone to the present-day feature called "Archbishop's News-Notes." Priests, brothers, and nuns in the mission fields used it as clearing house of news, inter-communication, and requests for help.

In 1939, Cardinal O'Connell, with a softer glint in his eye toward his Propagation Director, had little trouble in persuading Pius XII to make Richard Cushing a Domestic Prelate, or Right Reverend Monsignor. Two months later Cushing was made an Auxiliary Bishop.

The new Bishop never broke stride. "During World War II," Editor Lally tells us, "Cushing redoubled his efforts on behalf of the missions of the Pacific, sponsoring among other drives the Solomon Islands Mission Fund. After the war, this fund helped restore those missions in the South Solomon Islands which had been ravaged by the conflict."

A Medford businessman, George W. Rose, formerly a combat Sergeant of Engineers in the American Division campaigning through the Philippines, tells us he was cordially received by natives when they learned he was from Boston.

"You know Faddah Cushin?" he was asked.

"Many a GI," Monsignor Lally tells us, "owed his cordial reception on these islands, and occasionally his safety or his life, to the natives' warm response to the assurance by the GI that he 'came from Father Cushing's place in America.'"

CHAPTER VII

A True Friend at Court:
Spellman and Cushing

"If I were to summarize in my humble way your life as a priest in the episcopate and the college of cardinals, I can unhesitatingly say that you have been a source of consolation to Christ and His Church."—Cardinal Cushing on occasion of Cardinal Spellman's 25th Archepiscopal Anniversary

A friendly fellow lodger at Granby Street in the early days of Cushing's Propagation work was a distinguished young Roman, Father Francis Spellman. Home again in his own Archdiocese, remote from the heady atmosphere of the North American College, the stable and resilient Father Spellman was now under Cardinal O'Connell's flinty surveillance. First-off he was assigned to the job of drumming up subscriptions for *The Pilot,* a somewhat graceless task for the prize pupil and protégé of Cardinal Borgogini-Duca. His unrivaled tact and natural ability eventually led to Chancery work, however.

Fathers Cushing and Spellman hit it off well together. Opposite poles attract. The quiet diplomat was attracted to the lusty man of action, and *vice versa.* Cushing's failure to reach the North American College had engendered no bitterness in him. He retained, rather, admiration and respect for those who had that special advantage. There was a certain sure linkage between the two in their mutual admiration for Father Louis Kelleher. Kelleher, as previously mentioned, had been Spellman's Latin mentor at the Roman College, and Cushing's favorite professor.

Later, Archbishop Cushing was to choose Kelleher as his first Auxiliary Bishop. He must have known that this appointment would please Francis Spellman quite as much as it pleased himself.

Spellman, younger than O'Connell, older than Cushing, was a keen judge of men. He saw in Cushing a potential bishop and, contrary to all inane gossip and rumor, he was to do something to help make him that. In reminiscence, Cardinal Cushing speaks with warmth and candid gratitude of the man to whom Pope John once referred as "this bravo Spellman!" I have seen Cushing clustering his fingers birdcage fashion into his short-cropped gray hair and wrinkling his brow in thought about Spellman, when he was once asked about a chapter on Spellman in a possible Cushing biography. He finally came out of the regions of memory with detonating impact: "Spellman got me this job! Pius XII himself told me this!"

He also intimated that Spellman helped him become Auxiliary Bishop. This looked like the place for a journalist to ask: "Who else was trying to get it—the Boston Archdiocese, I mean?" We are sure we heard the Cardinal say: "Mooney."

The matter was not pursued further. But a later, routine check revealed that the then Archbishop Edward Mooney of Detroit was not made a Cardinal until 1945, one year after Archbishop-designate Cushing was installed as spiritual leader of the Boston Archdiocese.

Earlier, on a crisp October evening in 1963, we had first talked with Cardinal Cushing about Spellman in terms of Father Gannon's interesting, if almost completely laudatory, biography of the New York Cardinal published in March of 1962. Cardinal Cushing had written a lengthy review of that work for the national Jesuit weekly, *America*. At that time this writer had read neither the biography nor the review.

When asked what he thought about the book, the Cardinal did not revert to his published review, but, grimacing thoughtfully, he said in bronchial tones and with his intense blue stare: "Political image."

Cushing said he wouldn't want to hurt Spellman and he added with deadly sententiousness: "He's lost his power."

Pius XII, Roosevelt, Eisenhower—Spellman's benefactors—they had left the seats of world power, perhaps Cardinal Cushing meant.

It is well-known that Pope Pius XII wanted Spellman to succeed Cardinal O'Connell as Archbishop of Boston. Spellman, himself from Whitman, just outside Boston, knew the Boston Archdiocese, its priests and people. He would have made a superb Archbishop and Cardinal of Boston. But the death of Cardinal Hayes of New York in 1938 changed the Pope's inclination. World War II was at hand. Franklin Delano Roosevelt was President of the United States, and sooner or later, as Pius XII knew and everybody knew, the United States would have to enter the war. Roosevelt was a New Yorker. He would look with favor, increasingly, upon the charming, brilliant, steel-willed Spellman. This would give the Vatican an intercessor and contact at the White House. Francis Spellman was appointed Archbishop of New York.

Thus destiny also beckoned to Richard James Cushing. He no longer had to be in competition with the redoubtable Spellman.

In his review of *The Cardinal Spellman Story*, Cushing paid magnificent tribute to Spellman. He wrote that vocations grow out of holy family life. He described the "boy from a small town in Massachusetts, following the early example and directions inculcated by his family to serve God and country . . . who had the opportunity for so many decades to serve with both great loyalty and accomplishment."

Cardinal Cushing wrote that he had known Spellman "throughout my priesthood of forty years, and I am quick to say that he has been, during all this time, a devoted confrere—a true friend as well as an inspiration.

69

"From the very beginning of our friendship I was well aware that Father Spellman was destined for a great role in the life of the Church. He was tireless, an ardent student, available at all times to the humble and the poor, and yet capable of being at ease with those in high places.

"The formula of his unique way of life—I shall call it harmony of heart and head and hand.

"Cardinal Spellman would go anywhere to aid a friend, or to seek a forgotten soul or to be with someone who needed a helping hand to make all things new . . .

"There is so much that one cannot put on paper. Words are weak when we ask them to hear the things that can only be felt in the heart.

"For example, those of us who have known Cardinal Spellman over the years miss in these pages his natural wit and charm, which only a personal association could appreciate.

"The quick turn of phrase, the friendly repartee, the ready smile—all of these are familiar to his friends and acquaintances and reflect his warm-hearted character."

In the review, Cardinal Cushing talked again of Doctor Louis Kelleher, the late Boston Auxiliary Bishop. He spoke with glowing praise of Spellman's devotion and loyalty to his deceased friend. In conversation, he has several times mentioned Cardinal Spellman's annual pilgrimage to Boston to offer a death-day anniversary Mass for Doctor Kelleher.

Then came the final, monumental accolade:

"What these pages may not reveal, but what is to me an indisputable fact, is that here is the story of the greatest American churchman of this century."

Cardinal Cushing's heartfelt and prophetic compliment to his distinguished colleague could very well prove true. The judgment of history will decide. And that decision may well narrow down to a choice between two great Cardinals: Spellman and—Cushing!

CHAPTER VIII

"The Unparalleled Auxiliary!"

"In a sense, his funeral was the triumph of his life. The eulogies poured in, the tears flowed, thousands upon thousands came to look upon him and do him reverence. What he had accomplished was the living memorial."—Rev. Francis B. Thornton on William Henry O'Connell

The great Archdiocese of Boston was a prodigious, living memorial to William Cardinal O'Connell. Young Bishop Cushing, too, was O'Connell's "Living memorial." Pope Pius XII, prior to Cushing's official appointment as Archbishop, referred to the Bishop, then forty-four years old, as "the unparalleled Auxiliary." This imposing compliment was surely based on Cushing's fame as a world-wide mission fund raiser and organizer. But no doubt the Pope's high opinion of Cushing was also influenced by the brand-new shepherd of the New York Archdiocese, Archbishop Francis Spellman.

Cushing had been a Monsignor for a scant two months when Boston Auxiliary Bishop Spellman was appointed to wealthy, powerful New York. Richard James must have known his own designation as new Auxiliary was in the offing. Cardinal O'Connell told him so. Cushing insists he didn't want the appointment and declined the honor directly to O'Connell's face.

"You *take* it," Big Bill said, briefly and to the point.

The designation as Auxiliary Bishop came on June 12, 1939, and with it came appointment as Pastor to Bishop Spellman's former Parish, Sacred Heart Church in Newton

Center. On July 1, Cardinal O'Connell consecrated the new Auxiliary. Cushing's former seminary rector, Bishop John Peterson of Manchester, and Bishop Thomas A. Emmet, S.J. of Jamaica, West Indies, another native Bostonian, assisted at the ceremony. Archbishop Spellman was present, along with other luminaries of church and state. In the front pew, with his two brothers and three sisters, was the Bishop's mother, Mary Dahill Cushing, then eighty-one years old, and a widow since 1922.

"I always knew you'd be a Bishop," Mrs. Cushing said to her son after the ceremony. His mother could well be proud of him. He had gone from priest to Monsignor to Bishop in two short months. The promotion was, as one observer said in *The Pilot*, "a fit accolade of tireless, self-sacrificing service."

After the consecration, Cushing tells us, there was no fanfare, no parties. "I went right back to work."

Cushing was now to become well-known as "The Bishop of Franklin Street." For even as Pastor of Sacred Heart, he continued his unabated activity as Director of the Society for the Propagation of the Faith from his Boston office. Added to his duties now were confirmations and occasional ordinations. And he was deeply concerned with the spiritual welfare of Boston men and women serving in the armed forces. Many New England veterans of World War II remember with warmth the little green kits they received from Bishop Cushing as the result of a direct or indirect request. The kit contained a small missal and a well-made Rosary, along with a cordial personal message signed by the Bishop.

In May of 1940 Cushing involved himself in direct Chinese missionary work, right in his Boston backyard. He organized Boston's first Catholic Chinese Sunday School in the heart of the Hub's China Town in the South End. In an address to Chinese merchants, their wives and children, the Bishop urged them, with friendly bluntness, to "put aside your racial aloofness and become integrated in the life of the community." The indomitable Maryknoll nuns are now in Chinatown, established there at Archbishop Cushing's request, ministering to the children of Boston's Chinese behind the well-known red doors of their convent.

In September of 1940, while Bishop Cushing was preaching the sermon at the Mass of the Holy Ghost which annually opens Boston College's academic year, his mother died. Had she lived four more years, she would have seen him become Archbishop of Boston. But this was not to be. Cushing celebrated a solemn high requiem Mass for her in St. Brigid's, South Boston, which all the Cushings had once known and loved as St. Eulalia's.

Surely the gone and golden years of his seaside youth on "O" Street, the pure fun around City Point and the Aquarium, the memories of the love and dignity of the Cushings' simple, God-centered home, must have been in his mind as he moved toward the inexorable "Requiescat In Pace" in the Mass for the Dead.

He had buried Patrick Cushing in 1922. Now he knew most profoundly the loneliness of high places in the Church, for his parents were no more, and even his love for his brother and sisters could not and would not bring him the distraction of family ties. No more for Cushing the "I will follow Thee, Lord, but first let me take leave of them that are at my house." He had long since taken leave; but death was the final parting. He would greet his parents next in eternity. Now more than ever, there was work to be done, singlemindedly.

The whirring months of ceaseless apostolic activity continued until December 7, Pearl Harbor! Within a year, Boston soldiers, sailors, marines, nurses, WAVES, and WACS had blended with their fellow citizens in training and combat areas all over the world. Bishop Cushing maintained communications with many of them and particularly with far-flung Boston chaplains who tried, catch-as-catch-can and often with surprising success, to keep some lines of liaison and supply open with missionaries and their war-torn establishments in the Pacific Islands, in Africa, and on the mainland of China itself.

Doughty old Cardinal O'Connell was aging rapidly. Cataracts had obscured his vision, and he walked with the aid of a heavy cane. At the Boston College commencement in June of 1942, the Cardinal was helped to the edge of the platform in the broiling summer sun and delivered a stirring impromptu address to the "war class." His great powers of eloquence had not dulled as he referred to this bright, new group of fellow alumni as "the flower of the flock" and ringingly called on them to defend their land, their liberty, and the great heritage of their Christian faith. It was an old-fashioned call to patriotism by a grand old patriarch, and it just suited the time. When he finished, there were few dry eyes in Alumni Stadium. The aged Cardinal O'Connell in this unprepared address had outshone the distinguished speaker of the day.

In New York City and at bases around the world, Bishop Cushing's predecessor, Archbishop Francis Spellman, in his role as U.S. Military Vicar, was winning fame as a globe-girdling religious emissary. He also became the author of best-selling books of war poems, diaries, and meditations. Moreover, Archbishop Spellman, with the favor and blessing of both President Roosevelt and Pius XII, was able to act as liaison in certain diplomatic areas of particular concern to the Holy See.

As for Bishop Cushing, he clearly and definitely kept the home fires burning. He willingly remained at Franklin Street and continued to serve at the beck and call of the fast-failing Cardinal O'Connell. The old Cardinal had no co-adjutor, nor did he want one, and Cushing was his only Auxiliary Bishop. Cushing stayed in Boston, close to the old Cardinal who needed him, despite the accessibility of military air travel and his lifetime interest in the missions which beckoned him to visit many mission locations now under the protection of the American flag. His Boston character and fierce local pride were to be even more deeply etched in him by his confinement to Franklin Street during these exciting and embattled years.

In the Spring of 1944, the Angel of Death was to strike twice in the personal life of Richard Cushing. The Angel left behind in Cushing's heart a painful loss; he also drew Cushing another step forward in his destiny. In late March, Cushing's much loved former seminary Rector, the Bishop of Manchester, New Hampshire, Most Rev. John Bertram Peterson, died. "Take your priesthood seriously, never yourself." This lovable and practical style of priesthood had become so much a part of Cushing's life that he took the phrase into his own conversational coinage.

It was fitting that Bishop Peterson's most outstanding pupil should deliver his eulogy in St. Joseph's Cathedral, Manchester, on March 21, 1944. "Even as we think of him, a cedar of Lebanon before the altar of God, honoring the vestments of holiness, we are led to think, too, of that sobering pronouncement of Holy Scripture, 'nothing defiled shall enter heaven.' "

But the stout and industrious Cushing was, within a month, to deliver another funeral oration. This time it would be for the Cardinal of Boston. By mid-April Cardinal O'Connell, eighty-one years old, lay gravely ill of pneumonia. The wonder drugs developed in wartime had not come into commercial civilian use in time to benefit the redoubtable but failing "Number One."

Keeping the death watch in the Cardinal's bed chamber, along with O'Connell's personal staff, was his rugged Auxiliary. On the polished oak floor of the big, master bedroom, on the second floor of the Cardinal's residence, Bishop Cushing knelt, saying the Rosary. The Cardinal, sporadically conscious, seemed at that moment in a coma. Cushing continued telling the beads and the old Cardinal opened his eyes and looked at him with certain recognition. Bishop Cushing then asked him for a blessing. O'Connell

75

did not speak, perhaps could not, but raised his right hand and placed it directly upon Cushing's head—precisely what Archbishop Williams, at the hour of his death, did to William Henry O'Connell.

Thus Cardinal O'Connell still pursued his dream: a Boston priest, a St. John's boy, in the Archepiscopal chair. After his death, an aide revealed that it was the Cardinal's wish to have Cushing preach his eulogy; and that Cushing would be appointed Archdiocesan Administrator.

"I had no direct indication from the Cardinal that he desired me to deliver his eulogy when he had passed along," Cardinal Cushing asserts. "However, I believed my informant from the late Cardinal's staff and prepared my sermon."

Bishop Cushing's first statement regarding the Cardinal's passing appeared in the columns of *The Pilot*. It was prefaced with the scriptural passage: "No man liveth unto himself and no man dieth unto himself." The tribute reads:

"With perfect resignation to the Divine Will we may yet mourn his passing as a public loss to the church on earth and an infinite loss to ourselves. We may sorrow in an impersonal way that a Master of Israel is no more; that a burning and shining light is quenched, that lips which discoursed divine knowledge are sealed in the silence of the grave."

The Cardinal had died on Saturday, April 22, 1944. On the following Thursday, April 27, the new Administrator of the Archdiocese, appointed by a council of Archdiocesan officials, was celebrant of the solemn high mass of requiem for the distinguished patriarch who had once called him "Tunney."

A multitude of the great and small in national, state, and municipal life attended the funeral. Bishops, Monsignori, priests, and religious knelt in or near the sanctuary; lay dignitaries from all walks of life sat in the benches. Thousands of ordinary lay folk filled the rear pews of the great Cathedral, or stood outside mournfully waiting. They had loved their late Cardinal despite his often haughty aloofness.

The great O'Connell, lying there in funeral state, could not have cared whether the electric sound system was on or off when his lusty Auxiliary climbed into the high pulpit and there delivered his impassioned and eloquent praise and farewell. Bishop Cushing took as his theme an arresting and perceptive passage from Ecclesiasticus: "Behold a great priest, who in his days pleased God, and was found just and in the time of wrath was made a reconciliation."

Cushing spoke of O'Connell as his mentor, highlighting his conception of universal charity and his sense of the universal church, "Missionaries are keeping his memory sacred before the crude altars of jungle chapels and in the stately sanctuaries of Oriental cathedrals. 'Remember,' he frequently admonished me, 'this is God's work; keep it in God's Hands.' "

The loneliness of high place in the Church is a recurrent theme in Cushing's conversation. Cushing told us once, in the winter of 1964, with a poignancy not quite concealed in brusqueness: "I have no close friends. Because of what I have to do, day in, day out, I go it pretty much alone." He saw this same loneliness in O'Connell. He said that day, in the Cathedral of the Holy Cross: ". . . any man exalted above his fellow men, most of all in ecclesiastical life, can have few intimates. In an extraordinary degree, Cardinal O'Connell succeeded in combining a genuine love of his priests and people with a detachment which kept him from the softening consolations of their friendships; but he paid the price for this magnificent service to God and country with a lonely life and a no less lonely death."

Bishop Cushing concluded the eulogy by citing a piece of verse, the author of which is not named. It is a genuine and accurate tribute to Cardinal O'Connell's memory:

> Were a star quenched on high,
> For years would its light

77

Still streaming from the sky
Fall on our mortal sight.

So when a great man dies,
For years beyond our ken,
The light he leaves behind him lies
Upon the paths of men.

And that was the farewell the heir-apparent said to his first superior, William Henry Cardinal O'Connell.

BOOK THREE

The Pride of Boston

CHAPTER IX

Happy Interlude

"Somebody said to me when the election was known: 'Now you will never hear the truth again.' Everybody in high place stands in a room full of mirrors and sees himself multiplied without end by a servile reflection.' "—Diary of Cardinal Manning

Throughout the vast Archdiocese of Boston there was happy expectation and awe among the faithful at the prospect of Auxiliary Bishop and Administrator Richard J. Cushing becoming their permanent spiritual shepherd. The genuine sorrow at the death of Cardinal O'Connell was being replaced with a certain lightness of heart, now that the almost grim solemnity and pomp of the O'Connell regime was no more. Observers could not help sensing the similarity of this change to the vast family joy of Democrats in Boston when Franklin Roosevelt succeeded the Hoover administration in 1932.

The sense of growing awe had much to do with an increased awareness on the part of the faithful of the boundless energy, the indefatigability, and the generosity of the lean and burning stentorian Irishman on whom they kept their eyes.

As Administrator, Cushing continued to maintain living quarters at the Sacred Heart Rectory in Newton Center. He had left Franklin Street, however, and now kept office hours at the Chancery just down the hill from the archepiscopal residence.

There was some talk around rectory dining rooms about Archbishop Moses Kiley of Milwaukee receiving the archepiscopal appointment. Kiley was originally from Somerville. Men like Louis Kelleher and Monsignors Phelan, Minihan, and Splaine were also mentioned. But O'Connell had wanted Cushing; Archbishop Spellman had urged Pope Pius XII to favor him—as indeed the Pope revealed years later, to Cushing himself. And most of all, the great majority of the Faithful of Boston wanted Cushing.

To end all rumor and uncertainty the electors of the Archdiocese cast their ballots, and by September 28, 1944, one of the most popular decisions in the history of the American Church was announced. The Apostolic Delegate, Archbishop Amleto Cicognani, called Bishop Cushing from Washington and officially notified him of his election. The Archbishop-elect almost immediately put in a local call to South Boston and shared his great happiness with his sisters and his brother.

Boston was electrified with happiness. *The Pilot* editorialist on September 30 called his election "an answer to many prayers." The editorialist referred to Cushing as "a priest's priest" and continued perceptively: "He will remain—we know this—utterly un-pompous. That's an invented word. But it is truly expressive of the reality. Wearing his honors with the dignity they require, Bishop Cushing will regard them only as an increased opportunity for service. But self-importance is alien, utterly alien, to this candid, straightforward nature."

Earlier that summer, still as Administrator, Cushing had experienced the great jubilation expressed by "Southie is my home town," when he paraded through South Boston on July 8 with Monsignor Augustine Hickey of St. Paul's, Cambridge, and Monsignor Joseph C. Walsh flanking him on either side. The occasion was the celebration of the 125th Anniversary of St. Augustine's Chapel in old Southie. Cushing walked jauntily behind a brass band, with flags flying and his own people cheering and calling blessings upon him, a tall, vigorous Irish-American Bishop with the brilliant summer sun upon him.

The magic of Cushing's presence in public parade,

among the faithful, was to be repeated in years to come, in this country, in Ireland, Rome, and in Latin America. Amid all of this, then and since, Cushing has been "utterly unpompous."

As Bishop-Elect, Cushing wasted little time in showing a group of the aged and ailing—one of his favorite groups —how informal and accessible he could be. He agreed to say Mass for 125 patients at the Holy Ghost Hospital for incurables in Cambridge. At his suggestion, so that bed patients could be close to him and the Mass, the benches were removed from the chapel and the bed-ridden were pushed in, along with those who could walk or be rolled in on wheel chairs.

At church dedications and confirmations, while still Administrator or Archbishop-Elect, Cushing would sweep into a country parish with great vigor and flourish. He sometimes had to wear his episcopal vestments in the car, he would cover so many places in one trip. His great cordiality and informality won over everyone. He calls pastors, curates, and laymen by their first names, slaps them on their backs, and bustles down church aisles with characteristic energy and informality. "O.K., boys," he even then said to newspaper photographers in the midst of a confirmation or dedication, "we'll call off the show for a minute and you can take your pictures."

On one occasion when he had time to change back into a black summer suit and a straw hat (the boater), he was met at the steps of the church by a group of women who were escorting a tiny old lady. She was ninety-eight, the oldest active member of the parish, and she greeted him, placing her bird-like little hand on his arm. Richard Cushing, who was to become renowned in Father Joe McInnis' phrase as "the clown prince of human compassion," tilted his boater rakishly and toddled along with her to his car. The newspaper photographers were alert as this temporary Maurice Chevalier of the episcopacy played one of the earliest of his droll, legendary charades.

"You won't forget me, Father, will you? You won't forget me?" the old woman pleaded.

"How could I forget you?" Bishop Cushing said, placing his arm protectively around her as the flash bulbs popped. "I'm your boyfriend!"

Bostonians and others the wide world over were to become stunned, then amused and touched, by these flashes of public drollery in the long career of the Cardinal-to-be. He danced jigs with sprightly old ladies and gentlemen at Thanksgiving Day dinners, sang "Sweet Adeline" in clerical quartets; he clowned publicly in all sorts of headgear: fire helmets, construction workers' iron hats, Red Sox caps, and once even donned an old lady's flowery Easter bonnet —these were to be the at-first shocking and then warmly familiar images of the Archbishop, both in the press and on television.

"Take your priesthood seriously, never yourself." He had learned that axiom well at the feet of the late Bishop Petersen.

The date of his solemn and festive installation had been announced for November 8, 1944. By that time, the entire Archdiocese had sensed in the establishment a change from a certain official oppressiveness to a rare and epochal fortitude and gaiety.

Meanwhile, discerning commentary on the Archepiscopal election continued. As close to the heart of the matter as any statement, personal or public, were the simple words of his colleagues at the office of the Propagation of the Faith: "Beyond the limits of the Archdiocese, yes even to the frozen north and the tropical islands of the Atlantic and the Pacific, in fact in any mission where the news has reached, there will be much rejoicing. All worthy of help have received the benefit of the mission zeal of the new Archbishop. No missionary begging help left without his burden being lightened. He was assured that back in Boston he had a real missionary who did not forget. It would be difficult for us to find any corner of the mission field where Boston has not aided the spread of the Kingdom of God."

The *Boston Herald* in the mid-forties was still the militant spokesman for the Republican Party and the Yankee Brahmin establishment of commerce and industry. The *Herald*, albeit, responded to the appointment of the rustic and rough-hewn Cushing with the utmost cordiality and vigorous editorial applause:

"Cardinal O'Connell was a cosmopolite and a keen judge of men regardless of their race or place of birth, but he had an amiable partiality for his own clergy. He considered them the best educated, the best trained, the most devoted, the most capable group of priests in the country. He wished dearly to have one of his own flock become Archbishop of Boston.

"He regarded Bishop Cushing very highly ever since ordaining him as a priest and consecrating him as a bishop. Reviewing, after the fact, the relation of the two men, Catholics will surmise that His Eminence so trained him that his achievements would somehow speak for themselves and that he would be well qualified for a high honor if the Holy Father should see fit to bestow it."

From the Epistle of the Mass for the Propagation of the Faith, the Archbishop-elect quite logically chose the Archepiscopal motto we have often in these pages had to cite: "That they may know thee, O God, as we have known Thee . . ."

His Coat of Arms celebrated Boston: a Trimount, symbolizing the three hills on which the city is said to have been built, and at its base waves, symbolizing a seaport town. Above the hills is a Cross tipped with fleurs-de-lis, in honor of the first Bishop of Boston and later Cardinal of Bordeaux, John De Cheverus. St. Richard of Chichester is represented by a book and pastoral staff; St. James the Greater, the Apostle, by the scallop shells traditionally borne by pilgrims to the famous shrine of St. James at Compostella in Spain.

85

Not least important are the symbols denoting the Archbishop's absorption in the Propagation of the Faith: The Cross symbolizing the Faith itself, colored the red of charity and zeal. The monogram of the Lord is inscribed on the open book of the Gospels. Boston, the foreign missions, Christ: Cushing's symbols.

At the Installation, Cushing symbolically received the Sacred Pallium, a narrow, white woolen band, the symbol of the union of the Archdiocese with the Holy See. When Cushing accepted his appointment as Archbishop, he petitioned Pope Pius XII, as a matter of form, for the conferring of the Pallium, and it was duly received. Boston had an Archbishop of whom it was proud, and whom it loved. The actual, official conferring of the Pallium, because of war-time conditions took place on Sunday, April 7, 1946, with Archbishop Spellman presiding.

CHAPTER **X**

The Sixth Bishop of Boston

"And he gave some apostles, some prophets, some evangelists, and some pastors and doctors, for the perfecting of the saints, for the work of the ministry, for the edifying of the body of Christ, until we meet unto the unity of the faith and of the knowledge of the Son of God . . ."—St. Paul to the Ephesians, 4, 11

"Go back and read my original sermon at the Installation!" Cardinal Cushing growled, as I was present, one wintry afternoon in 1964. "I held out my hand to all peoples." I asked him if he had a copy of the sermon handy which I could use.

His answer was typical. "No. I don't keep any records like that. Go down to the *Pilot* and get it."

The Cardinal continually repeats that he has not kept letters and manuscripts which would help construct an autobiography or biography. He expressed this view with a certain amount of regret. "I tore up a lot of letters and threw away a lot of things I should have kept," he once said.

As a man of action, Cushing was not working and striving, sacrificing and giving, just to sustain his image for posterity. One's respect and regard for him could only increase because he had not taken measures to solidify himself with the biographers and historians to come.

In his sermon at the Installation, as in most of his other projects and statements, the Cardinal constantly alluded to "the Universal Church." "All my money goes to the Universal Church," he will say when giving a list of institutions and schools he has built for religious orders, here and abroad. "These things pertain to the Universal Church," he will repeat.

The day of his Installation at Holy Cross Cathedral was Sunday, November 8, 1944.

The famed and powerful of Church, state and nation, the Archbishop-Elect's family, his friends, representatives of all the clergy and religious, the home missions, the foreign missions, and all the unknown ones who loved him, all who could jam into or around the back pews, side aisles, vestry, doorways, and the sweeping staircases of Holy Cross Cathedral, joined in fervid tribute to and surged with mighty hope for their anointed spiritual leader.

Seated in the sanctuary or aiding him in the ceremony were the Apostolic Delegate, Archbishop Amleto Cicognani of Washington, D.C., Archbishops Francis Spellman of New York, Francis J. Beckman of Dubuque, Edwin V. Byrne of Santa Fe, Moses E. Kiley of Milwaukee, William Edward Mooney of Detroit, John G. Murray of St. Paul, John T. McNicholas of Cincinnati, and Alexander Vachon of Ottawa.

Special love and admiration radiated from a front pew on the center aisle, where sat the blood of his blood and the bone of his bone. His brother John J. Cushing was there, and his unmarried sister, Elizabeth. Mrs. William Francis and Mrs. Richard Pierce were basking in reflected glory there, with their husbands. His nephews were there: William Francis, now a priest, carrying high his uncle's aspirations as a missionary in Cushing's St. James Society in Peru; and Richard Francis who works as a pressman for the *Boston Globe*.

They were all there—Governor Saltonstall of Massachusetts, Mayor Tobin of Boston. The war was raging then on all fronts, and many other bearers of famous names, who would have been among those present, were under arms: a legendary young naval hero named John F. Kennedy, and the late Bay State Governor Paul A. Dever, also a naval officer, a bold warrior of the armored divisions in North Africa, named Henry Cabot Lodge, and many others.

Most Rev. Francis P. Keough, then Bishop of Providence, R.I., delivered the Installation sermon. He took as his theme the quotation from St. Paul which prefaces this chapter: "And he gave some apostles, some prophets, some evangelists and some pastors and doctors, for the perfecting of the saints for the work of the ministry . . ."

Richard James Cushing was one of them, Bishop Keough eloquently expounded, given so richly to Twentieth Century Catholicism. "Apostle," yes, of the poor; "prophet," yes, of religious unity; "evangelist," yes, in the missions, and particularly in South America—"evangelist" of the Word but also of the corporal works of mercy, showering money, medicine, clothing, housing, churches, and institutions of staggering value on many continents—"pastor," yes, of Sacred Heart Parish in Newton Center, and personal, always approachable "pastor" to the entire Archdiocese; "doctor," not a man of scholarly inclination—without even a regular bachelor's degree, nor hardly a formal degree in Sacred Theology, but "Doctor," perhaps in his sense of the meaning of Catholicism in his time.

Then up into the pulpit climbed the new Archbishop. "Ut cognoscant te!" he began, "that they may know thee!" Surely he could have snapped off the sound system with despatch. He needed no microphone to carry his voice, his heart, his soul, to all the people there and all his beloved clergy, religious, and faithful in the Archdiocese who could not be physically present. The Archbishop held his hand out "to all peoples" in behalf of the Universal Church. "To Almighty God," he began, "I consecrate anew all that I have and all that I am, for his glory, for my own sanctification, and for the welfare of the souls entrusted to my care."

High above him, suspended from the rafters over the altar of the Cathedral, hung the wide-brimmed, round-domed Red Hat of the late Cardinal O'Connell. The new Archbishop may have sensed its presence. His own red hat would one day dangle from those rafters *In Memento Mori.* His booming voice spoke of ". . . thoughts drawn to the hallowed past and toward the hidden future. Both past and future meet in the text from which I have presumed to take the motto for the present."

Cardinal O'Connell: "His was the task of organizing and fortifying the House of God in this city, of revealing to the Archdiocese its own greatness as a unit of the Universal Church." He mentioned his other forebears, the Bishops of Boston: John De Cheverus, Fenwick, Fitzpatrick, Williams. "To this end the Master has set a new servant over His household. Here where others have builded and made strong and have stored the fruits of their toil, that new servant has his work to do.

"It is for him, for me, to kindle anew and to spread the blazing fire of supernatural life. This is the fire that Our Lord came to cast upon earth, the fire of spirituality. Only spirituality can work the miracle that will raise our self-slain world from the bloody grave.

"That is our aim, spirituality, love, based on knowledge, in every walk of life. For with all our current Catholic activity, we have too little of Catholic living, knowing and loving first things first. 'Seek ye first the kingdom of God and His justice.'

"Not until a dynamic army of Catholics is actively engaged in an all-out pursuit of sanctity can we hope for progress. Nineteen hundred years ago the Lord gave us the infallible remedy for every ill now affecting civilization. That remedy is heroic personal sanctity, distilled from the knowledge of a personal God. 'Now this,' said Our Lord in His Prayer, 'is everlasting life, that they may know Thee.'

"Almighty God is not merely a principle and a force: He is a personality, one God in three Divine Persons, a constant, unending source of intellectual delight and of loving companionship. To know Him, however, takes time and thought. Out of the twenty-four hours of every day, which God has made and given to us, we must reserve some time for undivided attention to Him. The Church offers the means, and a wealth of aids, but it is for us to take and use them."

The Archbishop then extended a special message to his priests, religious, laity, respectively:

"*Ut cognoscant te:* That you and I, my brother priests, may know God so well that all men will recognize us, not only as His ambassadors but as reproductions of His Divine Son. That is our vocation; we dare not fail. The light must shine, the salt must season, the shepherd must lead.

"*Ut cognoscant te:* That you and I, my dearly beloved religious may know God so well that we shall become the very likeness of God, responding to His will as a shadow responds to the movements of its substance.

"*Ut cognoscant te:* That you and I, my dear brethren of the laity, may know God and in every act of ours fulfill that word of His: 'You are to be perfect, even as your heavenly father is perfect.' "

Now, in the climactic moment of his thundering keynote sermon the new shepherd held his hand out to all peoples, as he was to do all the days of his life: "For the knowledge of God and for the love of God and neighbor that flows therefrom, I give myself this morning to the priests, the religious and the Catholic laity of the Archdiocese of Boston, and to all others to whom I can be of help.

"Pray for me please, not that I may attain the heights of learning and the pinnacles of visible success, but that I may be saturated with, and help others achieve, that spirituality which flows from the knowledge and love of God."

Thus spoke the Sixth Bishop of Boston, now only forty-nine years old. A fabled new era of democratic administration, monumental fund-raising, endless building and expansion, bottomless personal generosity, and unparalleled warmth among religious groups, was begun, not only in the Archdiocese of Boston, but wherever and whenever Richard Cushing could exert his influence throughout the Universal Church.

After the ceremony the new Archbishop held a festive lunch for the visiting prelates, Monsignori, and priests at the Copley Plaza Hotel. Specially invited also were the pastors, and one curate, from each of the three hundred parishes in the Archdiocese. In every convent, in every religious institution throughout the Archdiocese, simultaneously with the Copley Plaza affair, nuns, priests, monks, and brothers were Archbishop Cushing's guests at a mid-day meal.

Some from among the diocesan clergy who are now inclined to remark that Cushing "favors the layman" might recall that the brand-new Archbishop ran the Copley Plaza dinner strictly for religious, with no laity in attendance. When this opinion of some of his clergy was mentioned to the Cardinal recently, moreover, he seethed with controlled anger, and denied that it had any sound basis in fact. He warmed to his conviction that he had always been good and generous to his clergy, and as the anger left him, he talked affectionately, lavishly, of what he was still going to do for his priests.

He talked of the huge modern and commodious apartment-like home now complete in Boston for retired Archdiocesan priests. "This will be my personal gift to them—a kind of legacy that will comfort and shelter them after I'm gone," the Cardinal said. He strode around his office with that long, princely grace, which he seems to have acquired and charmingly developed since he became a Cardinal. "I'm gonna throw them a big party at a downtown hotel—all of them—on my twenty-fifth anniversary as an auxiliary bishop." He was walking me to the door, loading me up with books, records, pictures, as is his bountiful way—especially, one will note, after he has been angry about something or other.

"Will you give them a drink at the dinner?" we asked somewhat impishly.

"More than one," he said with his typical rasp and his fetchingly crooked smile.

At the private dinner for the clergy after the Installation ceremony in 1944, some of the new Archbishop's remarks at the head table were recorded by the late Joseph F. Dineen, ace Boston reporter, top national journalist, and a novelist who had a droll, astute understanding of what makes the Boston-Irish tick. One of the few newspapermen present at that exclusive luncheon, Joe Dineen, reported Cushing's remarks for the *Boston Globe*. In this case, the notes are invaluable. The Cardinal said: ". . . a new order is in the making, and although it would be rash to predict what it will be like, it would be a neglect of duty not to read the signs of the times and to anticipate intelligently the situation confronting us. Intellectual skepticism and moral indifference are already on the horizon. They do not attack Christianity; they ignore it. Individual souls can be reclaimed only by truth.

"The postwar world is likely to have less respect even than the present-day masses for official status. In the democracy of the future, the clergy will doubtless be asked unceremoniously for its contribution. For example, Chaplains in this war have told us they are recognized as 'men among men.' It is for us to win recognition as Christ-like men among men. We should welcome a state of things that will bring home to us in sober fact that although being shepherds, we have to lead our flocks, yet we are not by right the overlords of our people, we are their servants."

This was quite a revolutionary statement for the Archbishop of Irish-Catholic Boston, where priests and pastors —in an embattled atmosphere of survival against stubborn Yankee Protestant hostility and bigotry—were stern masters of their flocks and for years could do or say no wrong. Perhaps this was, after all, the first public manifesto of Cushing's partiality to the layman. For here, surely, in the presence of his pastors, fellow bishops, many curates, he clearly "held out his hand" to the layman and, in no uncertain terms, urged his peers and subordinates to do likewise.

Later, in a general press conference, as a climax to what must have been an exhausting, if joyous and solemn day, the Archbishop made a rather paradoxical set of remarks. Such statements were to become characteristic of him. He opens with a stunningly liberal remark, and then, with easy *non-sequitur*, hews closely, emotionally, to what he still is, a quite provincial, almost chauvinistic Bostonian: "I'm against every anti. I was born in Boston, I was bred in Boston, I love Boston. I'm for everything that will promote Boston's welfare."

Cushing began as he has continued: against ideology, for people—especially for Bostonians. He is almost perfectly consistent with himself, however out of step, at times, with others.

CHAPTER XI

Whence the Money?

"The Archbishop's residence on Commonwealth Avenue, known as an exclusive place in the days of the old Cardinal, was now a vibrant center of hospitality and charity."—Rev. Francis B. Thornton on Richard J. Cushing.

It has been well-said that Pope John XXIII threw open all the windows in the Catholic Church when he became Pope, letting in an enormous amount of desperately needed fresh air. In the Archdiocese of Boston, by way of letting in fresh air, Archbishop Cushing figuratively tore the roof off the Church.

As a fund-raiser for the missions Cushing had preached in each parish of the Archdiocese at least three times. He had predicted that O'Connell's successor would have to build at least eighty-five new parishes and raise millions of dollars annually. "I don't know where he is going to get it," he had said. Now he was that successor, and he would have to lead the new building and fund-raising himself, on a vast, unprecedented scale. And, indeed, by natural gifts and long years of training, he of all churchmen was equal to the task. He knew there would also be a need for many new institutional buildings: schools, homes for the elderly, hospitals, orphanages, residences for religious orders. But what he did not know, according to a spokesman at *The Pilot*, was "the deplorable state of disrepair and ruin of many of the buildings in which various institutions were functioning." The challenge of repairs required a major fund-raising program in itself.

The great result for the Church of the Allied victory in World War II, as Cushing saw it, was expanded missionary activity abroad and more socially conscious religious activity at home. Cardinal O'Connell had not encouraged the establishment in the Archdiocese of new and diverse religious orders. A Dominican in a white cowl, a brown-robed Capuchin in sandals, a black-hooded Benedictine, would have seemed like strange birds to many of us growing up in Boston in the 1930's. Many of us simply had never seen or known members of certain storied religious orders which we had read about in the history of Europe. The old Cardinal leaned heavily and long on familiar local groups—rich in history themselves, of course—like the Jesuits, Passionists, Redemptorists, the newer Maryknoll fathers; among the orders of Brothers, the Xaveian and Christian Brothers; and the School Sisters of Notre Dame, the Sisters of Notre Dame of Namur, the Sisters of St. Joseph, the Grey Nuns at the Holy Ghost Hospital, and the Good Shepherds who have for a long time looked after Boston's naughty girls. These orders and a few others did all the work of the old Archdiocese, in the fields of education, medicine, the missions, social and spiritual rehabilitation.

But World War II and the postwar social, economic, educational, and religious problems were increasing in mathematical progression. The vineyard needed more workers. Archbishop Cushing lowered the O'Connell curtain, threw open the door, and steadily invited units of almost all the religious orders of the Catholic Church into the Archdiocese. The hard-nosed Boston-Irish Church many of us knew as children swiftly began to become the warm, expansive Universal Church of which we'd read. As fast as he could buy, build, rent, or lease institutional and residential accommodations for them, Archbishop Cushing kept the religious orders coming.

"My principal chore, in cooperation with them, was to build and raise money—all for the Universal Church," Cardinal Cushing said in an interview, recalling the first influx of new religious orders and institutions into the Archdiocese, back in 1945. Between 1945 and 1950 twenty-eight new orders of priests, brothers, and nuns were invited into and established in the Archdiocese. Among these were the Paulist Fathers, now so prominent at their downtown center and chapel on Park Street and on various greater Boston university campuses; and the Capuchins, whose commodious Arch Street Shrine and endless, considerate religious services for busy downtown workers and shoppers are now a Boston institution. Among others invited in during that period were the Ursuline Nuns, the Salesian Fathers, the Dominican Fathers of Dover, and of Providence College.

Between 1951 and 1962 thirty more religious orders, including hoary old veterans of the Church militant like the Benedictines, the Christian Brothers of Ireland, and the bright and resourceful Holy Cross Fathers of Notre Dame University in South Bend—all these and others of Apostolic distinction were invited into and established in greater Boston by this Episcopal colossus of America. In less than a twenty year span Cushing had brought in at least sixty religious orders to aid and abet the endless charitable, educational and social work of the Archdiocese, the nation and the world.

"All these communities sponsor projects identified with the Universal Church," Cushing says over and over again. "All my money goes to the Universal Church," he repeats with dogged consistency.

The river of psychic energy was swelling within the Archbishop at its broadest crest during the late forties and all of the fifties. How else explain the multiplicity and diversity of his formal and informal acts of charity, many of them the subject of his intense, personal ministrations: the daily radio broadcasts of the rosary and, later, TV masses for shut-ins; the incessant, jolly visits to his cherished hospitalized groups: the ailing old, the afflicted young.

"Few men *will* anything very strongly, and out of these few, only a tiny minority are capable of combining strength

97

of will with unwavering continuity," Aldous Huxley tells us. "It is for this reason that a strenuous and unwearying will sometimes becomes so tremendous a power, almost a hypnotic force." Cushing, who disparages any references, public or private, to his personal holiness, has a holy, inexhaustible energy which reminds one of the inspired furioso of men like Francis Xavier, Saint Martin de Porres, and Good Pope John himself. "I live, yet not I, but Christ liveth in me!"

Meanwhile V-J Day came and went. The nations knew a precarious peace. Archbishop Cushing's boys were coming home from all over the world to take up some semblance of a normal social and religious life. Said the Archbishop on the day of the Japanese capitulation:

"Our first thought in this hour of relief must be of God. In Him we have trusted, by Him we have not been confounded. May He save His people and bless His heritage. May he govern them and lift them up forever. May He keep us this day without sin. May no decent person anywhere on earth ever have reason to regret that this victory is ours."

Cushing needed millions of dollars a year to pay for the Rome of America which he himself was sponsoring: the new parish churches, parish schools, regional schools, the convents, rectories, hospitals, colleges, orphanages, seminaries, monasteries, and many other religious institutions which he was fostering because of the endless post-war challenge and demand. He saw the Universal Church as the only spiritual force in the world which had the organization and resources to challenge the peculiarly spiritual dynamics of world Communism. This task was of crucial urgency in the post-war world.

"Where is he going to get the money?" he had hypothetically asked, concerning O'Connell's successor, back in the thirties. He was, in truth, asking that question of himself. This was now his problem, the first problem of the New Rome which would aid the Old Rome: millions of dollars in an endless flow. Perhaps Cushing was again alluding to his own central financial problem when he wrote the following about Saint Martin de Porres:

There can be no doubt that Martin De Porres needed large sums of money to finance his charity to the needy. He was seldom refused, even when he asked for large donations. It has been estimated that his weekly disbursement of supplies to the needy cost in the neighborhood of two thousand dollars, a fabulous amount in 16th Century Peru. The reason he was able to get it was that everyone knew that whatever was given to him would be spent in its entirety for the purposes for which he begged it.

In 1962, as a Cardinal at the second session of the Vatican Council, His Eminence, with typically disarming candor, revealed to newsmen what his daily disbursement was, in marked contrast to Martin De Porres' weekly disbursement of $2,000. Under pressure to return somewhat early to Boston, to honor his financial commitments, Cardinal Cushing made the public statement that his Archdiocesan obligations required him to raise about $35,000 per day. That's about eleven million annually.

Where *does* he, and where *did* he get this kind of money? It isn't as complex or as staggering a question as it may first appear. The Cardinal freely acknowledges that most of his money comes from the obvious source: the folks in the pews, the Faithful in the 325 parishes of the Archdiocese of Boston.

The parishes are regularly and specially assessed over the calendar year and most of the Faithful simply get the money up. Boston Catholics (and Roman Catholics in general) know what's coming when the priest climbs into the pulpit at Sunday Mass and reads a letter just before the reading of the Gospel and the sermon. In Boston, such letters begin: "To the Clergy and Faithful of the Archdiocese of Boston, Health and Benediction . . ." These epistolary appeals are usually special ones on the part of the Archbishop: Peter's Pence, the annual collection for the Pope; the annual collection for St. John's Seminary; for the national shrine of the Immaculate Conception in Washington; for the Bishops' Relief Fund; for the Society for the Propagation of The Faith, the foreign missions, and so on.

The Archbishop eventually handles all this money, flowing into him centrally, and he and his trusted Auditor, a layman, John J. Drummey, know exactly what to do with it.

Yet, regularly, like clockwork, the Pastors meet their assessments; and this great, stable source of financial supply comes out of pew money, the weekly envelopes, the annual collection, bazaars, parties, parish reunions, smokers, theatrical entertainments, in all the parishes. The Pastors, whether smiling or sad, get the assessments up, and they get the cash from the people out there in the pews. The bigger the parish, the bigger the assessment.

But obviously for institutional and educational building, and for this incredibly expansive Cardinal's many charitable projects, foreign and domestic, this basic reservoir isn't adequate. Like the cities and towns, like the state and nation itself, the Church, whose tithe-payers are every bit as dependable and negotiable as tax-payers, and whose tax-free buildings and land are gilt-edge assets, could command the unlimited credit of the great financial and banking houses of the world. Diocesan securities are among the safest in the nation.

Moreover, such is the power and authority of the Archbishop, such is the love and confidence reposed in him by his priests and people, that if he walks into the First National Bank, or any other financial establishment, the very great and powerful Archdiocese of Boston also walks in, incarnate in him.

Some say the Archbishop also has to borrow short-term money. Some vehemently insist he does not. The latter point out that the Cardinal is in control of very substantial permanent funds, like the Perpetual Care money and other static cemetery monies, which he can borrow "temporarily" from himself, i.e. the Archdiocese, to amounts exceeding half-a-million dollars at a crack. This type of account-

100

switching could well mean that Cushing does not often have to go to banking houses for even short-term loans.

Early in his career as Archbishop, Richard Cushing announced that it was his "financial policy to complete payment for each building under construction, so that when placed in service, it is free of debt." The quotation is from a *Pilot* release, and its substance is widely acknowledged as representative of the Archbishop's views. On the surface this sounds like good economics; it looks like the steady course of a tight, financial ship, and one would hope it would not disturb the dreams of some future Archbishop of Boston, whoever he may be. It could be a very good procedure—if it is really in practice, and if it really works! But it is no discredit to the Cardinal Archbishop to suggest that the whole concept may be largely a hope, or a public relations oversimplification.

Since when does one who may well be a 20th Century St. Paul, one who gives and gives to the poor, the ailing, the educable, the missionaries, with boundless generosity, one whose only frugality is with himself, one who is personally penniless by personal vow, one who has extended this spirit, it would seem, with some undoubted pain to himself, to the possible deprivation of his relatives—since when does such a personage deal successfully in economic theory? And if any cynic or sophisticate possibly doubts the fierce integrity of Cardinal Cushing with regard to voluntary personal poverty, as it concerns both himself and his family, let that person follow this procedure: Seek out any knowledgeable individual in the Archdiocese of Boston who has a love for the comforts of money and the overlordship of power, and candidly ask this question: "To whom would you rather have been directly related? To Cardinal O'Connell or to Cardinal Cushing?"

It may well be that all these Archdiocesan buildings, the land, schools, hospitals, residences, and so on, are individually free of debt by the time they are in service. But

101

credit is basic to our deficit-spending economy. Property of the might and scope of the Archdiocese is eminently negotiable for credit in any of its direct or indirect forms. It would be entirely possible for the Cardinal-Archbishop to borrow as much as twenty million dollars in one fell swoop. There has been an unconfirmed report around that he did borrow that much money, however cleverly or indirectly, in 1963.

The philosopher Jean Jacques Rousseau, at a far removal from Richard Cushing in time and tidings, said something once which may well apply to South Boston's eminent philanthropist Archbishop: "When a man dies, he carries in his clutched hands only that which he has given away."

Archbishop Cushing, because of his money-raising genius, his fetching personal charm, and the spiritual power and force of his being, can and does raise millions of dollars from sources outside the formal diocesan administration. He tells us he has spent two hundred million dollars on new parishes, hospitals, schools, seminaries, and other institutions since becoming Archbishop. "I handle about eight million dollars a year." (The figure is probably closer to eleven, we are told by a layman quite close to the Cardinal.) "I pay no income tax, simply because the money is not mine. I keep it moving, don't possess a dime." And then he repeats another item on which he has never wavered. "Long ago, I took a vow of poverty."

He repeatedly gives the Faithful full credit for all this available money and all this construction and charity:

"We didn't do it. The people did it. And why? They've got confidence in me and the work of the missions. They know that I look upon the Church as primarily a mission church!"

But, again, we know that many millions of this amount were raised because of the charm and force of the Cardinal himself, over and above the devoted thousands in the pews, beyond what is totalled up in the Sunday afternoon clink of the counting parlors in the rectories.

102

"I don't know of any wealthy individual from outside the state who has helped me," he once said. Then he tells the story about the most "unique"—and certainly one of the most generous—benefactors he ever had. The Cardinal fondly remembers a Baptist Republican, an immensely successful businessman, the former Governor of Massachusetts, the late Alvan T. Fuller. "He was an honest, business-like, plain-spoken Yankee," the Cardinal said, "absolutely just, absolutely loyal." The Cardinal relates that Fuller's grandchildren are Catholics and had been out of town when Cushing administered Confirmation at their home church. The Archbishop said he'd be glad to confirm the eligible children in his private chapel.

After the ceremony, the Cardinal tells us, Governor Fuller said to his son—probably Peter—"Let me have that envelope." Therein was a check for one hundred dollars, made out to the Archbishop of Boston. The Governor scrutinized the check, took out his pen and added three zeros to the figure. He also revised the written figure, changing it to "one hundred thousand dollars" and initialing the change: "A.T.F." "From a hundred dollars to a hundred thousand," the Cardinal said. "For any charity I wanted."

He continues: "And every year thereafter, he would invite me to lunch, and at the side of my plate he would put an envelope. He would say nothing about it and in that envelope was one hundred thousand dollars. That is a fact. And there was no publicity on it, none at all."

The Cardinal also revealed that this bountiful, annual gift continued until Governor Fuller's death a few years later.

The following sidelight is also given us by a veteran lay observer of Catholic charities in the Archdiocese. Governor Fuller's widow, the former Grace Davenport of Somerville, is a very devout Catholic. The Governor was most respectful of her religious belief and had agreed to the traditional compliances of mixed marriages, such as raising the children in the Catholic Faith. It is said that every donation given to Protestant denominational charities by the late Governor was matched by an identical sum given to Catholic charities by Grace Davenport Fuller. Her devout and generous influence can thus be discerned in the handsome donations given to Archbishop Cushing by Governor Fuller.

Where else did he, and does he, get the money to help keep the Apostolic Church solvent? Where else did he get the cold cash so mundanely necessary to "make the Encycks click," if we may make an odd use of the phrase of Peter Maurin of the Catholic Worker movement.

What other personal benefactors have been prominent in Cushing's mammoth and incessant fund-raising? The names of Joe Kennedy, the late President Kennedy, the Kennedy family, come quickly to mind.

The Cardinal tells us that the first child he baptized, as a young priest, was deaf and dumb. This profound and moving experience is indelibly etched in his consciousness. Later, the Kennedy family, with their own heart-aches for a retarded child, joined their own solicitude in the field of child rehabilitation with the Archbishop's. Cushing gathered a million and a half dollars for handicapped children. There is a rumor to the effect that Joe Kennedy got up about a third of this amount. But Cardinal Cushing has several times given public credit to Joe Kennedy for the full amount, and who will deny him?

We know for certain that in August of 1946, according to the Boston *Pilot,* Rose Kennedy and a lean, boyish young man named John F. Kennedy presented the Archbishop a check for $600,000 for a retarded children's hospital in Brighton to be called the "Joseph P. Kennedy Jr. Memorial." At the presentation, the future President of the United States, who, astutely enough, was just about to run for Congress, made a brief speech in which he spoke of the family's happiness concerning the Franciscan medical nuns who were to staff the hospital. This group was well-known

104

to the Kennedys, and it was pointed out that the nuns had made the baby clothes in which the late Joe Junior was baptized. The Archbishop repeated this story in his remarks of acceptance, and in the *Pilot* photo we see two of the nuns, along with Rose Kennedy, the svelte young Jack, and the thick-set, strikingly full-faced Archbishop, so much in contrast to the long, gaunt Cardinal of present familiarity.

The loyalty and devotion of the Kennedy family to the Catholic Church and their Boston Ordinary needs no eulogy here. Their personal closeness to the concerns of the Boston Archdiocese goes back through Cardinal O'Connell to Archbishop Williams in the family trees of both the Kennedys and Fitzgeralds. It is easily understandable how Joe, Rose, and the children would take to Archbishop Cushing, and he to them, although some observers say this closeness was due mostly to the late President and the deep, personal friendship which developed between him and the Cardinal from the time of his wedding to Jacqueline.

Joseph Kennedy, Sr., and Richard Cushing—the political *savoir faire* of East Boston and South Boston were of mutual interest and charm. One master fund-raiser must have generated easy and profitable shop-talk with the other. The poor boy from "O" Street, now come lately to ecclesiastical barony, could not help relishing the opulent drawing rooms, sparkling lawns, golden sand vistas, gently swelling cabin cruisers of Hyannisport, especially among handsome, expansive, cultured people of his own race and creed, who were easily the social and cultural match of any Boston Brahmins. There were weddings, baptisms of grandchildren, and other festive and solemn days of note to be presided over by the Archbishop. The Kennedys were indeed, in the late Gov. Paul A. Dever's acute epithet, "the first of the Irish Brahmins." It was normal and natural for their Archbishop to honor them with his presence and friendship, in the sunshine of their glory. To him, and to many of us, they were and are the symbol of Boston-Irish ascendancy beyond the toils of immigration and lowly social, cultural, and economic status.

We will have more to relate about Cushing and the Kennedy family in later pages, particularly with reference to the Cardinal-Archbishop and the late President whom he still calls, without reservation: "My best friend."

With regard to the Kennedy Memorial Hospital, the Kennedy contribution was "only the beginning." Constant care for 150 retarded children, staff and salaries, hospital maintenance and repairs, plus extensive research into the causes of retardation, sponsored by the Kennedy Foundation, were financial considerations that ended up directly in Richard Cushing's lap. The Cardinal will tell you quite candidly, meanwhile, with a characteristic rasp of irritation, that he had to turn around and raise three and a half million dollars to fulfill and expand the entire hospital and research project.

Cushing, in short, raises thousands, perhaps hundreds of thousands of dollars from personal benefactors whose names are legion. They are the contributors, old and young, Catholic and non-Catholic, who mail him checks, money orders, currency, coins, whether spontaneously or in answer to one of many of his special appeals. Their contributions range from less than one dollar into the hundreds. Cushing has for many years acknowledged all contributions in the form of warm, personal letters, enclosing pictures, prayers, or any religious premium he may have at hand like medals, relics of saints, a reprint of something he wrote or preached about Pope John or John Kennedy, in colorful format and on expensive stock.

In a normal business day, we are told, Cushing starts dictating letters at eight o'clock in the morning, and, barring interruptions for personal appointments and engagements, keeps answering letters after lunch, and even after the supper hour until ten P.M. This long and indefatigable routine necessitates two shifts of secretaries who split the assignment of shorthand and typing between eight in the morning and ten at night. It appears that contributors get the same warm greeting and gratitude for one dollar as for a hundred or a thousand, since Cushing assumes that they have given according to their ability no matter what the amount.

One simple secret of the Cardinal's financial success in fund-raising by mail, then, is that people are pleased and grateful for his painstaking acknowledgements, and they keep on sending him money. This is another example of what we call his "unwavering continuity" as person and priest. It is, of course, not at all similar to his glaring intellectual and at times social "inconsistencies." But the latter are among the valleys in the fertile spread of his spirit and personality. Above the valleys loom his qualities, and they will one day make his peccadilloes seem only matter for a warm amusement, which is very close to love.

Betimes, at the office, the Cardinal is liable to be on one of several of the Residence telephones and extensions. And if you're lucky enough or important enough to have his private, unlisted number, which he seems to hand out to people he likes with complete trust and generosity of spirit, he is very likely to pick up the phone himself with a vocal blast that may unseat you: "THIS IS THE ARCHBISHOP!"

Strangers and the guileless who try to get hold of him by phone usually end up talking to some one on the published Chancery line. At that number you're liable to get some devout lady who may have been there when Cardinal O'Connell was big boss. There you'll get the protective bit which is quite prevalent in second or third echelons: "What is it you want to talk to the Cardinal about?" These echelons in the Chancery and at the Residence are also a source of daily information for "the palace guard," who in the routine of the Cardinal's surpassing informality sometimes

107

get no information at all until some Archdiocesan change of policy is a *fait accompli,* known to all the world but them.

For example, when the Cardinal got home from the second session of the Vatican Council he decided to do something about increasing the number of Sunday evening masses. Traditionally, if you were a night worker or late Sunday sleeper in the Archdiocese, you could make early evening masses in downtown Boston at St. James' Church and the Jesuit Church, St. Mary's in the North End. Later, the Franciscans at the Arch Street Shrine and the Paulists at their Park Street chapel also got into this accommodating and lucrative act. The Cardinal, however, was now aware that some members of the Saturday night set, largely younger Catholics, were sleeping late on Sunday mornings and not getting to Mass. Genuinely exhausted workers, businessmen, housewives, too, he told us, might have good reason to sleep on Sunday mornings and might not want to make the effort to go into Boston for evening Mass. He spoke of the senior citizens, the old folks, and of how so many of them had the problem of time on their hands and actually would go to an extra evening Mass on Sundays if there was one nearby.

He said he didn't want to get involved with the Chancery in a discussion of the administrative and local problems connected with such a move. So, very much like his great patron Pope John, he waited for a timely church gathering and bluntly announced that from now on all the parishes had his permission to celebrate Sunday evening Masses if they so desired. He heartily urged Pastors to avail themselves of the permission, and many did so. In some parishes it works and in some it doesn't, as far as attendance shows. But for those who find evening Mass easier, it has been well worth the Cardinal's effort.

If your telephoning business is serious and intelligent, you're very likely to end up with the Cardinal's present Secretary, Monsignor Joe Maguire. Formerly, you'd hear the pleasant voice of Father Lawrence Riley. And back in the late forties and early fifties you could have been talking to a famous former Secretary, Father John Wright, now Bishop of Pittsburgh.

And of course Richard James Cushing himself might just pick up that phone and talk to you—depending on his mood or the state of his health—with cold gruffness or with the solicitous warmth of an old Irish uncle.

Among the current and outstanding lay benefactors of the Cardinal Archbishop, two can be mentioned who are as friendly with Cushing as most. They are Joseph E. Sullivan, age seventy, "same as the Cardinal," a well-heeled Lowell printer; and Middlesex County Sheriff Howard Fitzpatrick, in his fifties, who runs a prominent and widely successful catering business in Greater Boston. Both are long-time supporters of Cushing from their own personal wealth, and both have been even more helpful to him when a fund drive is on, because of their affable and thoroughgoing money-raising ability. Both could also be classified as "B.C.L.'s," Big Catholic Laymen, for their hearty, handshaking, head-table style. Yet it is Sullivan who is perhaps closer to the Cardinal in the more intimate family ways of Holy Mother the Church.

Howard Fitzpatrick, a seemingly invulnerable bachelor, has been prominent in many of Cushing's fund-raising activities. Much of his good work in Catholic charities is often obscured by the hoopla and cigar smoke of big-hotel-orientated political fund-raising for the Democratic Party. But the Archbishop knows what Fitzpatrick does for the Church, and that seems to be satisfaction enough for the High Sheriff of Middlesex.

Joe Sullivan, the widowed father of nine children, enjoys quite a reputation as a humorist and raconteur. He is the brother-in-law of the late Monsignor Tom Reynolds, former Rector of Holy Cross Cathedral and one of the former and very exclusive Consultors of the Archdiocese. It was at the Cathedral that wise-cracking, big-hearted Joe Sullivan met Father Dick Cushing. "His room in the Cathedral Rectory was right next to Tom's and I used to drop in and visit him a lot when he was with the Propagation of The Faith." Sullivan, a Knight of Malta, Knight of the Holy Sepulcher, and honorary degree holder from Boston College, also enjoys a close friendship with Francis Cardinal Spellman. He is known as a great advocate of better human and community relations on the part of religious orders and institutions.

Sullivan tells this rather wry anecdote about something that happened to him and Archbishop Cushing: "Boston's Archbishop Cushing gave $100,000 to a hospital drive I was running." (This could mean that Sullivan helped Cushing raise the money, or gave him full credit for raising it.) "The day of the dedication I arrived at the hospital with His Excellency fifteen minutes early. I asked Sister Superior to assign one of her nuns to escort the Archbishop to a room where he could vest. The Sister had us climb three flights of stairs. Both His Excellency and I were then sixty-three years of age, and there are three elevators in the hospital. Sister escorted us to the men's room."

Joe Sullivan is probably responsible for getting the Executive Director of Rockingham Park, Lou Smith, and his enthusiastic wife Lutza, actively interested in the Cushing Charity Fund. Rockingham Park is a major New England track for thoroughbred horse racing and harness racing, in picturesque Salem, New Hampshire. Joe Sullivan and his sons print twenty-five religious magazines, some of them for free. But they make most of their money running off pari-mutuel tickets and racing programs for seventy-seven horse and dog tracks throughout the country. It is said that Lou Smith was Sullivan's first race-track printing customer. It figures, then, that Sullivan got Smith interested in Richard James Cushing and his need for funds.

For several years now, Lou and Lutza Smith have given an annual party for Cardinal Cushing's "exceptional children" at the Kennedy Hospital. At this affair the Cardinal

110

is annually presented a substantial check. Most of the money comes from ticket-selling for a chicken barbecue and big-name entertainment—which is offered by the Smiths on a mid-summer Sunday afternoon at Rockingham Park.

Contributions are also solicited from their many friends in the sporting world by the easy-going Lou and the persistent Lutza. Any owner or trainer of thoroughbred horses, stabled at Rockingham, is by now well aware of Cardinal Cushing's "exceptional children." It is almost legend, the way Lutza hunts down every last Rockingham possibility in behalf of the Cardinal's fund. "Here comes Lutza!" is something of an alarm bell among horsemen and habitués of Rockingham Park, between races. But great credit is due Lutza and Lou for the fund-raising they do, and do well for their non-sectarian fund for crippled children, most or all of which is administered by Cardinal Cushing.

The Smiths are among the pioneers from the Jewish community in contributing to the Cardinal's financial needs. They had their own little ecumenical movement going, it would seem, long before the brotherhood break-through became the thing to do.

From such hints, then, we get an answer to the question of normal, wide-eyed curiosity: "Where does he get all that money?"

Richard Cushing undoubtedly has other sources, great and humble, but the money comes largely: from the people in the pews; from people like the Fullers, the Kennedys, the Joe Sullivans, Howard Fitzpatricks, the Lou Smiths; from his personal, vocal appeals; from his person-to-person direct mail operation; and from almost any one who comes in personal contact with him and is fetched by the bigness and the charm and the fire of the man.

CHAPTER XII

The Political Image:
Emergent and Dissolving

"I cannot find language strong enough to bear the burden of moral judgment that must fall upon those individuals who poison politics with dishonesty and corruption. These are genuine subversives who turn to wickedness the good order of society."—Richard Cardinal Cushing, "Moral Values and the American Society": 1961

Those from outside the Bay State who look on Boston and Massachusetts generally as a kind of political jungle must wonder about Cushing's relationships with politicians, most of whom, in a predominantly Democratic state, are practising Catholics of Irish or Italian extraction. Did they help him get his building and fund-raising programs off the ground? With influence? With money? The chances are the Cardinal might now say a vehement "No!" But the politicoes, both elected and appointed, may well have helped him in the first decade or more of his Archbishopric.

Even though Cardinal Cushing has by now achieved an identity, long desired and long pursued, as a man concerned with Universal charity and the Universal Church, he is still sensitive about any accusation or even passing association with "a political image." Benevolent and admiring as he is in his public and off-the-cuff remarks about Cardinals O'Connell and Spellman, he seems to deplore mention of any crass political association or projection which might threaten to detract from the spiritual depth, administrative skills, and other talents of these two distinguished men, one living and one dead.

For his own part, with the blood and bone of South Boston so integral to him, one would think Cushing would have more political savvy born and bred in him than O'Connell and Spellman put together. But he didn't. And he doesn't. Cushing is still naive, guileless, completely open-hearted with journalists, special pleaders, rank opportunists of all stripes. He tends to trust people over and over again, and has been burned repeatedly for it—often in the daily press—and in who knows how many other areas?

His earliest baptism of fire with the press probably came when newsmen attracted by his approachability would phone him directly, upon hearing rumors of various parish and administrative changes. The trusting Archbishop's answer would go along these lines: "Well, it's going to be in *The Pilot* Saturday, anyway, so I suppose I can tell you . . ." What the Archbishop didn't quite realize was that he was giving veteran newsmen a beat of which they were going to take advantage, unless specifically forbidden to do so. Newsmen live by news, and if they have information, they are supposed to let it out before their competitors; they—and their city editors—could hardly be expected to sit on what, with the Cardinal, was often practically an open secret. Naively enough, the Cardinal's assumption in those early years would be that the newsman wouldn't use the information prematurely. But it sometimes happened, of course, that such news broke in the daily papers before the Pastors or administrators involved knew about their fall from, or ascent to, glory. This could wreak havoc, and the Archbishop would be the first to resent the unfairness and the uncharity of it when members of his clerical family were involved.

This same openness and approachability was, of course, very magnetic to the politicoes. The stunning, initial popularity of the new Archbishop was both personally and pragmatically attractive to elected and appointed Catholic officials in the State House and in the cities and towns of Greater Boston, if not throughout the entire Commonwealth. The grim reality of the great financial and construction needs of the Archdiocese in the fluxing, tumultuous post-war world was just then falling on the Archbishop's shoulders. He needed the help of all his people, the politicians included. And they needed him: the normal friendship and normal gratitude which could be earned or cultivated with their big, cordial, generous Archbishop was vastly important to civic executives, law-makers, and the law enforcement leaders who were, in a sense, associates with Richard Cushing in preserving and improving traditional standards of public security and morality.

Immediately ahead of the Archbishop in the vital, late forties and deep into the nineteen fifties lay his great program of finance and construction. Through that period, three Roman Catholic Governors, all Democrats: Maurice J. Tobin, Paul A. Dever, and Foster Furcolo, were to be in office. Furcolo, a two-term Governor, and the first Italian-American to hold that exalted office, would be followed in 1960 by another Italian-American, but this time a Republican, John A. Volpe, who is perhaps the most devout and active Catholic Churchman of all Massachusetts Governors. These Governors proved loyal, devoted, and generous to the Archbishop, whether he actively sought their help or not. But then so were the people of Boston and of the Commonwealth in general. There was a time, of course, when things were the other way around in Boston and throughout the Bay State. Irish immigrants and their descendants still have twinges of bitterness about the old Yankee-Protestant overlordship in city, town, and state (as the Italians now have somewhat the same feelings about the Irish). The Irish and the other early immigrants couldn't out-buy the Yankee Republicans, but they did outbreed them in Boston and across the state. The present numerical superiority of Democrats over Republicans in Massachusetts represents in large part the mathematical progression of Democratic offspring through three or four generations.

The bitterness and reverse prejudice against Yankee

114

Protestants is now almost a thing of the past. Greater Boston has become more and more a cosmopolitan community. The many cataclysmic shiftings, interminglings, and intermarriages of World War II; the impact of personages like Cushing himself; the symbolic rise of the urbane Kennedy family and others like them; the phenomenal progressive stirrings of the Universal Church—all these factors have changed the face of Boston. This spreading ecumenical spirit, at once religious, social, economic, has fostered warmth and brotherhood which is beginning to penetrate the darkest corners of ancient and stubborn prejudice, on all sides. Archbishop Cushing was not slow to discover, among the first of the Irish to do so, that the post-war Catholics of his Archdiocese were recast in a brand new melting pot in which Irish and Italians, Polish, French, Armenians, Greeks, and so on, were to be augmented by many new racial and religious varieties. Defense workers, war brides, students from out of state and from foreign lands, professional people in the electronics firms and the hospitals, came to like Boston and permanently settled there. Many of these newcomers were good, practising Catholics, but they were not all bred in a tradition of unquestioned obedience to Irish spiritual leaders. The post-war Archdiocesan faithful did not figure to be a monolithic group, bending with the glances of some spiritual "Number One." It is to the credit of the new Archbishop that he sensed the change and seemed to understand it.

Moreover, the Irish themselves were changing, and so was the hierarchy, at least in the person of Richard James Cushing. He had said as much in his semi-private remarks to his clergy at the Installation luncheon: ". . . we are not by right the overlords of our people, we are their servants."

Politically, Cushing did not cotton to the idea of being "Number One" as Cardinal O'Connell had been at the State House on Beacon Hill. Cushing tells us informally, as we mentioned earlier, that O'Connell would have been a churchman of greater renown, had he not involved himself in "controversial subjects," which we may surely translate to mean, at least partially, by "politics."

In his review of Cardinal Spellman's biography, *The Cardinal Spellman Story*, Cushing expressed a regret at not finding in the book more of the charming, personal side of Spellman which he knew and admired in the man, and which he believed thousands of readers would want to experience vicariously. This seemed to be his way of saying that the Spellman biography, willy-nilly, tended to project somewhat of a political image.

Since Cushing seems today hypersensitive and discerning concerning the danger of political involvement, it could well be that he was exposed to this danger in the first resilient decade of his Archbishopric. For it is a matter of public record that some of his lesser but nonetheless remunerative fund-raising projects derived a certain legitimate impetus from direct and indirect political influence in city, county, town, and state, within the Archdiocesan borders. To give one symbolic example: cylindrical cardboard coin containers began appearing on Greater Boston bars, sponsored by the "Caritas Guild," which is composed largely of Catholic liquor dealers and other beverage workers in Greater Boston, banded together presumably to raise the ethical standards of their profession—and also to help the Archbishop raise money for charity. Their motives are sincere and their devotion to the Archbishop is admirable. They gained a certain respectability for their profession, of course, in these fund-raising projects; who would deny them that?

Any one who knows politics, however, will understand how many political strings are tied to the commerce of alcoholic beverages, from distillery to consumer, at home, or over the bar. To get coin containers on the majority of Greater Boston bar tops, for example, would seem to require clearance, or at least good will, from the state Alcoholic Beverages Commission, the bartenders union, the teamsters' union which delivers the beverages, and, of course, the police and local licensing officials who sometimes with maneuverable haloes are always involved in the lucrative calisthenics of the liquor trade.

In recent years the Archbishop's coin containers seem to have disappeared from the bars, although the Caritas Guild apparently continues to do yeoman's work in the Cardinal's periodical charity drives. It is entirely conceivable that as Cushing became seasoned as Archbishop he became more sensitive to the danger of the earlier types of promotion, however well-intentioned. For there have been other coin containers on those bar tops in behalf of various secular charities like cerebral palsy, the Jimmy Fund for child polio victims, etc. But only in an overwhelmingly Catholic community like Greater Boston could one get away with such an overtly pro-Catholic, pro-Archbishop, money-collecting drive.

Through the late forties and into the fifties, the Archbishop also became identified with a project called "The Archdiocesan Waste Paper Drive," which probably picked up some of its practical momentum from the waste paper drives which were part of the homefront war effort. The Archdiocesan version got to be quite an elaborate, regularly scheduled project. Announcements came periodically from the parish altars at Sunday Mass, telling the Faithful of "St. Swithin's Parish" when they were expected to bale up their old newspapers and magazines to deposit on their sidewalks.

A press release from Monsignor George M. Dowd of the Catholic Youth Organization appeared, for example, in the pages of *The Pilot* in the fall of 1946. "The same procedure as on the last two Sundays will be followed and householders are requested to bundle their paper securely and place it on the curb by 1 P.M." The drive will "make possible a big contribution for the Archbishop Cushing Charity Fund and replenish stockpiles at New England paper mills." The release said the C.Y.O. was "seeking the donation of trucks to assist with the working of collecting the paper and hauling it to freight yards. Truck owners

117

willing to donate the use of their vehicles for a few hours are requested to communicate with the rectory of the parish in which they live."

So the trucks would come around, on a Sunday afternoon, manned by the C.Y.O boys, and the bales of paper would be roared at full throttle down to the freight yards —by-passing the junk yards—and on to the paper mills. A lot of good-natured ribbing about the whole operation became current; some of it was not so good-natured. In the early fifties the highly controversial Father Leonard Feeney, while raging and storming about "No salvation outside the Church" at his revival-like Sunday afternoon meetings on the Boston Common, used to refer to Archbishop Cushing, with all the sulfuric deadliness of his Irish wit, as "The Archdiocesan Ragman."

At one time, moreover, there was considerable grumbling among junk collectors and junk dealers, and perhaps some danger of religious bitterness since most of the old-time junk men definitely did not come from County Cork. There may have been happiness in the Arab League over Cushing's waste paper drive; there was none among the professional junk men. Still again, hired and donated trucks were involved; non-union help did the work—teen-age boys filled with an enthusiasm and ebullience left over from the Crusades. Local officials were involved: police and sanitary officials had to handle complaints from irate non-Catholic neighbors, who voiced their social and religious displeasure at the sight of stacks of ugly newspapers set up along front lawns, and the racket of great, noisy trucks groaning through hushed, elmy streets on the Sabbath, which they had been taught to keep holy.

The Archdiocesan Waste Paper Drive was a very profitable venture, regardless of its droll and sometimes awkward community relations. Here are the published figures: In the Spring of 1946, 3500 tons of paper were collected, yielding $53,555 to the Archbishop's Charity Fund; in the Fall of 1946, 4200 tons were handled, bringing in $64,500. The

Spring drive in 1947 yielded 5200 tons, for $90,460. The hope was expressed, at that time, that the Fall, 1947, drive would achieve the high-water mark of $100,000. And as the radio jingle lyrically used to insist: "No over*head!* No over*head!*"

There was little, if any, harmful publicity about the waste paper project, but the word was getting around in political circles, and questions arose about whether the solid, but not indispensable financial return was worth all the bother. Highly placed people sometimes had to get on the telephone to smooth things over with those who complained too loudly. The present, more sophisticated Cardinal is no longer the sometimes overzealous young Archbishop; and we may wonder if he'd have anything to do with the paper drive, on such a vast scale, were he to face it all over again. Of course, in a much lower key, the waste paper drive still continues, is perhaps tolerated, because of the well-intentioned who are willing to put their time and effort into it for the C.Y.O. Presently, the faithful who still wish to help out, bring their tied-up old newspapers to Catholic school-yards on certain appointed days and hours. Bales of rags and old clothes are also collected in the school yards—still to the dismay of the junk dealers, of course.

The coin boxes and the bales of old newsprint did not prove to be a serious involvement in politics. They were all part of Cushing's colorful development from the lusty, provincial Boston-Irish Bishop to the world-figure of fearless conviction and monumental humanitarianism which he is today.

Over the years, however, the Archbishop attracted the friendship and fund-raising devotion of a few well-intentioned political Irishmen who later were involved in serious public scandal. The Archbishop was hurt in two ways by these unforseeable events: his good, loyal, compassionate heart was involved; and his own image as Archbishop may have temporarily suffered.

One of the officials who was to scoot briefly across the

path of Cushing's steady climb, early in his Archepiscopal career, was a high, local Internal Revenue appointee of President Harry Truman. This jolly fellow, let's call him "Mr. Shamrock," was a very popular Irish tenor on the banquet circuit of the politicians. The cold roast banquets of Yankee Boston had by now been replaced with the hot, raw roast beef and rubbery chicken of the political banquet circuit. Picture the difference. The parlors and sun porches of the well-to-do Irish were well-heated in winter-time: a guest could have more than one drink, and even get to see and know everyone that lived in the house. On the other hand, an Irishman who visits a wainscoted Yankee town house or country estate completes his social or business call with the master of the house in a sedate drawing room, fully aware that there are all sorts of people in the cool recesses of that establishment whom he will never get to meet, precisely because some or all of those others decidedly do not want to meet him. Now Mr. Shamrock was a type of the highly personable, talented, opportunistic Irishman making his way to the top via politics. He was in great demand as an Irish tenor at various civic and charitable dinners and was lionized, too, in the gatherings on the "Irish Riviera," the South Shore colonies of Scituate and Cohasset.

At these public festivities, there used to be a cocktail party in a private room for guests of head-table rank, while *hoi polloi* roistered at an open bar in some large room adjacent to the grand ballroom. Later the head-table guests would file into the ballroom for dinner, while the orchestra played sprightly music. If the Archbishop were there, as occasionally he would be, though rarely if the event were political, he might give the invocation. Some one like Mr. Shamrock would then sing the "Star-Spangled Banner" in a great, blasting Irish voice—defiant of, and soaring over, the blare of the band. Then everybody sat down to eat, or kept on drinking, or both.

Later, Mr. Shamrock would render a few popular Irish

ditties, in good and lusty voice, not without, however, a delicate, fetching tribal whine. It never failed. "My Wild Irish Rose," "Galway Bay," and "When Irish Eyes are Smiling" can seem grossly vulgar and shallow in the cold light of day. But sitting there, suffused with the warmth of a few amber glasses, with the rich roast beef running crimson before them, in a festive company, in a kingly hall, the politicians thought it was the very singing of the angels.

Then someone like the wily and seemingly indestructible Massachusetts Governor's Councillor, Patrick "Sonny" McDonough, who has run successful fund-raising parties for the Cardinal, would get up and tell a few of his patented funny stories. Sometimes they really were funny, and truly made even those laugh out loud who didn't go for portly, red-faced Boston-Irish politicians.

This same McDonough and a goodly number of pols and political hangers-on still spend a lot of their time at a Beacon Street oasis formerly known as "The Boston Club," about which there is this story. The political image of the establishment once became so pronounced that a new owner, riding the publicity of a Hollywood movie, changed the name to Tiffany's. A freshet of office girls and matrons was attracted to the refurbished huddling spot for a while. But the older crowd prevailed, the seekers after new restaurants drifted away, and occasional tourists and newcomers who wander in are still mildly curious about the name. The answer, of course, is that a new movie has quickly become an old movie, forgotten by all but the sentinels of the late, late show. A recent Supreme Court decision, petitioned by Tiffany, the famous New York jeweler, has ordered this restaurant to drop the Tiffany name.

Meanwhile, at Tiffany's not too long ago, Sonny McDonough ran a fund-raising party for the Cardinal. The new owner, Ben White, who also races horses, began with a lavish spread of hot and cold *hor d'oeuvres* and choice liquors, at Sonny's request. All had a fine time, a substantial sum of money was raised for the Cardinal's charities, and

121

Ben White ultimately presented a bill to Sonny for $1100.

Sonny handed the bill back to Ben. "This is your contribution to the Cardinal Cushing Charity Fund," he said.

"If I had known that," Ben told this writer, "I'd have put on an even bigger splash, and made the party much more deductible in taxes."

This little story is significant in that it gives some insight into how some of these fund-raising affairs were handled, though even the Cardinal was unaware of it. The Sonny McDonoughs and the Mr. Shamrocks, like most Irishmen in Boston, professional and otherwise, are passionately devoted to their Archbishop and to their Faith, each after his fashion.

In order to help Cushing raise funds more definitely, Mr. Shamrock once collaborated with the Archbishop in a lyrical and prayerful St. Patrick's record album which enjoyed a certain commercial and popular success throughout the Archdiocese. Bostonians away from Boston received this old-type record album—I remember receiving it in Chicago in 1949—and it aroused great nostalgia for the churches and tribal rites of Irish Boston. The Archbishop's doughty portrait adorned the album folder, against a background of green and shamrocks. Mr. Shamrock's photograph may have been on the jacket somewhere also, if memory serves us rightly.

The recordings were abundant with great-voiced readings of the prayer of St. Patrick by Richard Cushing, against a background of Irish martial music played on a meandering but vigorous piano. There were also popular Irish ballads, like "Galway Bay," stoutly rendered by Mr. Shamrock.

The album may well have raised some money. The initial phase of the Archbishop's regime was in full swing, and that first great glow of love and support for him must have found a practical outlet in things like the purchase of this album. But not too long after this unfortunate lyrical honeymoon, Mr. Shamrock was sent to the Federal penitentiary for using his influence a little too assiduously at the Bureau of Internal Revenue, and the albums disappeared from the market.

A contrast leaps to mind today between the lyrical, commercial St. Patrick's record album of the trusting young Archbishop and a later long-playing recording sponsored by the great, world-renowned Cardinal in 1964. At the Memorial Mass for the late President John F. Kennedy, the entire majestic proceedings were recorded in Holy Cross Cathedral by RCA Victor. From Mr. Shamrock to the Boston Symphony Orchestra, in less than fifteen years!

Thus did the Archepiscopal political involvement, through no serious fault of Richard Cushing, wax and wane.

This involvement, under the sporadic impulse of local and national events, was to grow and glimmer again in the late fifties and early sixties: in the turmoil of the Boston mayoralty election, in 1959; in the glory of the Presidential triumph of 1960; in the comic opera tragedy of the Key Shop Bookie Raids in 1961, involving the Boston Police and the Archbishop's ill-fated friend, Police Commissioner Leo Sullivan. But all this was for Boston and his own kind. The Cardinal was to show his love and loyalty throughout, unworried about the loss of a political image and, in the final analysis, triumphant over it. But he has remained sensitive to reminders of the old type of image, concerning O'Connell, Spellman, and, yes, himself!

CHAPTER XIII

Into the Fifties: Warrior of the Pulpit

". . . a youthful David, a shepherd of Christ's flock and a man after Christ's own heart . . . In this fateful hour of history, such a man and leader God has given to this beloved Archdiocese of Boston."—Francis Cardinal Spellman on Cushing, April 7, 1946

The liberalism would come later, the checkered liberalism, if you will. But in the late forties, and on into the mid-fifties, Archbishop Cushing was decidedly a man of his time: a flaming and awesome crusader against Communism at home and abroad. He denounced the Reds constantly, identifying them totally with the Devil, in all their works and all their pomp.

Liberals and liberalism, to him, and indeed to most priests and Bishops, were dirty words. Tito, Archbishop Stepinac, Red-fronting Protestant Ministers, Henry Wallace, Louis Budenz, the Dies Committee, Nixon and Hiss, Whittaker Chambers, J. Edgar Hoover, and the oncoming dark angel of anti-Communism, Senator Joe McCarthy— these were among the feudal names of the times, and Cushing was alert to them, for and against, depending on their posture on Communism, liberalism, fellow-travelling.

Even years later, in March of 1964, as a great Prince of the Church, Cushing was to say in reference to Fidel Castro: "When I see a bird that walks like a duck, and swims like a duck and quacks like a duck, I call that bird a duck." Perhaps earlier he had not the grace and sophistication to sum up his attitude so succinctly, but basically his outlook was the same. Although now more resilient toward liberals,

124

both in politics and religion, his rigid hatred and ferocity against Communism has been, for him, marvelously consistent over the years. He was "agin" it, and "agin" anybody and everything associated with progressive movements which in any way were parallel, tangential, peripheral, concentric, orbital, or even legitimately conscious of the debt that the New Deal, the Fair Deal, the Welfare State owed to Socialism and Communism.

This attitude eventually brought Cushing into some uncomfortable positions with Robert Welch, the John Birchers, Senator McCarthy, and others, it is true; but his heart bled for Stepinac, Mindzenty, and the others; he felt outraged and helpless before the imprisonments, tortures, confiscations, and ejections of Bishops, priests, nuns, and brothers in the formerly great and fertile Catholic missions of China. The "fiend of righteousness" was in him and he allowed it to speak out with eloquence in newspaper comment on the events of the day. "A youthful David . . . ," the great Bishop of New York had called him, at the formal conferring of the Pallium in April of 1946. Spellman, more quiet and methodical in his approach, was himself one of the world's most convinced adversaries of the Marxists and the Pinks. Spellman, wilier than Cushing in the interest of the Universal Church, was perhaps responsible for unleashing Cushing's antipathy toward Marxism and the general blight of materialism which surged through Europe, China, and America itself. Cushing was Spellman's protégé, one who would reach to the heights of the master in more matters than that of Communism, and who would surpass him in many.

Meanwhile, less than a year after he was consecrated Archbishop, Richard Cushing was to recommend the beloved and scholarly Rev. Doctor Louis J. Kelleher for appointment as his Auxiliary Bishop.

In this recommendation, we can recognize Cushing's remarkable admiration for, and vicarious pleasure in, honoring men of intellect and scholarship. Master of the rough-hewn pose with prosaically-minded cronies, Cushing is nonetheless unfailing when a tribute or good act toward men of goodwill and intellect is due. He could have chosen his auxiliary from a number of others. Secretaries and intellects of impressive clerical stature surrounded him, the vigorous and seasoned survivors of Cardinal O'Connell's palace guard; men like Monsignors Minihan, Stapleton, Splaine, McKenzie, Fathers Walter Furlong and the onrushing John Wright. The last named, especially, was steeled with the determined will of ambition, urbane and charming of speech and manner, dazzling with rich continental wit and erudition. But Cushing chose Kelleher, the noble Roman, the scholar. It was a happy choice: the former lector at St. John's Seminary conferring the dignity of the episcopacy upon his professor. Moreover, the appointment made the Archbishop of New York quite happy, for, to Spellman, Kelleher was more than an intellectual mentor, he was a close and abiding friend.

Archbishop Cushing remarked when the designation from Pope Pius XII arrived: "I am naturally profoundly grateful to the Holy Father for providing our busy diocese with an Auxiliary Bishop. The Bishop-Elect is a former professor of mine at St. John's Seminary. As a professor he was one of the best. He always aspired to the highest ideals of the priesthood. He has been an irreproachable priest." A pundit, concurrently, conferred a wry accolade: "Dr. Kelleher's style is often noted for a rugged simplicity, original thought, an abundance of ideas presented with an economy of phrase. His purity of style is not unlike that of the public addresses of the late President Calvin Coolidge."

Surely, the style of Dr. Kelleher would not allow the folksiness of Coolidge's laconic public statement. We recall, for example, that when Coolidge was asked the topic of his minister's sermon at the preceding service, Coolidge answered: "Adultery."

"What did he say about it?"

"He was against it," Coolidge replied.

A far remove from the academic eloquence of Rev. Dr. Louis Kelleher.

This same pundit—in the *Pilot*—must have benefited as a seminary student under the humane Bishop-Elect Kelleher. He wrote tersely: "He was in charge of the Philosophy Department, and was willing to look the other way on minor infractions of the rule." Had Seminarian Richard Cushing experienced this aspect of Professor Kelleher's character? Very likely.

Dr. Kelleher's remarks of acceptance were, however, Coolidge-like in their brevity. Said the Bishop-Elect: "I do not possess the boundless energy of Archbishop Cushing and I am far short of the driving force of his leadership, which has caught up and carried with it the admiration and enthusiastic loyalties of our Catholic people. What strength is mine, I pledge to him to be absorbed in his unwearied labors for the flock."

"Do not possess the boundless energy . . ." said Bishop Kelleher, who was to become the deeply revered pastor of the hilltop parish of St. Catherine of Genoa in Somerville. His health may have been fading even then. He was to be dead, suddenly, within a year and a half, November 26, 1946, at the age of fifty-seven. Yet he lived long enough to travel to the Roman Consistory in March of that year and stand beside his friend, Francis Spellman, to read the official letter from Pope Pius XII which declared the latter a Prince of the Church.

Archbishop Cushing's statement at his Auxiliary's abrupt demise was simple and moving: "The sudden death of Bishop Kelleher has shocked and grieved us all. I have lost a devoted co-worker in behalf of souls. Bishop Kelleher was an exemplary priest and Bishop and in him the entire community venerated an eloquent spokesman of moral idealism."

The Archbishop, before and after Kelleher's death, maintained his startling and original pace. Early in March of 1946 he gave the universal church a harbinger of what mission technique he was to use in Latin America. He lent five priests to the Bishop of Sioux Falls, South Dakota. On the 29th of June, in a colorful and moving seaside ceremony, which has become an annual event, he blessed the fishing fleet at Gloucester.

Twenty-two years later, he was still keeping the tradition. On the 29th of June, 1964, in the week of his 25th anniversary of consecration as a Bishop, he blessed the fishing fleet, amid a wild demonstration of parade and tribute. After the ceremony he sailed up the coast to the Boston Fish Pier in an ungainly old fishing trawler. He ate lobster aboard with Portuguese and Italian fishermen and lustily cracked open the claws with a monkey wrench.

In the late forties, Cushing began to tune up for Tito and the Communists, pinks and fellow-travelers in general. In a speech to 3000 members of the Veterans of Foreign Wars who attended mass at the Holy Cross Cathedral, during their convention in Boston, the rising episcopal stentor declared: "We are probably the only nation in the world that permits, tolerates, and at times blesses the parlor pinks, the fellow travellers, and out-and-out Communists who thrive in our midst." He referred to such persons as "moral Quislings."

One must here recall the temper of the times and realize that Cushing could make uncomfortable a lot of honest, non-Communist liberals, who nonetheless had strong and unshakable convictions about Civil Rights for all political parties, about aid to Yugoslavia and other Balkan countries, about the high-living, free-spending autocrats, General and Madame Chiang Kai-shek, who knew how to manipulate American-bestowed money and supplies for private gain. Among anti-Communist liberals there were a good percentage of Catholics who considered themselves loyal and devout sons of the Church. Many of the latter in Boston and elsewhere were members of the academic community, journalists, lawyers. Blanket anti-Communist condemnations from church and political pulpits very often cast a pall over them, whether intentionally or not. Speakers at Holy Name Societies were notoriously loose in their sweeping condemnations of Communists, fellow-travelers, and those who did not agree with the speakers themselves.

At a Holy Communion breakfast one Sunday in the late forties, for example, I remember an irate Holy Name Society speaker, who paid tribute to Archbishop Cushing's anti-communist crusade, refer to those liberals who had protested the picketing of a movie by the Catholic War Veterans—it might have been *Forever Amber*—as "the pinkoes and the stinkoes!"

Liberal Catholic journalists, teachers, and lawyers—those who contributed or subscribed to *The Commonweal*, for example—bore much of this abuse in the late forties and early fifties; they were never sure whether they were thought of as the pinkoes or the stinkoes, but they knew their views weren't popular.

Before he finally found the range on Tito, whom he was to shower with bitter and uncompromising invective, Cushing led his flock on the first of several pilgrimages to holy places. This one was relatively short, to Quebec, at the shrine of St. Anne de Beaupré, from July 23 to 25. His piety was of an old, traditional style. His piety and his politics supported one another: holy places of the past and anti-Communism.

In what we consider to be two of Richard Cushing's greatest public addresses, one in July and one in September of 1946, we see the young Archbishop at the height of his oratorical power. At the invitation of Cardinal Spellman, Archbishop Cushing traveled to Maryknoll, New York, late in July and, with Spellman presiding, delivered a departure address to seventeen young Maryknoll missionaries. In the address Cushing summed up the very essence of his philosophy of the missions, and it is to be emphasized that here, on the subject of the missions, he has ever been consistent:

129

We call you the best of Americans and say that no one can possibly do as much for America as you are going to do. Yet here is the strange paradox of your relationship henceforth to your native land: No one serves America so wonderfully as you do, and in no one must love for one's own people be so strictly disciplined and personal patriotism be so subordinated to other loves and loyalties.

You are the finest possible representatives abroad of your nation; you are its most convincing goodwill ambassadors. But you must never act out of mere patriotism nor ever directly seek the promotion of the national interests of your fatherland.

Above all, you must never mix politics with the preaching of the supra-national gospel. You must never enforce upon others the institutions or the language or the tradition of your own nation. Yet by your very detachment and your Catholic universalism you will cause the true American character to be first respected, then loved, then imitated by all who come to know you.

No political state has any right to ask you to do its work for it in the mission fields but, strangely enough, when you do your own work as Catholic missionaries you will win more friends for the America which produced you than any other group of Americans could possibly win.

This address by a young American Archbishop, back in 1946, almost sounds like a charter for The Peace Corps of 1960. Echoes of a solid liberal and international attitude are heard in this code of conduct for young missionaries sojourning to the undeveloped nations.

In September of 1946 at the consecration of Most Rev. Daniel J. Feeney as Auxiliary Bishop of Portland, Maine, Cushing delivered a remarkable talk on what it means to be a Bishop. This address is worthy of an anthology, not only because of its eloquence, but because of its sense of tradition. It identified the trials of the past with those of the present. Archbishop Stepinac of Yugoslavia was in custody and on trial for the monstrous and ludicrous charge of treason; the Primates of Poland and Hungary were in the shadow of the gaol. It was an appropriate time to analyze the meaning of what it means to be a Catholic Bishop, when three-quarters of the world was as hostile as history had ever seen.

Cushing's view of his own vocation shines through his words. The address may not have pointed to the collegial powers of the bishop, shared with all the bishops of the world. Yet it was somewhat individualistic and juridicial in its conception of all powers coming from the Pope to individual bishops. On the other hand, Cushing revealed a remarkable sense of the community of bishops down through history. It was the historical rather than the present bond of unity that attracted his imagination. And he was passionately American:

What does it mean to be a Bishop? Theology tells us that it means the acquisition of a new and special relationship to Christ, the Good Shepherd of Souls. It means the possession of the fulness of the priesthood and a participation in the powers and privileges of the Apostles. It means to possess a new and special relationship to the Vicar of Christ, the chief shepherd of Christendom; for all Bishops exercise offices, of orders and of jurisdiction, under the direction and authority of the Sovereign Pontiff and in due submission to his primacy.

It means the exercise of new and wonderful powers in the Body of Christ which is His Church; powers of preaching the Gospel and of teaching the Faith; powers of transmitting the priesthood from generation to generation; powers of blessing and consecrating, of guiding and guarding, of confirming, comforting and ordaining, which are proper to the office of a Bishop alone and which are supremely essential to the life of the Church.

History knows that to be a Bishop of the Catholic Church means to be one of a mighty company, one of the men of God who in every Christian century and in all the nations of Christendom have transmitted from Jerusalem to the ends of the earth that Apostolic Succession which like a golden chain, links every Catholic altar to Calvary and every Baptized Catholic to Christ.

It means to be one with such High Priests as St. Cyprian, first great exponent of episcopal dignity; one with St. Irenaeus, Bishop of the infant Church in France and great episcopal champion of orthodoxy; one with the venerable bishops of Alexandria, Caesarea, Constantinople, and of every Pontifex of every ancient See in the days of the Fathers of the Church; one with Augustine, greatest of the Latin Fathers and once an auxiliary bishop; one with Ambrose, acclaimed a bishop by the admiring populace; one with Fulgentius

131

in Africa, Gregory of Tours in France, Isidore of Seville in Spain, Boniface of Germany, Patrick of Ireland, Thomas A. Becket and John Fisher of England. Yes, indeed, my beloved, to be a bishop of the Catholic Church is to share the dignity and enjoy the lustre of High Priests born in every century and famed beyond the seven seas.

A priest who is called to serve as a bishop in our country also takes his place in the glorious litany of the American Hierarchy. A Catholic bishop in America belongs to the company of John Carroll, John De Cheverus, John England, the Kenricks, John Baptist Purcell, Peter John Loras, John Joseph Hughes, John McCloskey, the great brothers Blanchet, John Baptist Lamy, John Baptist David, John Neumann, Louis Joseph De Goesbriand, James Gibbons, John Joseph Williams, John Joseph Glennon, John Ireland, John Lancaster Spalding.

I do not think there have been greater bishops in modern times than these and other bishops in America whom you may recall to mind. There have certainly been no greater Americans in all our national history than these illustrious bishops of the Catholic Church.

Cushing did not mention William Cardinal O'Connell, George Cardinal Mundelein of Chicago, or Francis Cardinal Spellman. He did mention his late contemporary, Cardinal Glennon of St. Louis, who died returning from the Consistory at which he had received the Red Hat. But no living bishops were mentioned. His thoughts of the living were confined to those like Mindzenty in Hungary, Wyzinski in Poland, Walsh in China.

In the days of the Apostles to become a bishop meant to become a candidate for martyrdom. So today, to be a bishop, indeed to be a priest should mean to have a cheerful readiness to die and certainly to live entirely for Christ.

The Church in her long and varied human history has seen times in which her bishops could be great patrons of the arts, scintillating personalities in society, urbane and cultivated associates of the culturally privileged.

The Church in the course of her earthly development has seen times when her prelates could live without the danger of scandal, in the relative ease expected in prosperous days of all who hold places comparable in dignity to the exalted rank of bishop. But we do not now live in such times.

The priest who today dons the mitre and accepts the sacred oils of episcopal consecration, if he wishes to be a bishop in accordance with the needs of the Church, must have a far more disciplined and devout, yea, a more truly divine concept of his calling.

There is no place today for priests or bishops with gold. There is only room for the golden variety that shines with humility, poverty, detachment and an overpowering love of God and souls.

As ever, Cushing deplores the materialism of the clergy. He reveals his own ideal of personal poverty, despite handling millions, and in this, again, he is the man of "unwavering continuity." His address concludes:

My mail is largely a court of appeals, from bishops with only one possession—a supreme torment of souls. For ours is a day when bishops are languishing in prison for Christ.

The language is like that of Georges Bernanos. The hectically busy Archbishop, with the hectically busy building and fund-raising program, in the hectically busy politics-ridden Archdiocese of Boston, just for a moment, sounds like someone from *Diary of A Country Priest*. One wishes, nostalgically, just for a moment, that all Cushing's sermons, statements, pastorals would echo this note.

Bernanos, Bloy, indeed the country Curé himself would applaud Cushing's final assessment of what a Bishop should be, what Cushing is himself and what he will always be, no matter what his alarums and excursions:

" 'Have they made Thee a ruler?' cries the inspired author of the Book of Ecclesiasticus, 'Be not lifted up; be among them as one of them.' "

On Wednesday, September 25, 1946, Cushing paused, typically, to say the Mass of the Holy Ghost at the inauguration of the first college of the Madames of the Sacred Heart in the Boston area. What the Jesuits had traditionally been to the sons of the wealthy in Europe, the Madames are to the daughters of the well-heeled in America. Cushing was glad to have the impeccable Madames in the Arch-

133

diocese. He was not immune to the value of a touch of class here and there.

"You are pioneers," he told the first Freshmen Class of the Newton College of the Sacred Heart, "but remember that it is not stone and buildings that make a college. The GIs are living in tents to get an education because they appreciate what is ahead. You may not enjoy the fullness of college life in the same way as those who will come after you, but I hazard the opinion that the experience of these primitive days will be a joy that will not be had by those to come after."

In 1963 Cushing was to return again to Newton. One of "those to come after," a rather heavy college girl was to share a laugh with him at a reception. The gruff and earthy Cardinal had just blessed the thin-spired new chapel at Sacred Heart College. "Don't kiss my ring," he said to the girl as she began to kneel, "you're too heavy to pull up!" At this solemn and festive chapel dedication, the Cardinal also paid salty tribute to Mother Sweeney's fund-raising ability. Said the rose-garbed prelate to his many listeners: "She's had more gall than I have. And that's a lot of gall!"

In October, 1946, when Archbishop Stepinac had been sentenced to sixteen years of imprisonment at hard labor on Tito's trumped-up charge of collaboration with the Nazis, Cushing was angry:

Archbishop Stepinac is guilty of one crime and one crime only: it is the crime of being an Archbishop of the Catholic Church. That is enough, in the eyes of Red Fascists to warrant his persecution and that of his followers. Anyone who has read the murderous history of Marshall Tito's regime and the inspiring story of Archbishop Stepinac's resistance first to the Nazis and now to the Red Fascists need not be told that the accusers of the Archbishop lie.

The tragic fate of Yugoslavia is another warning to us, it is a bloody and barbaric practical proof of the wisdom with which the late Pope Pius XI uttered this prophetic warning:

"Communism is intrinsically evil and no one desirous of saving Christian civilization will collaborate with it in any undertaking whatsoever."

Strong medicine for a strong time, uttered before the development of a United Nations organization, before UNESCO with which a certain Cardinal Roncalli, later Pope John, was to serve as a liaison officer. It was a decade before Khrushchev and "peaceful co-existence," before the astronauts and the resulting exchanges of data on outer space, before the Test Ban Treaty and the wheat deals executed on behalf of peace and better relations by Cushing's "best friend," J. F. K.

On Sunday, October 13, 1946, the Archbishop of Boston spoke from the pulpit of Holy Cross Cathedral, again in behalf of Stepinac. The flame of his compassion for a beleaguered fellow bishop and of his righteous hatred for the tyranny of Communism flared up before the congregation and the world:

. . . today as I stand in this Cathedral a free bishop, preaching under the protection of a free government, with the inner ear of our common faith, I hear as strongly as if he stood before me the voice of Archbishop Stepinac speaking through me to you and saying: "I serve Jesus Christ Who is God. His is the kingship of David, not Stalin. This is my Gospel in which I suffer even to bonds, as a criminal."

But I am not discouraged and neither must you be. The word of God is not bound and I, though bound, continue to preach it if only in the silence of my sufferings. What I preach in chains, you must use your freedom to preach from the housetops. If we have died with Christ we shall also live with Him; if we endure, we shall also reign with Him; if we disown Him, He also will disown us.

Secretary of State Dean Acheson, who never was very popular with anti-Communist crusaders, and whose later involvement with the Hiss case did not endear him to the American Catholic Hierarchy, did not appear to be vigorous in his protestations against the Stepinac proceedings. The following words of Archbishop Cushing's sermon seem directed against the cool urbanity of the State Department and perhaps also the detachment of the British government with regard to Stepinac's fate.

135

The Communists have the right to fight for their materialistic theory, so we have the right to fight for Christianity. We shall not be silenced, even though others, the political leaders of the world, give the tacit approval of their craven silence to the things that are happening under the Red terrorists.

About ten months later, on Tuesday, August 19, 1947, the Boston Archbishop loosed what may have been his final arrow against the Stepinac injustice and those whom he discerned to be the friends of Tito, in our American back-yard. There was little ecumenical spirit abroad in those tense post-war years, which were only a prelude to the witch-hunts and the anti-Communist hysteria of the early fifties. It would almost seem impossible for the present Cardinal to blast off against a group of Protestant ministers now, in the wake of the understanding he came to share under the late Pope John. But after a committee of American Protestant ministers, some of whom may have been, in fact, Communist fellow-travelers, visited Yugoslavia and blandly issued a favorable report on religious freedom in Tito-land, the sixth bishop of Boston took himself wrathfully to the hustings.

He referred to this committee of American ministers with holy indignation as "the clerical friends of Tito" and "the innocents abroad." ". . . I know full well that they have betrayed their orthodox brethren. But how in the Name of God shall they answer to their freedom-loving Protestant brethren for involving the Protestant name in the Red Fascist scheme to enslave the Christian East?"

The question of Stepinac gradually faded into the background. But Cushing's anti-Communist crusade was on. The men who were to make ruthless political capital of the witch-hunts: the Nixon-Mundt committee, Senator Joe McCarthy, Roy Cohn and G. David Schine, etc., were waiting just around the corner of history.

136

CHAPTER XIV

The Rise of Bishop Wright—The Feeney Case

"Manning had his Newman, Pius XII his Montini, O'Connell his Spellman. It is possible that history will show that Cushing had his Wright."

The rising young secretary of Archbishop Cushing, Father John J. Wright, who had also served on the secretarial staff of Cardinal O'Connell, seemed to reflect the clerical temper of the times when he made these *then* palatable, but *now* somewhat unhappy remarks to the League of Catholic Women at the Copley Plaza, Boston, in February of 1947:

Several easy rules on: "How to Spot A Communist . . ."
Observe the attitude of persons under suspicion toward certain nations. If one objects to Franco and not to Tito, he is a Communist.
The Communists can be recognized by certain over-worked words and phrases: "liberal," "friend of Democracy."
If anyone tells you he suspects a certain prelate of being a fellow traveler, there you have a Fascist.

Such rules were perfectly in keeping with the panic-gathering clouds of the times, but they would not now be uttered by the sophisticated, erudite, and politically astute Bishop of Pittsburgh.

When he made the above statement, John Wright was already, at thirty-eight, a Domestic Prelate with the title of Right Reverend Monsignor. The following May he was to fill the vacancy left by the late Doctor Kelleher, to become Archbishop Cushing's second choice as Auxiliary

137

Bishop. John Wright had a meteoric rise to the dignity of the Episcopacy. Like O'Connell, he scooped up many of the scholastic, literary, and debating prizes at Boston Latin School and Boston College. He was also strong in theological and humanistic studies at the Gregorian University and the North American College in Rome. He became a secretarial aide to Cardinal O'Connell at the ripe old priestly age of thirty-three. The late Monsignor Walter Furlong, former Chancellor of the Archdiocese, and more recently pastor of Our Lady's, Newton, once told two stories about his dear friend, Bishop Wright. One of these was in connection with Cardinal O'Connell and the other concerned Wright's facility with the French language.

In the late fifties, with Archbishop Cushing's hearty approval, several active Catholic trade unionists, including labor journalist John C. Cort, the able and dedicated labor priest, Father Francis McDonnell, labor leader Edward T. Sullivan, and several others, including this author, arrived at the Chancery to see Monsignor Furlong. The group had almost accomplished the reorganization and re-invigorating of the stultified Archdiocesan Catholic Labor Guild. Monsignor Furlong and John Cort struck it off quite cordially, once they discovered a mutual interest in "bird-watching." It was on this occasion that Furlong told this bird-watching story about O'Connell and Wright.

The old Cardinal, a great walker, while strolling about the seminary grounds, encountered Father Furlong and invited him to join the walk. The Cardinal's habit was to walk silently, stop, and then talk. The Cardinal cherished a firm belief that walking and talking at the same time caused a strain on the heart. During one therapeutic pause for conversation, a bird trilled from a neighboring tree.

"Such a pretty robin song!" the Cardinal said.

Father Furlong, even then a rabid birder, rejoined: "That's not a robin, Your Eminence, it's a woodthrush."

"Father Furlong," said the Cardinal, raising himself to the top of His Eminence, "you may go!"

Ten years later, the Cardinal, walking along with the young Father Wright, spied a bird thrashing in a bird bath near the Residence. "Father Wright, just what kind of a bird is that?" the Cardinal asked.

"Your Eminence," Wright diplomatically said, "I'm about the last priest in the Archdiocese who could identify that bird for you."

"Well, you must ask Father Furlong," the Cardinal said with deadly off-handedness. "He'd know."

Meanwhile, at the labor meeting, Monsignor Furlong was showing the group through the Chancery building. He conducted them into the Marriage Court. Beautifully done in dark paneling, it looked like a toy municipal court room. Furlong gestured at a private elevator, "That reminds me of another story about Bishop Wright," he said. "Father Wright was showing several French nuns around the Chancery and Seminary grounds, among them the Very Reverend Mother, or *Tres Reverende Mere* as Father Wright called her. Father Wright in his masterful French was chattering away urbanely with them on various subjects and the nuns were swooning in the radiance of his charm. He then ushered the sisters into the elevator for a trip to the second floor. Suddenly the elevator door slammed shut and the contraption took off with the nuns aboard and Father Wright marooned helplessly on the first floor. The elevator went to the top floor and then started down again. When it reached Wright, he stooped to give instructions as it flashed by on the way to the basement.

"Très Reverende Mère . . ." he called, stooping, as the infernal machine went down. "Très Reverende Mére, push the first red butt . . ." (body action up).

"Très Reverende Mère . . ." (body action down) "push the red . . ."

After about a dozen "Très Reverende Mères," Father

139

Wright ran down to the basement and pulled the master switch, stopping the elevator and everything else electrical in the building.

It was at the eleventh Annual Congress of the Archdiocesan League of Catholic Women, on May 14, 1947, that Archbishop Cushing announced in Wright's presence that the mellifluous Monsignor had been appointed Auxiliary Bishop of Boston by the Holy Father. Monsignor Wright was the highly popular chaplain of the League of Catholic Women and continued on in that role with all those be-furred, be-jeweled, and be-bosomed Catholic matrons for quite some time. The ladies went into a complete tizzy of delight at the news and the Archbishop said some very nice things about the magnetic and scholarly Bishop-Elect: ". . . He is a kindly, priestly, earnest man of God, a young man who will continue to devote his time and energy going among the people, just as he has been doing throughout the years of his ministry, doing good in the service of Our Lord. He has been among my faithful helpers ever since I assumed the burden of my office; now thanks to the goodness of His Holiness he will be consecrated to help me in a very special and intimate way."

For his consecration as the new Auxiliary and Titular Bishop of Tegea, on Monday, June 30, 1947, Bishop Wright had chosen a Jesuit scholar to deliver the keynote sermon, the Reverend Gerald Groveland Walsh, S.J., at that time editor of the learned review, *Thought,* and Wright's former instructor at the Gregorian University. The new Bishop had taken for his motto: "*Resonare Christum,* Echo Christ."

When the ceremony was over, *Te Deum* was sung: "Leading us all in that exultant song will be the dear Father and Friend, Counsellor and Consecrator, who is to intone the opening words *Te Deum laudamus,* our beloved Archbishop Cushing, whose single and undiluted passion it has ever been 'that all the world may know Thee'—how shall he not rejoice that today another mitred apostle of Divine charity and truth has been given to help him in the task of teaching man's muddled and troubled world God's Way and Truth and Life."

The generous and benevolent Cushing was to exhibit, at least privately, a certain coolness and even jaundice toward his brilliant protégé in the oncoming years. This is not an extraordinary human vicissitude among the clergy as among laymen. Manning had his Newman, Pius XII his Montini, O'Connell his Spellman. It is possible that history will show that Cushing had his Wright. Strains on loyalty and difference of opinion among these prelatial duets did not negate a certain union of spirit and respect for each other's personal integrity. We should not be surprised, then, when we in our generation, in our country, witness an instance of a relationship history has often before produced: a patron who remains distant from his protégé.

In one of our long and exhilarating tête-à-têtes with the Cardinal in the winter of 1963-64, we asked him about John Wright in the days he was Cushing's secretary. The Cardinal said Wright was "nominally" his secretary, and he didn't say it in a very friendly manner. We also recollect him as saying: "He was never my secretary. He was all over the place. I could never find him." For Monsignor and then Auxiliary Bishop Wright was in great demand as both an academic and convention speaker. As an Auxiliary, he had confirmations, ordinations, and other ceremonial duties, to keep him busy. Moreover, Richard Cushing isn't the kind of man who could keep a personal secretary in a formal, consistent capacity. The Cardinal is and has been his own secretary, off the cuff, and out of his hat, in many informal but highly effective ways. He often answers the phone himself, and does not always list appointments in the appointment book; he dictates his own voluminous daily correspondence to various stenographers, and above all, he makes his own Archdiocesan policies and, as often as not, handles the press, radio, and TV himself. His arrangement of his own affairs baffles—and sometimes frightens—those nearest him. His wily *faits accomplis* and renowned shooting-from-the-hip, for public consumption, are, fortunately, 99 and 44/100ths percent on the side of the Angels. The other 56/100ths percent is his Irish loquacity as he freely admits himself, which occasionally gets him into difficulty.

Wright's successor, Monsignor Lawrence J. Riley, and the present Secretary, a young, former Boston College star athlete, Monsignor Joe Maguire, would probably admit that some of their loyal and devoted functions have entailed: the highly important role of door-tending against cranks and nuts; expediting many arrangements and items of business for the Cardinal by phone, and providing him the staunch and cordial companionship he needs at home or on the road.

We asked the Cardinal quite bluntly if there was anything to the reports that Bishop Wright had a touch of the Machiavellian in him and that, not unlike the young Spellman, he had very fancy footwork at climbing the political ladder in the Church and outside of it. The Cardinal looked at us, almost as if in agreement, but said nothing. Later on, when we were talking about the Kennedys, he did tell us about a telephone conversation he had with Governor David Lawrence of Pittsburgh, just before the Democratic National Convention in 1960. Cushing implied very clearly that he had some way of knowing that Bishop Wright (a long-time Republican) was sitting with Governor Lawrence at the other end of the wire. The Cardinal seemed quite sour about that other episcopal presence. This telephone conversation with Governor Lawrence, a Catholic, was probably relative to Kennedy's "Catholic problem."

Like Cushing, Wright was born and bred in Boston, knows its priests and people intimately, and with both his Roman erudition and American diocesan experience seems tailor-made as Cushing's successor. It is not idle talk to recall that Richard Cushing was almost counted out of the hierarchical dynamics and almost indeed out of life itself during and after his grave illness in 1953. There was strong

142

talk of the Pope naming a Coadjutor-Bishop in those days. And Bishop Wright in his neighboring new, midget diocese of Worcester was, whether he wanted it or not, one of the names being mentioned for the projected episcopal "partnership." But Cushing would have none of it. He miraculously bounced back with his old astounding vigor, even though an eight-pound tumor had had to be removed from his kidneys.

Much sand has run through the hour-glass since John Wright's consecration as Auxiliary in 1947. Why the perceptible coolness toward Wright on the part of Cardinal Cushing? Wright is the sophisticated scholar, the polished social diplomat; Cushing is the bluff man of action, unintellectual, constantly "rough-posing." Cushing reveres scholars and intellectuals in a generous almost wistful manner.

Meanwhile, another incident must be recorded: the Feeney affair. Cushing received bad publicity for the entire and infamous comic-opera heresy. Although history doesn't warrant it, Catholics in Boston and elsewhere still seem to be of the impression that the Feeney case delayed the conferral of Cushing's Red Hat. Francis Spellman was elevated to the Cardinalate in 1946 by his friend Pope Pius XII. The princedom was well-deserved: Spellman had been Archbishop of New York since 1939. Cushing, on the other hand, had only been Archbishop of Boston for a scant two years when that Consistory took place. Francis Spellman was due to be the top man East of New York for a while.

In any event, Cushing's failure to get the Red Hat in 1946 had nothing to do with the Feeney affair, since "the contumacious Irishman," as Evelyn Waugh once called the latter, did not become defiant of ecclesiastical authority until the early fifties. When we asked Cardinal Cushing about the Feeney case, he threw up his hands in wry alarm and exclaimed: "I had nothing to do with it!"

John Wright was close to Father Feeney, in the early days of St. Benedict's Center, across the street from St.

Paul's Catholic Church in the quaint backstreets of Harvard Square. It was a magnificent idea, the Harvard Catholic student center, culturally, socially, religiously. Feeney was eccentric but charming, a famous literary man; he attracted young people and utterly fascinated them; he seemed unshakably orthodox and, moreover, basically sane.

Many Boston Catholics—this writer included—were friends of Feeney and his brother, the whimsical, lovable fellow Jesuit, Thomas Butler Feeney, during World War II and through the late forties. The relationship was laudable and normal in those days.

Eventually, Father Feeney began saying and doing strange things; perhaps he was under exceptional mental strain. His rigid, fanatical emphasis on "No salvation outside the Church" was bad enough at first. Yet a nice matronly lady from Baltimore once said to me at a labor convention in the early fifties: "Father Feeney is preaching what we were taught to believe." She had attended a very proper nuns' academy in Baltimore and studied the same catechism we had memorized in the parochial schools of Boston. But Father Feeney's rigid fanaticism deteriorated steadily into bitter invective. He reduced the doctrine to the absurd, and so started a momentum in a more ecumenical direction.

We'll leave the theology to the theologians. But we know that the key word is the "Church" in the Father Feeney controversy. Formerly, being in the "Church" meant you had to be a baptized Catholic; there was "baptism" of water, desire, of blood, and if you qualified, under certain of these three categories, you were in under the umbrella of the elect. Now we're all part of the brotherhood of man, under the Fatherhood of God, which is fine, but in a way you can't blame Father Feeney and many, many thousands of Catholics who grew up in America in the twenties and before, for thinking the way they did about who gets into

Heaven and who doesn't. They were taught to think that way.

So, of all people, the eminent Bishop Wright of Pittsburgh, then of Boston, tried to do some solid good for the Catholic students of Harvard University and ended up stepping on a theological land-mine. That he has survived so well, socially, theologically, and ecclesiastically, is a tribute to his quality. Cushing himself was very compassionate toward Father Feeney and his followers. No lovelier sight do we remember than the Archbishop imparting his personal blessing to the then distinguished poet and master of the informal essay, Father Leonard Feeney, at the altar rail in the empty Church of the Immaculate Conception in South Boston, in the early years of World War II.

The war-fevered class of 1943 at Boston College had just attended the Baccalaureate Mass. Leonard Feeney gave a brilliant Baccalaureate Sermon. Archbishop Cushing presided at the Mass. Home on furlough from the army, we sat there watching from the pews as the Archbishop emerged from the vestry and calmly placed his hands upon the head of the famous Jesuit. Feeney received the blessing dressed in black Jesuit habit and black top-coat.

Later, after Feeney and his bookselling fanatics had been pressured out of St. Benedict's and Boston, and moved from Cambridge to the northern Massachusetts town of Harvard, Cardinal Cushing came close to paying a friendly visit to the eccentric, excommunicated group. Monsignor George Kerr tells us that as he and His Eminence were riding in the vicinity of the Harvard retreat of the Feeneyites, the Cardinal, attired in his robes and fresh from a neighboring parish ceremony, expressed the desire to drive in and say "hello." George Kerr wouldn't say whether he dissuaded His Eminence from turning in or not. But the Cardinal drove on and a completely unpredictable moment in local religious history aborted.

Anyone who has ever been to St. Benedict Center during the first days of deterioration, or to the Sunday "seances"

145

at the Boston Common during the final days, can recall some of Father Feeney's sick, horrifying rhetoric. Even in the early days, no difference of opinion, no matter how gentle or reasonable, would be tolerated. At St. Benedict's one of his young lady patronesses had given the Center a set of her family's valuable and heavy brass candlesticks; they stood imposingly on a pamphlet table. During one of Feeney's famous "one-way-street" lectures, this gentle soul had the temerity to demur from some point the leprechaun-like priest had made. Feeney pointed to the door and crisply said: "Out!"

The sensitive female votaries were, of course, completely devastated by this treatment and would react with tearful disbelief. This particular young lady, when she divined that he meant what he said, showed a good, healthy flash of Irish temper. "I'll go," she said, "but I'll take my candlesticks!" With that, she arose, rushed to the table, and with an effort embraced both huge candlesticks and walked slowly, bravely, out the door.

There are scores of droll stories about the pathetic and yet sometimes ludicrous Feeney religious revolution throughout the Archdiocese in the early fifties. The black-clad zealots, in a hymn-singing, sign-bearing, rosary-twining "spectacular," picketed the grounds of the Archbishop's residence, after they had all been excommunicated from the Church. They got into the garden at the front of the residence before the police cars arrived, undoubtedly called by one of the Archbishop's assistants who could not face the terrors of religious history come alive. It is believed that the Archbishop was away at the time. Father Feeney was not among the demonstrators. Within minutes, the grounds were alive with good-natured Boston-Irish cops, most of whom had been rigidly taught the doctrine which Father Feeney's assiduous followers were now publicly espousing: an exclusively Catholic Heaven!

To complicate matters, the doddery old Police Commissioner, Colonel Tom Sullivan, who had once been Cushing's boss on the Boston Elevated Railway, arrived on the scene in all his righteous fury. The police were hesitant about arresting or pushing and shoving the eager young Catholic extremists, many of them recognizable Boston-Irish types, who were insisting that all they wanted to do was say the Rosary on the Archbishop's lawn.

"Pull them up! Arrest them! Get them out of here!" the Commissioner shouted.

The Feeneyites, no dumbbells at public demonstration, immediately went to their collective knees, and following their lector, began chanting the Rosary with impressive fervor. The police were hesitant. Commissioner Sullivan directly ordered one of his sergeants to drag the Rosary leader off to the wagon.

"Commissioner," the head-scratching Irish Sergeant said, "this is one arrest you'll have to make yourself. It goes against my conscience to arrest people while they're saying their prayers."

The Feeneyites were then permitted to complete their Rosary, and when they had finished they arose and filed out of the Seminary grounds in orderly fashion.

So much for Father Feeney and the comic-opera heresy which now, in the full swell of the ecumenical era, seems like a nightmarish anachronism, dead upon the vine.

The new and tiny diocese of Worcester, meanwhile, was carved out of the Archdiocese of Boston in 1950, and Bishop Wright became his own boss.

The young Bishop had left his first mark upon Boston. The very distinction of some of Cushing's public addresses and sermons in the forties—and these are assuredly among his best—are said to be attributable to the "editorial assistance" of John Wright.

Many good and loyal Boston Catholics would be happy to see John Wright come back home again—if he comes back! In the chaffinch flock of American bishops, Wright still stands out like a golden eagle—the emblem of Boston College at that.

CHAPTER XV

Labor Spokesman and Pilgrim

"St. Paul, the Roman Citizen, had looked forward to Rome for many years. Here was the infant Church, here was Peter, and during those long journeys through the Mediterranean area, St. Paul longed for the day he might join the Church in the Eternal City."
—Welcome to Cardinal Cushing by the Paulists at Santa Susanna Church, Rome, December, 1958.

In the preface he wrote for Giordani's *Life of St. Paul* Cardinal Cushing speaks with admiration of "the nervous, wiry little Jew who was aflame with the love of Christ." Cushing himself is wiry now; he said recently he weighs only 147 pounds, a far cry from what he weighed before the major operation of 1953. How tightened and Lincoln-esque in frame he now seems by contrast with the burly, full-faced, six-footer we knew as Archbishop in the late forties and early fifties. In those years the young Archbishop was much like Paul in his reserves of nervous energy, and the tirelessness of his preaching. A fierce puritan, he flared up in reaction against the "emancipated" morals and manners of the "gentiles" here and across the world. He was Pauline with Paul's special liberalism, not that of politics nor that of social and religious revolution, but with the less utopian liberalism of love for people. The source of Cushing's liberal tendencies is his huge compassion for people in pain and trouble, people racked by the pressures, temptations, and confusions of our society.

Through the late forties and early fifties, Cushing was

148

always in demand as a ceremonial, convention, and commencement speaker. His Pauline ferocity of eloquence and his compassion for people drew him even further from his earlier, ecclesiastical pieties toward a sense for social justice, toward increasing relevance to the real moral issues of American society.

Compare the puritanical flame of his blast against Boston night-life immorality on New Year's Eve, 1951, for example, with his eventual social sophistication—but not tolerance—of evil in the late fifties and early sixties.

In a public statement to all the Boston press the two-fisted, young Archbishop lashed out at Korean War home-front morals on that particular New Year's Eve.

"Boston is a city that has sunk to the bottom with its filthy, immoral night life," he declared. The crusading young Archbishop then went on to condemn "Boston's vile burlesque theatres" and female impersonators.

Police Commissioner Thomas F. Sullivan was obviously upset when asked to comment on the Archbishop's diatribe. The old "Colonel" threatened to punch a *Boston Record-American* reporter on the nose, after being disturbed at home on a Sunday afternoon.

The Archbishop may have fired a righteous shot into a political hornet's nest because the pattern of evasion continued among public officials. Mary Driscoll, the late chairman of the Boston Liquor Licensing Board, that powerful state agency not under the control of the Hub's mayor, was also contacted by the press and proved bristlingly noncommittal. Walter Milliken, then the Boston City Censor, said evasively that he could only control shows on Sunday evenings because he had special licensing power only for the Sabbath.

In a major address to thousands of delegates and guests of the national convention of the Confraternity of Christian Doctrine, in the Boston Garden in October of 1946, Cushing strongly urged the canonization of Giuseppe Sarto, the

149

sainted Pope Pius X of Venice—forerunner by fifty years of good Pope John XXIII. The Apostolic Delegate, Amleto Cicognani, and Archbishop Spellman of New York were present as he spoke. But there was a surprise in Cushing's discourse. His eloquence burned brightly through the huge, barren barn of the Garden, touching its vast coldness with warmth and concern. For Cushing grasped the true nature of the renewal and reform begun under Leo XIII and continued by Pius X. Cushing's thought led him swiftly from the canonization of Pius X to the cause of organized labor:

And so, my dearly beloved brethren, we are met here this evening to dedicate our work in the Confraternity of Christian Doctrine to the saintly memory of the Pope of the Confraternity, His Holiness, Pope Pius X.

We dedicate it to him because we share the purpose which inspired him to establish the Confraternity: *"The restoration of all things in Christ."* We act in the hope that the spirit of devotion in which we pay homage to his memory may prove in itself a means unto his eventual beatification and canonization, for we are convinced that this would in turn prove another and heaven-inspired means to the speedier restoration of all things in Christ.

But if we hope to achieve this social purpose of the spiritual program fostered by Pius X, we must not merely quote his preaching, we must imitate his personal example, and restore ourselves in Christ, each in accordance with the needs and the nature of his vocation. Pope Pius X constantly said: *"Remember, I am a poor man and Jesus Christ is all."*

As Cushing spoke, he knew that a storm of reaction to the strength gained by organized labor under Roosevelt was gathering. Soon the national off-year elections would be held, and President Truman would find himself with a reactionary Congress hell-bent on strapping down labor with the punitive Taft-Hartley law. Cushing, whose heart was with labor, but whose money-raising often depended on the benefactions of business leaders and executives, must have been apprehensive of opposing the reform legislation. Or, perhaps without a thought, simply sensing the rightness of the situation, he continued:

Most of our Catholic people are in the ranks of those who labor in one or another of the crafts and trades and industries. (He spread his hands to his audience.) Never before in history has your dignity and your power been so great. Individually, and above all, organized in your trade unions, you are among the most potent figures in the shaping of our society. Through collective action you are able to determine the issue of momentous crises in the political, the social, the military and even the charitable activity of our times. Your power is unparalleled; precisely because it is new, it is exhilarating and therefore sometimes dangerous. But there is no danger, indeed there will be great good come with your power, if only you remember (with Pope Pius X), you are poor men and Jesus Christ is all.

There was a danger, however. Even the staunch friends of labor knew that the movement had become too big, too fat, too powerful, perhaps too arrogant to be assimilated by American society. The Taft-Hartley law seemed inevitable: this great *bête noire* which many of us fought so hard and feared so much. And yet the law turned out to be a good thing for organized labor; it was a bit and bridle for the magnificent but untractable workhorse of our society, organized labor. It even saved the steed from the glue factory: the death of unions which right-to-work laws would have meant.

Cushing seemed uncertain of organized labor and the labor barons in the early years of his episcopal career. In the movement's rise to power under Roosevelt, the hue of labor's dynamic leaders, particularly in the C. I. O., was decidedly pink. To point out the Communist infiltration in certain echelons of organized labor like the newspaper guild, the electrical workers, the leather and meat-packing groups, and the West Coast longshoremen—all affiliated with the C. I. O.—was more than just red herring. Moreover, names like Sidney Hillman, Bridges, Carey, Reuther, whether their owners were deep pink or simply progressive, were not about to arouse benevolence and enthusiasm among predominately conservative Irish-Catholic Bishops, particularly on the eastern seaboard. Even Auxiliary Bishop

Bernard J. Sheil of Chicago, who was almost alone among organized labor's episcopal spokesmen in the forties, was referred to by a prominent eastern Irish prelate as "the Red Bishop of Chicago."

But of course Cushing and the other Bishops had Catholic sons to sustain and fortify their basic regard for labor: men like Philip Murray of the C. I. O. Steelworkers, Dan Tobin of the Teamsters, and the rising, ultimate overlord of all organized labor, George Meaney. Such soundly liberal, honest, and courageous labor leaders, both of the A. F. L. and C. I. O., deserve everlasting credit for enduring the calumnies and witch-hunts launched upon them. They were long subject to the smears and hysteria of anti-Communist fanatics in the late forties and mid-fifties. Some of this invective came from Catholic bishops, monsignori, priests, powerful laymen. Even to speak out, in the name of charity, for simple justice and sound social reform, against the scatter-gun, irresponsible generalizations of the Dies Committee or Joe McCarthy, was sometimes to find oneself at loggerheads with the indiscriminate anti-Communism of many in the American hierarchy.

In Boston, too, it took a good measure of personal courage for a Catholic journalist, lawyer, teacher, or leader of organized labor to sign one of those public petitions which appeared as paid ads in the daily newspapers, and which protested against the blind and ruthless tyranny of Senator Joseph McCarthy. Catholics who allowed their names to be entered among the signers of such petitions were henceforth scrutinized with baleful eye, and the epithets "dupe" and "fellow-traveler" were all too quickly bestowed on them by their pastors and fellows.

Archbishop Cushing was by inclination partial to Senator McCarthy—to almost any vigorous anti-Communist. But he was able to see the concrete requirements of social justice, too. He gave several ringing speeches to organized labor, and particularly to groups of C. I. O. workers in convention assembled. Part of his insight into the needs of labor must have come to him through his interest in the reorganization of the Boston Catholic Labor Guild. The Guild believed in the then Archbishop and trusted his convictions. Particularly instrumental in winning the Cardinal's corresponding belief and trust in labor was John C. Cort, an able Catholic journalist, executive secretary of the Boston Newspaper Guild, and a layman of unusual dedication to and understanding of his Catholic Faith. Hand-in-hand with Cort was Father Francis McDonnell, who ultimately became the popular and highly successful director of the reorganized Guild and its labor school, both of which still flourish under the nationally respected Father Mortimer Gavin, S.J.

This reorganized Guild, with the Archbishop's hearty cooperation, gave the "deep-six" to the former, useless organization of the same name, which used to hold a splashy Communion Breakfast once a year, and spend the rest of its time worrying about Communist infiltration. It held no meetings, no elections. Ventilation and reorganization were inevitables, granted a sympathetic sponsor like Cushing.

Regarding the "unconditional release" of that moribund group's former moderator, Cushing once said to John Cort: "I told Furlong to call him up and tell him he was 'through!' "

The work of another socially-conscious organization in the Archdiocese, the St. Joseph's Workingmen's Retreat, developed by a Jesuit task force, under Father Paul Murphy, S.J., has also redounded to Cushing's credit. The Archbishop tried to understand labor, and labor responded with gratitude and affection. For Cushing was unleashing a new kind of Catholicism in Boston, socially conscious and willing to do the hard work of organization and political action by which justice is achieved in this country.

Meanwhile, in June of 1947, while the recently elected 83rd Congress strove to tie organized labor in knots and

153

to frustrate a program of progressive legislation, Cushing rallied the graduating class of Boston College to labor's cause:

> Most of you are the sons of laboring people; almost all of you are grandsons of laboring people; and you cannot isolate yourselves from the interests of labor without doing violence to your own roots and turning your backs on your own kin. In this country it was working people who built our churches and our colleges. In all the American hierarchy there is not one Bishop, Archbishop or Cardinal whose father or mother had been graduated from college.
>
> The blood of our college men is the blood of laboring people, and on that basis, if on no other, I ask that Boston College men, whatever the professions they may enter, develop an intense interest in the Labor movement for the good of the nation, for the good of the Church.

Boston College was an appropriate place for the Archbishop to propose his socially conscious Catholicism. For Boston College, afflicted with post-war growing pains, had been see-sawing back and forth between the hard-shell conservatism of the New England Jesuit province and the social progressivism of the papal encyclicals and the New Deal. Compared to the intelligent, active, socially conscious laymen which the Catholic colleges of Chicago feed into their city, Boston's Catholic Colleges seem gravely remiss.

Not long after the Archbishop's address, for example, a young alumnus of Boston College, named Joseph O'Donnell, now of the Harvard University Labor School faculty, and then an organizer for the Building Service Employees International Union, was chased off the campus by the Jesuit authorities for trying to organize a labor union among the college's kitchen help, grounds workers, and janitorial help. There was, of course, a Jesuit side to the story: the college in many cases gives gainful employment to older folk and people partially retarded, mentally or physically, who would not be able to make a living otherwise. Some aspects of the controversy did get into the newspapers,

154

however. The incident gave the Archbishop, and many others, pause concerning the true social-consciousness over at "Hail Alma Mater . . ."

In September of 1947 the Archbishop welcomed a group of Franciscan nuns from Jefferson, Wisconsin, to staff his newly established St. Coletta school for mentally handicapped children in Hanover. These "exceptional children" are very close to the Cardinal's heart, so much so that he wishes to be buried among them. He has established a cemetery plot on the lovely South Shore grounds of that institution where, with such children, he will take his rest.

In October of the same year, Boston was to witness a mass public demonstration of Catholic faith by the Holy Name Society. At their National Convention in Boston, the men of the Holy Name Society sponsored A Candlelight Holy Hour at Fenway Park, in which 60,000 men took part. Then, on the following Sunday, much to the wry curiosity of Boston's non-Catholic brethren, in an as yet non-ecumenical era, a parade of 100,000 Holy Namers marched through the streets of Boston.

It is interesting to speculate on just what such a public spectacle accomplished. Were these men, like Red Chinese armies, out to impress their neighbors that they just might be able to inundate them with force of numbers? The Holy Name Society, commendable for its motives, has always seemed inclined to an ambiguous, massive style of action. Reverence for the Holy Name of Jesus is a lovely thing, but to organize reverence so assiduously . . . ? In every parish, hundreds of men go to Holy Communion once a month, and then attend a breakfast afterwards, at which they are harangued—either literately or nonsensically— about Communism and dirty movies.

Until the Vatican Council and the serious work of renewal and self-criticism it has inspired, such societies of men had almost no positive program of study, and hence maintained the same style of activity unchanged for a generation.

155

It was not long after this demonstration, on the other hand, that the Protestants, too, were in the Boston streets, parading at an annual mass Communion Day. Oddly enough, in the spirit of the day, while the Catholics spent their fury on Communism and birth control, the Protestants and Other Americans United (POAU) worried about a Catholic power-grab. Paul Blanshard's books on Church and State, and the insidiousness of Catholic power were catching on. Protestant Bishops Oxnam and Pike fulminated against Catholic Bishops Spellman, Sheil, and movie censorship. In those days one could conjure up droll visions of columns of men having it out in the streets, European-style.

Cushing, however, told the 60,000 men at the Holy Name Candlelight ceremony at Fenway Park:

The only union which we Catholics seek in America and in the world is that for which the President of the United States pleads in his recent letter to our Holy Father: "I desire to do everything in my power to support and to contribute to a concert of all the forces striving for a moral world . . ."

As Al Smith once remarked: "the Catholics of the Country can stand bigotry. The Jews can stand it. But the United States cannot stand it; it is aimed at every clean concept on which the American pattern of life is founded."

Thirteen years later, of course, a classy young Boston-Irishman would campaign successfully for nomination and election as President of the United States. He would echo similar sentiments in his struggle against a revived religious prejudice. And then a new era would begin. Meanwhile, before the candlelight throng, Archbishop Cushing read a cordial and astute letter from Harry S. Truman, President of the United States. Harry had an Irish-Catholic secretary from the Boston suburb of Clinton named Matt Connolly, and Matt may have had a hand in the message:

The Holy Name Society is carrying on a praiseworthy work in accord with ancient tradition, commended alike in the Old Testament and the New. The Psalmist sang the praises of the Lord

156

from the rising of the sun to its going down, and St. Paul admonished at the mention of the Divine Name every knee should bow . . . May God speed and prosper the noble work to which this society is dedicated.

A sensitive tribute indeed, from a tough, old artillery captain and two-fisted Kansas City machine politician, who, even as President, could blister the paint off the White House walls with choice back-room epithets.

Next the Archbishop, coming into prominence as a friend of organized labor, addressed the Ninth Constitutional Convention of the C. I. O. Cushing had been invited by Philip Murray, President of the United Steelworkers of America, C. I. O., and a devout son of the Church. Cushing delivered his quite famous "I belong here . . ." speech, a theme which he subsequently was to invoke again and again before groups of organized labor. His maturing social consciousness is apparent:

I am glad to come this morning because Mr. Murray invited me. But I am also glad to come because I belong here. I am a priest, an Archbishop. As such, I am by office and should be by my every personal action the representative of One whom twenty centuries have hailed as their high priest.

Every one of our bishops and archbishops is the son of a working man and a working man's wife. That is one further reason why I belong here this morning.

In May of 1948, Cushing returned to this theme before the National Steelworkers' Convention, obviously at the invitation of President Murray, eager to claim him this time as speaker to his own men in the C. I. O.

A bishop of Christ's Church belongs with workers, first of all that he may bring Christ to them and them to Christ, but also in order that he may help achieve those moral and social objectives which should be the result on earth of the coming of Jesus Christ and of the work that He did in our midst.

I said that I belong here because mine is the Church of the working people. If anyone doubts that, let him take up his stand outside our churches and see who enter and who come forth.

I belong here—a bishop always belongs with the workers. But

that proposition is equally true when stated in reverse! You belong with me. The workers belong with the Church. Organized labor needs organized religion.

Workers of the world unite—with God—that under God you may the more strong and successfully and safely unite with one another!

It isn't difficult to imagine the reception this speech had from hundreds and hundreds of lusty steel-workers in gay yet serious convention, all their expenses paid, and a manly Archbishop identifying himself with them and with the noble causes of religion. The man from Southie, whose father had repaired white-hot street car wheels as a blacksmith over an open forge, brought the house down in resounding cheers, whistles and applause!

That previous winter, the army brass in the Pentagon, aided by several military-minded Congressmen, had brought the Universal Military Training Plan to a legislative head. The Catholic Bishops of America were against this wholesale regimentation of young men, who would be plucked out of home and school to pay for war-mongering hysteria, and batten a few generals and admirals on sweeping budgetary expansions and a headier military power. Ministers, rabbis, educators, community and business leaders sided against this foolish and untraditional plan of regimentation. In a ringing attack on the plan and its underlying philosophy, before the First Friday Club of Detroit, February 6, 1948, Archbishop Cushing gained national attention and warmed the cockles of American hearts everywhere.

The fact is that Europe, far from being made strong by Universal Military Training, was bled white by this paralyzing system—bled so white that the late Cardinal Gasparri once described Compulsory Peacetime Military training as the curse of Europe and the source of uncounted evils on that unhappy continent. . . . I ask you as taxpayers to discover what this radical and far-reaching venture would cost us in terms of dollars and cents. There are those who assert, and they appear prepared to back up their assertions, that the cost of this program will be between three and five billion dollars per year; the President's Commission has already admitted it will cost almost two billion.

Let me suggest some of the social improvements that could be obtained for half of our youth and which, to my way of thinking, would be more in the interest of young people than military conscription. There are over eighty counties here in the state of Michigan; the total number of counties in all the forty-eight states is, of course, enormous. But with the annual cost of compulsory peacetime it would be possible: (1) to construct a ten-room modern school building in every county in the U.S. each year; (2) to pay the full maintenance and tuition at college or technical school for one year for the 900,000 boys who would be conscripted.

I have been quoting quite often of late from the magnificent American and peerless prelate who was Cardinal Gibbons, America's famed Cardinal and a man who spoke the language you and I understand: "The oftener I go to Europe, the longer I remain there and the more I study the political condition of its people, I return home filled with greater consideration for our country and more profoundly gratified that I am an American citizen."

In his address to the Confraternity of Christian Doctrine in 1946, Cushing had pledged that he would personally lead a pilgrimage to Rome to further the cause of beatification of Pius X. In August of 1948, then, at long-last, it was Cushing's turn to saunter up the gangplank and wave at the beloved faithful he would leave behind him. The colorful, nostalgic opportunity to visit Rome, Ireland, France, and the shrines and holy places of all Europe, had finally come. How deservedly rich and golden, how warmly fulfilling, for the man who could not go to the Roman college because of World War I, who cheerfully and industriously remained in Boston as the stalwart right arm of Cardinal O'Connell—while "Gangplank Bill" had embarked for Bermuda or Rome and while the glamorous Spellman traveled East and West around the globe.

Several thousand ebullient, sentimental Bostonians were at the South Station on August 13, 1948, when Cushing and his entourage took the train to New York. The next day, August 14, the Archbishop and his fellow pilgrims boarded

159

the *Queen Mary* and embarked for Europe on the 34th anniversary of the death of Pius X, whose cause of beatification the pilgrimage was intended to promote. The Archbishop, and with him some 400 pilgrims, visited Lourdes before going on to Rome. Their first Continental pause was in Paris, where Cushing was the guest of Emmanuel Cardinal Suhard, the world-renowned seventy-four-year-old Archbishop of Paris. Cushing had the privilege of climbing into the historic pulpit of the Cathedral of Notre Dame, to preach the sermon at a solemn pontifical Mass which was celebrated in his honor. He brought greetings, of course, from America, and he astutely praised Cardinal Suhard's great post-war pastoral letter, *The Church Today: Growth or Decline?*, which was a Catholic best-seller in the U.S.A. and enjoyed a wide vogue among laymen actively engaged in working for a Christian social order—whose very title, however, most of the well-heeled Boston-Irish who accompanied the Archbishop on his journey had no doubt never heard.

Bishop Wright, who accompanied his generous if mercurial patron, described in *The Pilot* the delightful incongruity of a Boston-Irish Bishop, a product of American freedom of religion, reverberating his eloquence against "the walls of a temple once defiled by an irreligious revolution."

New England priests and nuns, of course, had paid the price, in the old days, for freedom of religion; and their own temples had once been defiled by anti-Catholic bigotry. One does not have to be a historical scholar to recall the tarring and feathering of priests, and the ruthless burning of the Ursuline convent in Charlestown. The Archbishop had his own traditions of New England religious defilement to remember, within the hallowed and once-desecrated walls of Notre Dame.

Before going to Lourdes, the Archbishop was made an Officer of The Legion of Honor by Foreign Minister, and later Premier, Robert Schumann. Present at the ceremony were Bishops Wright, Edward F. Ryan of Burlington, Vermont, Edwin O'Hara of Kansas City, Missouri, and Matthew Brady of Manchester, New Hampshire.

Bishop O'Hara later led the procession up the side of the mountain at Lourdes, on August 22, while the Archbishop carried the monstrance and imparted the blessing. Many of the reported miraculous cures at the famed French shrine are suposed to have taken place during this ceremony. Lourdes seems to have a special fascination for Cushing. In his huge faith and endless charity he was to return twice with groups of his beloved mentally retarded children. The trips required a punishing physical effort on his part, and the miracle of Lourdes, so far as he is concerned, is that he has so wonderfully survived the physical and psychological drain of the illness under which he was even then laboring. There is quackery, fanaticism, and crass commercialism at both Lourdes and Fatima, of course; but Cushing overlooked those in order to bow his head and incline his heart toward the God such places honor.

Then, on a memorable September morning, the Archbishop entered the presence of a Pope for the first time in his life. Cushing had, of course, met Eugenio Cardinal Pacelli in Boston in the late thirties. But Pacelli was Pope now, Pius XII. Cushing's fellow bishops on the pilgrimage were with him in the audience chamber. But the Holy Father drew him aside for a few private words.

After the audience, the Archbishop went to Assisi, visited the American Paulists at Santa Susanna Church, which was later to be his titular church as Cardinal, and then it was time to go home.

"The best part of it is coming home!"

"Now back to work!"

These remarks are familiar to Bostonians as they welcome Cushing home. He seems to sense the frustration and delicate envy of the thousands who cannot travel as he can. He never draws attention to the glamor of his trips; he speaks of them only to share them as a father with his

161

flock. He invariably ends by asking all into partnership again: "There is still so much to do."

Cushing would go again and again to Rome, each time further up on a spiral of achievement and honor. He would be cheered by foreign crowds, and his hand taken eagerly in the streets by strangers; he would know all the honor the Church can give a priest, short of the papacy, and this would change him not at all.

CHAPTER XVI

Job of the Fifties

"In politics today as of yore, the plots and schemes that surrounded Caesar, the racism and persecution that Pharaoh employed,
these are the order of our day. There is no book about the troubled
life of modern man more up to date than the Book of Job."—Archbishop Cushing, Radio Station WNAC, Jan. 4, 1947.

The pilgrimages to Rome, Ireland, and the Holy Places
of Europe were to continue. The Archbishop's power over
crowds in Ireland particularly, increased with the brisk
pace of his expanding fame. Accompanied by Governor
Paul A. Dever of Massachusetts, Cushing was to lead 500
pilgrims on a festive "Come Back to Erin" pilgrimage one
year after his initial trip to Rome. Keys to the city, freedom
of the city, deference and obeisance from national and city
officials, and particularly the roaring adulation of the Irish
people, marked his steps as he returned to the towns of his
parents.

From the start of his Irish sojourn he was characteristically sensitive about sharing the trip with the folks at
home. "I'm happy to be going to the land of my ancestors.
I plan a Mass each morning for the people of Boston and
for those of Ireland, especially for the loved ones of Irish
immigrants, including my own folks, who helped build up
the Church in America."

Bishop John Wright was to write glowingly of this and
later pilgrimages—and of the fact that the Archbishop
brought the great Cunard liners back to the port of Boston.

Writing in a special supplement in the *Boston Sunday Globe*, Wright said:

When Cardinal Cushing, after World War II, undertook the apostolate of pilgrimages, he gave us new reasons to be proud. For one thing, he gave an example of the kind of temporal influence a spiritual shepherd should seek to exercise in the political and economic community within which he does his work of religion.

Wright went on to point out that the docks which had only recently been the scene of sad departures of troop ships were now merry with the laughter of peacetime pilgrims.

Reflecting back on the great pilgrimages of the late forties and fifties, from the perspective of the sixties, one cannot look upon them as major accomplishments in the career of the great Cardinal. As journeys of good will and piety, they are not to be lightly dismissed, and the Consistory trips and the voyages to the Vatican Council are of great historical moment. Still, it has always been his absorption in Archdiocesan business to which Cushing eagerly hurries home.

It is interesting also to reflect on John Wright's eloquent and cleverly-aimed tribute to Cushing's career, on the Sesquicentennial-of-the-Archdiocese. Wright wrote of Cunard liners and pilgrimages—was this emphasis intentional or just accommodating to a large metropolitan weekly supplement? Could not one who was looked on as the finest clerical intellect in the Archdiocese, Cushing's Secretary, at times his ghost writer and thus, *alter ego*, could not the then Bishop of Worcester have had more to say in 1958 about Cushing's accomplishments than the utterance of compliments about helping the Port of Boston?

Cushing went to Rome for the Holy Year of 1950, and then again after his illness in 1954. And of course, most gloriously, as Cardinal-Designate in December of 1958. The 1958 visit to Rome and his Irish trip in August of the same year were so triumphant as to merit more adequate comment later on.

It is only recently, in June of 1964, that Cardinal Cushing has candidly discussed the nature and extent of his extremely grave operation in December of 1953. At that time, word got around that he had cancer, and a pall fell over the Archdiocese.

Cushing had had asthma for years and we can recall a mid-western Catholic Bishop asking us somberly in Chicago, how he was feeling? That was in 1950, and the talk around Boston rectories was that—since the oxygen mask, which he now uses, was not in use—he slept occasionally in the old-fashioned "oxygen tent."

This particular Auxiliary Bishop was sweating out a diocesan appointment and he was very much aware of the longevity of various Ordinaries, as ageing assistant pastors are aware of the "immortality" of irremovable pastors.

"Well, how is Cushing feeling?" the Auxiliary repeated.

"He's not feeling well at all," we answered somewhat ominously. "He has very bad asthma and he sleeps in a tent."

The Auxiliary Bishop laughed heartily and without malice. Dismissing the issue with a gesture of his hand, he said: "Those asthmatics live forever!"

But Cushing was in serious physical trouble in December of 1954, and it wasn't asthma, and no tent would give him solace.

Five months before he gave the information out generally to the press, he gave it to us at one of our tête-à-têtes in late February of 1964. He prefaced the information with this statement: "You need faith to understand this; how I survived, the Lord knows." He revealed that he underwent a prostate operation and had a malignant tumor removed, weighing nine pounds, an operation which stripped some fifty pounds off his frame and left him the lean and angular figure he is today.

He also revealed, confirming rumors which we had heard back in 1954, that church authorities wanted him to retire, or at least take on a coadjutor bishop—a camouflage for retirement.

He took a strong position—a strength presumably beyond his temporarily spent being—and retorted that he would retire when he was unable to work.

The revelations which the Cardinal gave to newsman Arch McDonald of Boston's WBZ-TV on June 29, 1964, are much more comprehensive than what he had earlier given to us. Part of his character is revealed in the way he has let this news come out. In the Spring of 1964, he suddenly abhorred all writers of articles and books about him. Then, just as suddenly, he seems to have undergone a benevolent change on the occasion of the twenty-fifth anniversary of his episcopal consecration in late June. All journalists who have experienced the "buzz-saw" of his sometimes unreasonable wrath rejoiced for Mr. McDonald and the press in general when the sun began to smile again.

We have no hesitancy at all in reminding the Cardinal that, for all his genuine greatness, it was the devotion and loyalty of many Boston newspapermen who lovingly and painstakingly, over the years, projected his qualities and achievements all over the world. He has always been newsworthy, it is true, but it takes two to make a story; the subject and the reporter. All this semiprivate raging and storming about "journalists, they're all alike" comes with less than good grace from a man whom Boston newspapermen have striven to cherish and protect for at least twenty-five years.

The Cardinal told Arch McDonald in a video-taped show that during his 1953 illness: "I had the prostate gland removed; then probably ten days after that I had a kidney removed on which there had been an eight-pound malignant tumor.

"And in those days I weighed 200 pounds. Now I weigh

166

about 146, but the weight that I had was due to the malignancy, to the inactivity of the kidneys, and my body was filled, it seemed, with water."

Then we get the charming profoundity of phrase which the Cardinal can occasionally get off, all by himself, without benefit of ghost-writers or anyone: "About eight years ago they gave me eight months to live. Somehow or other, God chooses the foolish to confound the wise."

Speaking of the "foolish," once the word had gotten around that the Archbishop's operation was a success, back in 1954, a general sigh of relief went through the Archdiocese and the wise-cracks were bruited about. One of the smart sayings went like this: "When the surgeon opened up the Archbishop's kidney, he discovered four corner-stones."

"Now that I am home . . ." was his theme of eagerness to resume work again, weak and gaunt, a shadow of his former strapping Irish-bull appearance, feeling the carefully suggested pressure to resign, sensing that few believed in his capacity to carry a full load of work. But still in him the dynamos of energy straining to start, the fire of psychic force flickering against the "old Adam" that wanted to give in and just lie there, sparking, catching on, guttering ultimately into steady flame.

"Now that I am home, a period of convalescence lies before me. How long it will be I do not yet know. If it were only a week I would naturally be impatient to be done with it so that I might be about my Father's business, to quote the divine phrase from this Sunday's gospel which inspires and consoles those of us who yearn to be always at work for the Kingdom and the King."

Those were his words when he returned to the Residence from the hospital on January 9, 1954. He longed to be again in contact with his flock, so many thousands of whom had prayed for him and written to wish him well. "Ere long the natural wonder of radio will give me opportunities to speak

167

and pray with you as a means of resuming, gradually but surely, our old intimacy in the supernatural business of the Father."

By St. Patrick's Day of 1954 he had rejoined the chase like some Hound of Heaven pursuing souls again, down the nights and down the days. Hosted by Bishop Wright, he traveled to Worcester for a mammoth celebration of the green—and suffered a serious collapse on the platform with his former Auxiliary right there to catch him. By some supreme effort, he got out of the hospital in a few hours and made his way home, as he was wont to do, like some noble, wounded lion, regathering, recouping, refreshing in solitude, that he might go forward to the struggles of the spiritual jungle again.

With a seeming miraculous resilience of recovery, after his collapse in Worcester, he appeared at morning mass on St. Patrick's Day, in Holy Cross Cathedral, with his Irish guest, Bishop Cornelius Lucey of Cork. His appearance before an anxious Boston congregation, who had heard of his Worcester relapse, was startling at first, and then gave way to whispers of sheer admiration.

Shortly after he became Cardinal in 1959, he was to collapse publicly again, at Kansas City, briefly, and with still more rapid recovery. Twice, then, he went down in the view of thousands. Is this how he will finally go, the man of endless spiritual good works and fund-raising, amid the public?

"Behold," says Job, whom Cushing greatly admires, "happy is the man whom God correcteth: Therefore, despise not thou the chastening of the Almighty: for He maketh sore and bindeth up: He woundeth, and His hands make whole . . . In famine He shall redeem thee from death: and in war from the power of the sword. Thou shalt be hid from the scourge of the tongue: Neither shalt thou be afraid of destruction when it cometh."

What is so rare as a day in June when a man could voyage to Rome and Lourdes after passing through the cold and agonizing winter of the shadow of death? Sweet must have been that journey, of 1954, with the Pope ahead of him, the pain and uncertainty behind him. Behind him the Senator Joe McCarthy controversy boiled, with the Senate vote of censure looming, and Catholics again taking sides for and against the strident, hipshooting Senator from Appleton and Marquette University.

Ahead of him, Cushing knew, there could not be a Red Hat. The sickly, yet valiant, Pius XII had not called a Consistory, nor did he seem especially inclined to garb the towering Boston spiritual leader with the princely red. Perhaps, in this instance, rectory and churchyard gossip was correct. The Pope thought the world of Archbishop Cushing, but he thought even more of Cardinal Spellman, and he simply may have wanted the Whitman prodigy to continue to be the more imposing of the two.

But Pius XII had a special honor to confer upon the spiritual Boston strongboy. It was the closest thing to the Red Hat. On July 4, in a special audience, the Pope named Cushing a Papal Count.

There's an interesting story connected with these days in the Vatican which we heard from the Cardinal's own lips. It's difficult to pin it down specifically because His Eminence has a way of telling you an intimate story once and then clamming up afterwards, perhaps deciding that he has already said more than he really wanted to say. This has much to do with his moods also: the buzz-saw versus the benevolent Irish uncle.

Anyway, the Cardinal told us he had a very strange experience with Pius XII which, in the sequence of his Vatican visits while Pius was alive, must have taken place on the 1954 trip. With a group of Bishops in a general audience, which must have taken place previous to his special audience, Cushing said he was asked by the ailing, perhaps absent-minded Pope: "You're from Boston, no? How is Archbishop Cushing feeling?"

The Cardinal said that he told the Pope: "He's feeling much better."

"Ah, good! We shall say a special rosary for him."

The Cardinal said he later knelt down as the Pope and a group of Bishops said the Rosary for his health, while he was actually present. He joined right in on that one.

It could well have been that the Pope simply didn't recognize the emaciated Cushing who had lost about fifty pounds and who had gone from "robust" to "gaunt." Surely, later His Holiness must have known his mistake when he conferred on him the honor of the Papal Count.

Before Cushing got to Rome there was a bit of a stir in the Roman press concerning a tribute paid to the Archbishop by Signorina Giuseppina Parolin, niece of newly canonized St. Pius X. This daughter of the sister of Giuseppi Sarto referred to Cushing as "My favorite American and the one whom my family must thank most for the early Canonization of my dear Uncle Giuseppe." She also told of the silver casket, donated by Archbishop Cushing and the priests of the Boston Archdiocese, in which the body of St. Pius rests at St. Peter's Basilica.

Home again, Cushing made this wonderful, nostalgic statement about Rome which could easily go on a book mark or a bronze paper weight: "Wherever you go, whatever you do, whatever you are recommended to do in the big things of life, always look to eternal Rome and you will always be on the right side."

The censure of Senator McCarthy was inevitable, but in a Washington statement, Cushing had given him the same curious yet consistent loyalty he gives to all vigorous crusaders against Communism. Witness his consistency, despite disapproval of their extremism and odd methods, in endorsing some of the anti-Communist aims of Robert Welch and the John Birch Society. Here, indeed, he may be called the "checkered liberal," which term would mean nothing to him and which, in fact, is obliterated by the

170

deluge of charity that manifests his great liberality of spirit.

In June, before his departure for Europe, and in typical seven-league boot fashion, he had visited President Eisenhower, in connection with the National Council of Catholic Nurses Convention of which group he was episcopal sponsor. Eisenhower had been scheduled to address the group, but because of the pressure of Presidential business had to by-pass the appointment. Graciously enough he invited the Archbishop and the nurses to call on him at the White House, which they did.

Presumably, the President was very much involved in the White House interplay and the backlash of the McCarthy T.V. hearings at that time. Eisenhower was, of course, very much in favor of an eventual censure move. He had patiently endured McCarthy's taunts and even insults.

Archbishop Cushing was confronted on the issue by White House reporters just after he left the President's office. He showed enormous personal courage and integrity in "sticking to his guns" in that time and in that place. Perhaps he was not unmindful, too, that a very sick young Massachusetts Senator lay then on his back in Miami and would be affected by a possible Senate vote. It was known that Senator Kennedy was not unfriendly with Joe McCarthy. It was also known that other Senators, very ill, had been carried in on stretchers to vote on issues which they thought urgent. Senator Kennedy, in Florida and genuinely ill with a serious back ailment, did not, or could not, or would not come to Washington and vote on the matter. This was unsuccessfully used against him by the Democratic liberals whom he later converted and even led. But at that time it appeared as if the future President "took a walk" on the eventual vote of censure.

But whether you agreed with him or not, Archbishop Cushing took his stand. Senator Ralph Flanders had just made a speech asserting that Senator Joseph McCarthy of

Wisconsin was dividing his country and his party, and had driven "a blundering axe deep in the heart of his own Church."

Archbishop Cushing told the White House reporters, and thus the nation, that he couldn't perceive any division in the country and added that Senator McCarthy "is certainly not dividing the Church." He said "there is no Catholic attitude on a subject of that kind and Catholics can go the way they will."

The Archbishop took a highly optimistic view of the entire heated McCarthy controversy. "As for the country as a whole, I think it will emerge from all this debate much healthier. Americans, as a people, like to argue. The televised hearings offer a good diversion and the people are enjoying it. They are being educated."

When asked by a reporter what he thought about Senator McCarthy, he answered: "In my personal opinion the whole thing depends on how you look at Communism. If you look up on it as one of the greatest evils that has attempted to undermine western civilization, naturally you do everything you can to save our way of life from the inroads of this evil."

Asked if this meant he was sympathetic to Senator McCarthy, he responded: "I sympathize with anybody interested in keeping Communism in all its phases and forms from uprooting our traditions and our wonderful opportunity of assuming the leadership throughout the world that is the only hope of oppressed people."

That's the way he felt about bludgeon-swinging, scatter-gun-shooting Joe who was wrong more than he was right and who wanted to throw the good, liberal baby out with the pinko bath water.

But the Cardinal, then and now, is consistent as a jewel on Communism and those who fight militantly against it. Witness again his 1964 statements—first against, and then, apologetically, for—Robert Welch and the John Birchers. He still applauds their sincerity and their anti-Communism efforts although objecting to the "society's methods." "What is needed is a more positive approach." Privately, the Cardinal thinks the Birchers are "a bunch of nuts" and "fanatics." But he still sticks with his friendship for Welch. He shares none of the hate and bitterness of these people, but doesn't seem to realize how strengthened in their fanaticism they were by his seeming approval in the past.

He could well have said that Senator McCarthy also "needs more positive methods." But the times have changed and the Cardinal has mellowed. One feels that he would certainly object to McCarthy's "methods" and call for a "more positive approach" if free-swinging Joe were in action today. But for his courage and his integrity, within the portals of Eisenhower's White House, while the anti-McCarthy cauldron was really at a climactic boil, the Archbishop deserves a good deal of belated admiration.

Soon, in November, he would celebrate his tenth Anniversary as Archbishop. In the Commemorative issue of *The Pilot* his praise of organized labor for its positive approach to the fight against Communism was duly noted. And, above all, his tenth anniversary message to the people of the Archdiocese, which no biographer or commentator can ignore, is both moving and comprehensive.

As is his wont, he goes right back to the people of the parish, rather than the priests of the parish, and gives them credit for all his success. After making his proper obeisance to Pope Pius for appointing him, he talks directly to the ones "who get it up" on Sunday mornings and divers other occasions:

To you, dear people, I give you my life and service. The history of the past ten years is yours, not mine. To you, after God, be all its glory . . . All of this has cost a great deal of money, every cent of which came from your open purses and your yet more open hearts . . .

And of course the money also came from, and keeps coming from, people like the Fullers, the Kennedys, the Joe Sullivans, the Howard Fitzpatricks, the good-hearted or guilt-stricken politicians and their satellites, and most of all, through himself, and his magic through the mails, on the platform, on the beaches, on land, on sea and in the air.

It is yours, my dear people of the Archdiocese, especially the modestly paid working men and women among you; it is yours, also, my friends not of my own faith. It has been an honor to formulate the details of its expenditures, the manner of its implementation.

He then mentions his motto *Ut Cognoscant Te*, That They May Know Thee, and describes its expression in his ten-year career as Archbishop as the "continuance of the mission that Christ gave to his Apostles: love one another as I have loved you. Unless we know God, we cannot love Him."

He pays due tribute to "the cooperation, good will, and hard work of pastors and their priestly assistants, of nuns and brothers . . ."

And then—a startling and reasonably true observation: "Our Lord is better loved, better served today than He was ten years ago."

Herein are the sources of my joy, and I take this opportunity of thanking you all, lay religious and clergy. As for myself, let me continue with work and prayer and sacrifice the labor of restoring all things in Christ. With my heart full of love and devotion to everyone, with a special measure for the poor, the shut-ins, the handicapped, I thank you for your prayers, your good-will, your generous support.

Pray for me as I pray for you. *Ut Cognoscant Te*.

It seems curious that earlier in this message he should express such great surprise at "the magnitude of the construction problems which were lurking around the corner, waiting for me to pull out the chair behind my desk." He says further, "on the occasion of my installation as Archbishop, I had no idea then of embarking on a great building program."

We know that he had preached around the Archdiocese as a mission fund-raiser at least three times and had said that O'Connell's successor would have to build many new churches, rectories, and parochial schools. It must be that his original generous estimate was understated because of the disrepair and ruin of all too many institutional buildings.

The bulk of the building and fund-raising had been done in that ten-year period, yet there was still much to do. He was thinking about hugely expensive regional high schools now, and had talked about Catholic men's colleges, much like Boston College, in the more remote ends of the Archdiocese. We were to see this fruition in Merrimack College in Andover, and in Stonehill College, North Easton, respectively staffed and administered by the Augustinians and the Holy Cross Fathers. (Though the Stonehill campus lies three-quarters in the Fall River diocese, and only belatedly did the Cardinal come to its aid.) There were also the many girls' colleges: Regis, Cardinal Cushing, Emmanuel, Newton.

Before the broad crest of history's wave swept him on to Pope John and to authentic world-wide fame in the late fifties, Cushing was to build one of his most cherished projects, Nazareth, a home for the homeless waifs of an anxiety-ridden society. At a mammoth fund-raising affair for this thoughtful and compassionate institution he spoke a piece that has been printed and re-printed and will serve as a lovely little anthology item as long as there is interest in him and his work. It certainly merits inclusion here:

"I am a great believer in the idea that trouble is the best thing that ever happened to us," he said at a Nazareth fund-raising dinner which yielded him a check for $125,-000.

If all the troubles in the world were eliminated and all the problems solved, we'd be more tired than work ever made us; we would be bored to death.

As you know, every bishop has a coat of arms. My coat of arms should include a wolf. The wolf to whom I am indebted and who has kept me going all my life is the old, familiar "wolf-at-the-door," and so he deserves a place on my coat of arms.

The wolf-at-the-door is not a restful animal like the house cat nor an attractive beast, like a favorite horse. But he has been a spur to achievement. He has been a warning against sloth, complacency and "taking it easy." He has kept us from going soft. People save instead of wasting, they improve themselves instead of going to seed, they become successful, spurred on by our old friend the wolf at the door.

Now the believer in God is a man who worries about the wolf at the other fellow's door. That's how he differs from the self-centered materialist or pagan. If there were no wolf at our door, we'd all grow fat, lazy and dull. If there were no wolf at the other fellow's door, we'd all grow selfish.

How can I despise the beast who gave me so many friends, so much pleasant work to do for God, so much opportunity to serve Him? Sometimes it is exhausting, the battle to keep the wolf from the door, but if we were having toasts at our dinner tonight, I'd lift my glass to the wolf-at-the-door, and say:

"I hope you never get so close that you can sink your teeth in my arm and keep me from working; but I hope you never go so far away that I can no longer hear you howl and thus be reminded of how much work there is to do for my neighbor, for the under-privileged, and for God!"

There is the real Cushing, the essential Cushing, not the political Cushing, the commentator on the affairs of state, the social interceder who confuses genuine feeling with the projection of a misunderstood image; this is Cushing the priestly man, the manly priest. It is the kind of thing for which he will long be remembered when the bar-top coin boxes, the shamrock record albums, the bookie key shops, the Joe McCarthys and John Birch Societies have glimmered out of history, and only the kindly, endlessly-giving Boston Irish Bishop will remain.

BOOK FOUR

Good Pope John:
The Big Break-Through

CHAPTER XVII

The Road to John

"Like John, I came from the poor, lived poor and saw in both our lives a total dedication to a cause. I recognized John as an apostle of love and later came to be convinced that John was the Lord's answer to the confusions and misunderstandings of modern times . . ."
—Richard Cardinal Cushing, in an exclusive interview.

The blurring pace of time for Richard Cushing was to pause and spin like a Kansas twister at key dates on the calendar of the year 1958. It was to be a twelve-month of momentous historical emergence for the rough-hewn Irish bucko from the dreary backstreets of South Boston. In that extraordinary year the following events were to mark his life: the Sesquicentennial Anniversary of the Archdiocese; the foundation of the Missionary Society of St. James for work in Latin America; a triumphal tour of Ireland; the death of Pope Pius XII in October and the accession of John XXIII; and finally, gloriously, in December the reception of the Red Hat from Angelo Roncalli, his roly-poly spiritual twin brother.

Cushing began that wondrous year preaching at the Paulist Fathers Centenary Mass in New York City; he ended the year accepting their welcome in Rome at his cardinalatial church, Santa Susanna, staffed by American Paulists.

In New York, speaking of their convert-founder, Cushing said: "The Paulists have become specialists, first of all in the work of making converts. It was a saying of Father Hecker that he would help Catholics with his left hand but that he would reserve his right hand for those outside the Church. To the Apostolate of the Spoken word the society quickly added that of the press."

In subsequent addresses the Cardinal showed that he liked to extend Hecker's idea that the "right hand" may be used for those outside the Church. Cushing sometimes emphasizes the idea that "most priests spend their time saving the saved," as he said at the Centennial graduation exercises of Boston College High School in June of 1964.

In the early months of 1958 he spoke at a Sports Night held in one of his huge new regional high schools, Archbishop Williams, Weymouth, and made remarks both humorous and serious. He spoke of athletes who bless themselves before the start of sporting events: "Signs in Sports are the Signs of the Cross. Athletes of all ranges make signs of the cross at crucial times in so many different ways. A Jimmy Piersall draws a cross on the ground with his bat at the plate." He also mentioned basketball players Bob Cousy, Easy Ed Macaulay, and track star Ron Delaney. "There are two good reasons for all of this," the Archbishop continued. "One is religious. The other is practicability. An athlete faces two pressures at times of crisis: the roar of the crowd and the physical conditions of the crisis itself. So he turns momentarily to God and finds both the desired relaxation and the necessary concentration."

He then warned his goodly company of parents, teachers, and athletes not to push the religion thing too far in sports: "Overdisplay in anything is always distasteful." Then he told an old joke about a C. Y. O. boxer who crossed himself over and over again just before the bell. "Will that help him win?" someone asked the C. Y. O. chaplain. "Sure," the priest answered, "if he can fight."

The Archbishop reminisced about his idea of founding co-ed regional high schools. He said he wanted to extend this idea and build several co-educational Catholic colleges, not in Boston but the outlying places of the diocese. He spoke of his hopes to build one "somewhere right here in the South Shore."

This hope has perhaps been obviated in the establishment of Stone Hill College by the Holy Cross Fathers, on the old Ames Estate in Easton, on the South Shore. Up North there is the imposing and co-educational Merrimack College at Andover. Stonehill College is already co-ed, and even Boston College, so long an almost monastic educational establishment for males only, has opened its doors to women in some departments.

The Cardinal has dotted strategic areas of the Archdiocese with large, modern, co-ed and non-coed regional high schools. To mention a few, there is the vast Cardinal Spellman regional high school in Brockton, a new Jesuit high school in Concord, a new Xaverian Brothers secondary school in Westwood, and most recently the three-million-dollar central high school, named for Bishop Fenwick, on the Salem-Peabody line. The latter marked the sixteenth central or regional high school which Cushing has established since becoming Archbishop.

In the winter of 1958, in the comparative calm before the historical storm, Cushing continued his love-feast with all who are militant against Communism. He met, for example, with J. Edgar Hoover, Chief of the F. B. I. Hoover presented the Archbishop with an autographed copy of his new book, *Masters of Deceit*. The inscription reads as follows: "To Archbishop Cushing whose magnificent fight against atheistic Communism has inspired the writing of this book."

Hoover, while not a Catholic himself, is devoted to former agents who have become priests. He conscientiously attends their first masses, and keeps in touch with them— one of them, for example, is Father Joe Nolan, a Boston College graduate and former F. B. I. agent, who is now a young pastor in the diocese of Kansas, and a journalist and liturgist of distinction.

Characteristically, Cushing seized the opportunity of this high compliment from the arch-fighter of Communists to publicize an educational idea which he was later to implement, "I have always advocated the teaching of Communism as an evil, in our secondary schools and colleges. We must teach it, I maintain, as we teach the evil of sin in the moral order, or cancer in the physical order."

April was a month of particular joy for the Archbishop and the people of Boston for it marked the 150th anniversary of the Archdiocese. *The Pilot* and the Boston metropolitan newspapers were both profuse and scholarly in their memoirs of past bishops and tributes to the present one. The *Boston Globe,* the *Herald,* and the *Sunday Advertiser* published at great labor and expense, colorful and comprehensive magazine supplements on diocesan history. The diocesan weekly, *The Pilot,* also had a special edition which was a tribute not only to the Archbishop but to its scholarly and journalistically able new editor, Monsignor Francis Lally, and his staff.

Most observers would agree, however, that the *Boston Globe* Sunday supplement under the editorship of veteran religious newsman William R. Callahan was the journalistic triumph of the year. The long-time efforts of Bill Callahan as a religious newsman earned this success, which he, genuinely modest and retiring, will not seek to have attributed to himself. His painstaking and loyal coverage of the Archbishop over the years, along with similar protective journalism on the part of Hal Clancy, Dave Farrell, Gene Moriarty, and John Manion of the *Herald-Traveler,* Eddie Holland and John Brooks of the *Record-American,* and many others like them in Boston journalism, have, despite the Cardinal's occasional irascibility and raw ingratitude toward newsmen, steadily, loyally projected his well-deserved image on the horizons of the world.

In the diocesan press, Cushing has been the beneficiary of three astute priest-editors: John Sexton, historian and scholar, now a pastor; Francis Moran, a pioneer liturgist and sponsor of inter-faith harmony, now living at the Cathedral rectory and engaged in editorial research for the Cardinal; and the present editor-in-chief, Monsignor Francis J. Lally, a topflight journalist, and a man of many social and political talents.

Monsignor Lally deserves some space here, not only because of his promising future, but because of his key and at times equivocal position with the Cardinal.

Lally, somewhat like his friend and patron, Bishop John Wright, is also a clerical meteor. He is forty-five years old, a graduate of Boston College where he was a contributor to the college magazine, *The Stylus*. He wrote able literary essays about writers like Agnes Repplier, seemed shy, retiring, studious. He was graduated in 1940 and went on to St. John's Seminary. He took his post-seminary studies at Laval University in Canada, returned to Boston, and after a brief period as a curate at St. Paul's parish, Wellesley, became an assistant editor of *The Pilot* under Francis Moran. The sporadic illness of Father Moran and his inevitable retirement moved Lally more and more into a position of editorial responsibility, and he was not slow to take up the reins. In 1953 he was assigned by the Archbishop to accompany Gregory Peter XV, Cardinal Agagianian, Patriarch of Cilicia of the Armenians, the spiritual leader of 200,000 Armenian rite Catholics, on a trip throughout the U.S.A. The charming, witty, talented young clerical journalist had found his "Eugenio Pacelli." Agagianian was so taken with him by the end of the trip that he asked Archbishop Cushing if he would cooperate in an effort to have Pope Pius XII make Lally a Papal Chamberlain. Naturally Cushing went along with it. And shortly thereafter, at the age of thirty-five, the brand-new editor-in-chief of the *Pilot* became a brand-new Very Reverend Monsignor. Lally was Agagianian's choice, not Cushing's as Spellman was Pacelli's choice, not O'Connell's.

As the journalistic right arm of the Archdiocese—and a

183

very strong and competent one it is—Lally progressed rapidly in impact on the diocese and on the American Church. He is recognized as one of the outstanding religious newspaper editors of our time. His active interest in the liturgy and his pronounced liberal views on the ecumenical movement thrust him forward as one of the most enlightened among the Boston Irish priests.

Monsignor Lally was soon on the executive board of the National Council of Christians and Jews; the national committee for UNESCO; he lectured and wrote widely; he succeeded his friend and patron, Bishop Wright, as spiritual director of the posh League of Catholic Women; and due to the enthusiastic sponsorship of the distinguished Catholic journalist, John Cogley, he was appointed to the executive board of the Fund for the Republic at $2000 annually and occasional expenses. Lally has also been awarded the Legion of Honor by the French Government, and now serves as Chairman of the controversial yet forward-looking Boston Redevelopment Authority, by appointment of Boston's former Mayor John Hynes.

Lally's membership and chairmanship on the renewal board has raised more than a few Catholic and non-Catholic eyebrows, even in, at times, priest-ridden Boston. The Archbishop must have thought it was a good idea in the beginning or he wouldn't have let him serve. But the juggernaut of reconstruction in "the New Boston" has uprooted many helpless families in its path of demolition and caused a lot of heartbreak, however legitimately, among bewildered and defenseless little people. In the name of progress, redevelopment, and renewal, more seizure of land and demolition is to come. At the controversial Boston area public hearings which the law requires the Authority to hold, genuine, pathetic pleas are heard—as well as the strident complaints of anti-renewal nuts. Monsignor Lally, as Chairman, sits on the platform with a gavel and handles some of these meetings. He has to gavel people into silence and even threaten them with expulsion from the hall.

Whether they be genuine pleaders or lunatic fringers, it seems rather obvious that this is no role for a Catholic priest, even in Boston.

We are proud that a new and glorious Boston is rising and will continue to rise from some of its decadent areas. The towering insurance buildings, the federal, state and municipal skyscrapers, the high-rise apartment houses catering to the well-heeled (and to call-girls), are replacing and will continue to replace simple family tenements. All this architectural grandeur will remain long after Monsignor Lally, Urban Renewal Director Edward Logue, and the recent Mayors of Boston are dead and gone.

But how long will it take to dissolve the bitterness and hatred against the Church, which can be engendered among simple working people because a man with a Roman Collar wields a controversial municipal gavel? What does the Cardinal think of urban renewal and, by indirection, of Monsignor Lally's involvement in it? He says nothing directly, but apparently without consulting Monsignor Lally, he blasted urban renewal in the South End, while speaking at a Protestant Church in the Spring of 1964. He blasted the Authority's delays and also expressed the hope that Churches could be spared and that compassion upon little people would be exercised. The statement appeared in the metropolitan press but no mention of it was made in the next issue of *The Pilot*. Be it also duly noted that in the most recent issue of the Catholic Who's Who, 1964-65 edition, the biography of Monsignor Francis Lally, written by himself as is the practice, does not include any mention of his connection with the Boston Redevelopment Authority, of which he is exalted chairman.

Redevelopment and renewal is, of course, inevitable, but to the helpless people who are without political guile and influence, the program means demolition and relocation. No matter how inevitable the program is, there is no question that the great heart of Cardinal Cushing bleeds for the victims of this municipal juggernaut.

In the *Boston Globe*'s Sesquicentennial tribute to the Archdiocese, a quotation from the Book of the Apocalypse was set as a preface. The quotation seemed an apt description of Cushing:

I know of all thy doings, thy faith, thy love, thy generosity . . . See I have set before thee an open door. There is no shutting it. I know how little thy strength is, and yet thou hast been true to my message, and has not denied my name. Thou has kept true to my lesson of endurance, and I will keep thee safe from the hour of trial which is to fall.

The Archbishop had been through severe illness and many trials, personal and public, and had, so far, emerged triumphant. His mettle would soon be tested again in local and national politics, in Church reform, in the seemingly bottomless pit of missionary needs in Latin America; but henceforth he would stand front and center, and in spotlight, on the vast stage of the world.

In his commemorative sermon at the Sesquicentennial Pontifical Mass in Holy Cross Cathedral, April 21, 1958, the Archbishop said:

We do well to thank God for the qualities He has given our diocese through the men who shaped its corporate personality and who still give us so much of themselves even to this day: the long-suffering heroism of Pius VII, the genial patience of Cheverus, the urbane erudition of Fenwick, the aggressive valor of Fitzpatrick, the mellow stability of Williams, the Roman cosmopolitanism of O'Connell.

And the next generation will add: the universal compassion and charity, the availability, the old-shoe fatherly concern of Richard James Cushing.

In 1946, the young Archbishop had made a dramatic and perceptive move by lend-leasing five Boston priests to the curate-shy diocese of Sioux Falls, South Dakota. It was an apostolic mode of action which Cushing later would develop internationally, as he himself developed in his sense of world needs. For example, he later explained the need for "Apostolic Target: Latin America" in a national magazine:

These countries to the south of our borders with a population destined to surpass that of the United States were brought into the Church centuries ago by explorers and missionaries from Spain, Portugal and elsewhere. Then after revolutions brought forth about twenty independent nations, they were left to themselves. For some thirty years they were without any bishops. I admit it was an impossible task to save them. The message of the missionaries did not go deeply enough. The numbers were not multiplied sufficiently until the time when the visible Church could be governed and staffed by a well-formed native hierarchy and clergy.

What is the result? Today millions of Latin Americans never see a priest and millions more wait years for the Sacraments, the channels of grace. Those who possess wealth in abundance have lost contact with the Church and have never been trained to share their abundance with the poor whom they have exploited, or with the Church that has the potential to save them from false prophets and dictators. The Popes in our times have warned us about the incredible possibility of losing millions of Catholics to Communism.

The Archbishop then revealed with climactic force: *"Pope Pius XII told me to send priests to Latin America."*

Cushing was almost ready to obey in the early summer of 1958. He wrote in his Archdiocesan News-Notes in a June issue of *The Pilot:*

In this column I have mentioned before that I plan to send some of our young priests who volunteer to work in countries of South America where priests are so direly needed. When these priests return after three or five years of service in South America, most of them will, I am sure, have an excellent knowledge of the Spanish language. They will be of incalculable assistance in our own Spanish-speaking apostolate in the Archdiocese.

The missionary group would be called The Pious Society of St. James the Apostle, known popularly as the Missionary Society of St. James. The Archbishop disclosed that he already had fourteen volunteers from the Archdiocese and one from another diocese. He said the first departure would

187

take place in February of 1959 and that he himself planned to visit the territory in October. The death of Pius and the accession of John were to delay that visit.

He also disclosed that the territory assigned to the Society priests was in the Prefecture of Yauyos-Cuarochire, which was formerly part of the Archdiocese of Lima, Peru. And he told of a letter from Giuseppe Cardinal Pizzardo, Roman Prefect of the Sacred Congregation of Seminaries and Universities in which that Cardinal wrote: "The project of Your Excellency helps to meet the great concern of Holy Mother the Church for the future welfare of the Republics of Central and Southern America. We are pleased that Boston, so abundantly blessed by God with vocations, will help less fortunate areas." The Primate of Peru, Archbishop Juan Landazuri Ricketts of Lima, added that he considered "the sending of U. S. Priests to South America a work of continental apostolic coordination."

There were already signs of apostolic hope in Lima. There, during the past twenty-five-year period, men attending the sacraments increased from thirty to forty percent. This renewal was ascribed to the Eucharistic Congress of 1935 and subsequent new regulations permitting afternoon Mass and a liberalizing of fasting regulations.

Cushing said that on his next trip to Rome he would petition the Holy Father for formal approbation of the new apostolate. It was his optimistic belief that the Society would be effective not only in Latin America but in the Philippine Islands and other areas where there are large numbers of Catholics and a shortage of priests. "It is my opinion," Cushing wrote, "that the Church of this country needs a challenge not only to help foreign and home missions but to save the faith in countries where it needs to be revivified." The Archbishop's concluding sentence went right to the heart of the matter of foreign missions and their effectiveness in the latter half of the twentieth century: "To strengthen our Faith, we must do more about spreading the Faith by *personnel,* as well as alms."

The new Society priest-volunteers settled into a sustained study of the Spanish language and Latin American customs, little knowing that their departure in February would be highlighted by the blessings of both a new Pope and a new Cardinal.

One of them, the Cardinal's nephew, Father William Francis, labors now in Lima, Peru. Cushing seldom, if ever, mentions in public this dedicated son of his sister Anna. About his family, Cushing maintains silence and humility, and is most sensitive to turning the public eye on them. Like Pope John's obscure peasant family, there is in the unselfconsciousness and withdrawal of the Cushings a lovableness not recognized in other families of great prelates past and present. There is so much, even indirectly, the great Cardinal could do for his family, if he chose to. Others have done this: O'Connell perhaps, who accrued considerable personal wealth; and perhaps one or two of our contemporaries who have made helpful moves for their close relatives.

Cushing's brother John has a good job at the John Hancock Insurance Company, nothing extraordinary; another nephew, Richard Francis, is a pressman at the *Boston Globe*. The Cardinal's relationship with his family fits his whole life like a T-Square. It is almost as if the Cardinal has compassion upon the petty and the carping in advance, for he gives them so little to be petty and carping about.

The glorious feature of the Archbishop's August voyage to Europe was his triumphal sojourn in Ireland. He had visited Rome and the ailing Pope Pius, then had gone on to his beloved Lourdes. At that great Marian shrine on Wednesday, August 20, 1958, he said:

If the sword of the spirit, the love of which the human heart, enriched by God's grace, is capable, prevailed throughout the world, we would be living in an earthly paradise. That to me is the real meaning of Lourdes. Come to God through His mother. Here is the lesson of love.

189

The press coverage of this trip, particularly in Boston, was newsy, intimate, and comprehensive. This was undoubtedly due to Monsignor Lally's emergence as a mature editor and coordinator of news releases. A regular newsletter written by the Archbishop, or sent at his direction, kept the faithful right on top of things in the pages of *The Pilot.*

The scheduled feature of his Irish visit was the conferral of the Degree of Doctor of Laws at University College, Cork, on August 27. The Archbishop wrote:

All dressed up in the colorful academic gown and wearing the great flat hat, I felt like the well-known picture of St. Thomas More, the famous Lord Chancellor of England. Mr. DeValera the Prime Minister and University Chancellor conferred the degree and I have never witnessed a scene of more academic magnificence.

At least one of the remarks Cushing made in accepting the degree is well worth quoting: "I stand here today as a man of action among men of ideas. I end by reminding you how much we need one another in times so perilous." Here again is a sign of his innate reverence for the intellectual, the scholar, with an understanding of his own different talent.

His receptions along the route of his travels through Cork were tumultuous and flowing with rivers of loving humanity. Previously he had visited Mallow Station and Glanworth, the home of his father. There he was met by Bishop John Ahern of Cloyne, and he tells us: ". . . the whole town was streaming with banners and a brass band was out to welcome us in the square opposite the Church."

He tells us about the "lovely Marian Shrine on the precise spot of my father's old home and the new parish school, Cushing Memorial School, in honor of my father, Patrick." He had the great experience of meeting an elderly man who had known his father and remembered saying farewell to him.

Shades of J. F. K.'s visit to Ireland, as President: The Archbishop motored to the city of Cork in a pouring rain.

And even in the inclement weather some 5000 well-wishers jammed the streets and forced the Archbishop's party to abandon their cars, cross the bridge over the River Lee on foot, and make their way to City Hall. There he was greeted by the Lord Mayor and twenty members of the City Corporation garbed in handsome red cloaks and fur-trimmed hats. The Lord Mayor made him a "Freeman of Cork" in a solemn and memorable ceremony.

When it was time to go home to Boston all the inhabitants of Cork turned out to bid him farewell. Cushing himself tells of his parting, movingly and well.

The entire city of Cork, once known as Queenstown, seemed to have assembled on the terrace and hills overlooking this beautiful cove as we boarded the tender to take us to the liner anchored outside the harbor. Row after row of children and adults gathered on the hillsides that stand like sentinels in gorgeous green overlooking one of the world's beautiful ports.

All the Irish seemed to cry out: *"Come back again and walk once more among us!"*

Habitually when he debarked in Boston, from plane or train, there were the usual low-key bromides: "Glad to be back! I hate to travel! Coming home is the best part of it!" Words like this always followed the most fabulous and fascinating journeys.

It was mid-September when he returned. He would never see Pius XII again and he would return to Rome and be greeted by a new Pope in a few short months. On October 9 Eugenio Pacelli died. In the wings of history, Cushing's man of destiny, Angelo Roncalli, awaited the call to the throne of Peter.

The Archbishop, like many another world dignitary, reminisced and paid noble tribute to Pius XII:

It was my great privilege to have a private audience with His Holiness less than two months before his death, and to present to him the group of priests who accompanied me on my pilgrimage to the Holy City. As we knelt before him we all felt close to Christ Our Lord, Who had chosen him to be His Vicar on earth. How majestic he was in the dignified circumstances of his exalted position! Little did we suspect that we would be among the last to be received by him, and that he would soon be called to the presence of his Divine Master to receive the reward which his long and fruitful service of the Church so richly deserved.

I met the Pope for the first time when he visited Boston in 1936. I shall never forget the holy enthusiasm of his beaming countenance, the penetrating directness of his sparkling eyes, the reassuring frankness of his conversation, the completeness of his grasp of the mentality and outlook of the American clergy. I have often reflected on the wisdom of Divine Providence in directing his steps towards this country so soon before he was to be elected Pope. He thus brought to the See of Peter a first-hand knowledge of the condition of the Church in the nation whose strong faith and abundant material resources have proved so important for the growth and security of the Church in modern times.

Those who attended Boston College in the thirties when the gracious and graceful aristocrat, Cardinal Eugenio Pacelli, then Papal Secretary of State, visited the college campus, heard often the story about the "free days" which he gave the students. Cardinal O'Connell was there at the convocation and perhaps Father Cushing himself, who was then making a name for himself as Director of the Propagation of the Faith for the Boston Archdiocese.

After Cardinal Pacelli addressed the students in English, however richly accented, the Boston College boys whooped it up with applause and whistles, and chanted football-style cheers. The future Pope was immensely pleased and Father-Rector was smiling amiably if discreetly. Cardinal Pacelli raised his hand benevolently, calling for silence, which was given him. He then exercised his ancient prerogative:

"I give you one day off!" he said.

Father-Rector again smiled amiably, and the students whooped it up with even greater enthusiasm.

Pacelli motioned for silence again, glowing with pleasure and affection.

"I give you *two* days off!" he exclaimed, raising two fingers.

Cardinal O'Connell was beaming broadly, but Father-Rector was now smiling thinly. The students really took off and roared out their gratitude.

"I GIVE YOU *THREE* DAYS OFF!" Cardinal Pacelli said, raising three fingers

The students were out of their seats again and so was Father-Rector, signaling the end of the convocation and politely making overtures to escort the two great Cardinals off the auditorium stage.

Archbishop Cushing in his final summation of the significance of Pius XII said:

History could well evaluate Pius XII as one of the greatest of them all and one of the few outstanding leaders in an age lacking leadership. He dwelt alone on a summit close to God where strife faded into peace, hatred into love. And yet he was one of the most accessible of all Popes. All men became children before him—his children. Wherever he walked, whenever he spoke, charity prevailed. He mastered many languages but he knew best the language of the heart.

Pius was gone. The papal throne was vacant. Cushing was shortly to meet a brother in spirit, a brother in style, on the throne of St. Peter.

"Who's Cushing?" Cardinal O'Connell had once asked brusquely.

"Who's Roncalli?" many of us would query in bewilderment when John was elected Pope.

Archbishop Cushing and all of us were soon to know.

O'Connell had had his Merry Del Val and Pius X; Spellman had his Pacelli, his Pius XII; Richard James Cushing would now have his beloved Pope John.

CHAPTER XVIII

The Red Hat

"Here was the infant church, here was Peter and through those long journeys through the Mediterranean area, St. Paul longed for the day he might join the Church in the Eternal City."—Father James C. Cunningham, C.S.P. on Cardinal Cushing at Santa Susanna Church, Rome, 12-19-58.

In his simple, light, and readable biography of Pope John, Cardinal Cushing sums up the swift and dynamic early weeks of Roncalli's reign and makes some interesting observations on Giovanni Battista Montini, the present Pope Paul.

The holy splendor of the Papal Coronation took place on November 4th. Now the man of action moved. Within a month of his election he created twenty-five new Cardinals, raising the membership to seventy-five. This broke a tradition that was four hundred years old.

One of the first to be named was the Archbishop of Milan, Giovanni Battista Montini. Montini had been a close aide of Pius XII before becoming Archbishop and had been prominently mentioned as a Papal possibility. He was famed far and wide as a friend of the workingman who espoused strong liberal thinking in the social order and in the Church itself.

Physically he resembled Pius XII, lean and burning with fervor for the good of man and the glory of God. But in a deeper way he resembled the plump and jolly Pope John. That was in the sense of the times, of the need for change in the Church in order to compete with the swift and efficient paganism of the world.

In the mind and as a man of action, to sum it up, Montini was very close to Pope John. The Penguin and the Arctic Tern, you might say, but each alert to the best interests of the Church in a ruthless, carnal world. 'This Montini could have been Pope,' it was said. Pope John generously kept alive that possibility by promptly making him a Cardinal.

Two American Archbishops were among those receiving the Red Hat at that time—myself and the late Archbishop O'Hara of Philadelphia.

On Sunday evening, November 16, the news of his cardinalatial designation was communicated to Cushing by the Apostolic Delegate, Archbishop Amleto Cicognani, who had at long last been made a Cardinal himself. The poor boy from South Boston was now to be a Prince of the Church. He was pretty much alone with the news, except for a call or two to his relatives and some communication with his household staff. The wire services did not announce the great word to the world until 6 A.M. the next morning. The Cardinal has said that in the late, dead hours of that Sunday evening, any one whom he would look upon as a press advisor—Monsignor Lally, or Father John Grant, or his secretary—was either asleep or not around.

In any case, the Archbishop had long been his own man before the press and in public relations, and would continue to be so. He lived with the great fact, nostalgically, mellowly, perhaps with an occasional touch of terror and uncertainty, until morning.

His thoughts then must have looked ahead to his future role. He told us in the winter of 1964: "I never wanted to be a Bishop. While doing missionary work for the Society of the Propagation of the Faith, I was the happiest priest in the United States. When I became Cardinal, they got a Cardinal who didn't know what it was all about. I didn't know Italian or any other modern language. I had no friends in Rome. When I went over there to get the Red Hat I couldn't even talk to them. All I could do was keep reminding myself that I was only a *tool of God*. I could not see myself as a Prince of the Church, but rather as a slave of Christ. So, if the Holy Father wanted to give me the Red Hat, it was all right by me as a tribute to the people, the

195

wonderful people and their priests that I was representing. I was thrilled that the Holy See recognized them by giving them a Prince of the Church."

This was the tenor of Cushing's remarks in the excitement of press, radio, and TV interviews on Monday, November 17, the day after he had heard the news. He spoke in this fashion at a scheduled diocesan affair which he refused to cancel that evening. He held to the theme on through the Consistory.

Of course, Cushing was very much taken with Pope John right from the start, and John with him. Motives and circumstances which we have touched on seemed to indicate that Pius XII was not in a hurry to make Cushing a Cardinal. Besides, the Father Feeney affair could not have been a big boost toward a Red Hat. Cushing was not at fault, but the rumpus had occurred in his Archdiocese.

It took Pope John to recognize Cushing, and he did it quickly, knowing Cushing hardly at all personally, but knowing him well through his world reputation as a man of the people and a priest dedicated to the Universal Church.

Cushing's private remarks about John again follow a certain pattern, but they are more warm and intimate in texture than some of his better-known public commentary. "I had never heard of him before he became Pope. Then when I saw him going to the prisoners, to old folks, to the laborers, even to the Communists, I said, 'Good God, that's my man.' For this is my own concept of the priesthood. My methods are somewhat akin to his. I go around to prisons and go about every place where somebody is in need of a word of encouragement or a helping hand. That is the best contribution I can make: to preach the gospel of love and heal the contrite of heart. I identify myself with all kinds of projects despite my limited ability."

Then the Cardinal added: "Like John, I came from the poor, lived poor, and saw in both our lives a total dedication to a cause. I recognized John as an apostle of love and

196

later came to be convinced that John was the Lord's answer to the confusions and misunderstandings of modern times, between those of other faiths and Catholics, and, equally important, between believers and those who have no religion at all. If the world is to be saved, it is men of goodwill who will save it, all men of goodwill."

Then he made a few tangential remarks about Billy Graham, tolerance, Communism.

"I like Billy Graham. He does a lot of good in the world. The compelling need of the world today is to meet on a level where we can live. How any one who believes in God could be anti-Semitic or anti-Protestant, or anti-Catholic, I don't know. But since Communism aspires to suppress all religions, those who have inherited the faith of their fathers should form a united front against that conspiracy."

There is a touch of the *non sequitur* here; Cushing invariably goes into remarks on his pet subject, the evil of Communism, when words fail him or an image crosses his mind.

These things were said in a mood of reminiscence, in 1964. Back in that exciting and triumphal December of 1958, Cushing was preparing to go to Rome where he would meet Pope John and take his seat in the August Senate of the Church. Everybody was after Cushing's handshake now; he had arrived; and it seemed that everybody wanted to go to Rome with him. He seemed wary of people he had never heard from previously, who now wanted to get in on the reflected glory. Some of these people wanted now to participate in some great, commemorative event which would yield money for his charities. He had his answer ready, one both charitable and reasonable.

He can be most candid in his weekly "News-Notes" in *The Pilot*. This half-page of devotional, financial, epistolary *potpourri* is not only a catch-all for previews of his coming projects, but a place where he is likely to reprint little paragraphs or poems which people send him by mail. As is

197

his custom, he usually has some needy writer helping him put the column together each week, and he or she, as the case may be, gets a pretty good monthly fee. There are times when the men down at *The Pilot* hardly touch this column at all. When he sends it down, they just run it as is. In the opening paragraphs of the column which are often pure Cushing, he can let go with a pique and candor which regular readers of the News-Notes immediately recognize. For example, writing recently about raising money and the endless drudgery required, he says, chidingly:

I am tired of appeals for help. How often have I heard or read that complaint. To those who make that or like statements let me answer that for almost 44 years in the priesthood it is time that I was tired of making appeals for others. Truth to tell, I am tired but not from begging, rather from the conviction that so few help me or respond in any way to my constant efforts to support an extensive spiritual, educational, charitable and missionary program of a large Archdiocese.

You can bet your "galero" if you have one—that wide, flat, much-tasseled red hat that Cardinals receive and never wear—that Cardinal Cushing writes the candid News-Notes himself, alone. No broken-down former stars of the Catholic literary revival, no underpaid Catholic professors with too many children, no brilliant whiskey priests, no holy, destitute maiden ladies—all types of which he compassionately and generously patronizes—nobody "ghosts" or researches that kind of writing for His Eminence.

And when he wrote in the News-Notes about his forthcoming trip to the Consistory, he directed his remarks right to the point and with the same candor:

Many inquiries have been made concerning the possibility of going to Rome for the public ceremonies connected with the Consistory and to visit the sacred edifices and places of the center of Christendom. The only answer I have is that anyone and everyone is welcome insofar as I am concerned. But you must make your own arrangements. Write to the Chancery Office, 1 Lake Street, Brighton, Massachusetts, and ask for reservations on one of the planes leaving the airport, December 9th or 10th etc.

Others have inquired about a collection, a drive or some other kind of campaign for a gift to the Diocesan Charity Fund. I would not be interested in any project of this kind. The same people who are always giving to me would be asked to give again and again. Our Charity Fund functions every day in the year. Contributions to it can be made anytime.

With regard to receptions on a large public scale, here again, I am not interested. I shall be moving about as usual in all parts of the diocese when I return from Rome and in that way I shall greet and meet more people than I could meet in any stadium or auditorium. Furthermore in place of one central gathering we shall arrange a special spiritual service for every deanery. In this way we can cover the entire Archdiocesan area and greet the faithful in all sections. Let us take it all in stride. God doesn't need us. But we can do nothing without Him. The Kindgom of God is not of this world.

And he did exactly as he said he would, when he returned from Rome. He showed himself in what he called his "glad rags" on TV, referring scripturally to himself: "Fear not, it is I." He knew the great enthusiasm and healthy curiosity of his people about the "Santa Claus" costume and he showed himself in full or partial regalia to the extent his busy, regular schedule permitted.

Could Cushing take the trip to Rome in stride? Four great planeloads of dignitaries and friends, including Cushing, Cardinal-Designates Amleto Cicognani of Washington, D.C., John O'Hara of Philadelphia, Bishops Wright and Minihan, Mayor John Hynes of Boston, Monsignori Lally and Sennott, and of course, the Cardinal's family, took off from Logan International Airport on December 10.

Wild enthusiasm, cheering, cardboard signs marked their departure and a no less enthusiastic reception awaited them at Ciampino Airport. To the press Cushing repeated his theme of gratitude to the Archdiocese and its people: "If it will help me to do more for others, I personally am content to assume this honor and all the obligations. I regard it as being given to the Archdiocese of Boston rather than to myself. I feel very grateful to His Holiness John XXIII for the great honor which I happily accept, not because of anything exceptional about myself, but for the wonderful priests, religious, and faithful of Boston and New England."

On December 16 a reception was held at the North American College where 1100 prelates, priests, and laymen had gathered to honor Cushing, O'Hara, and Cicognani so that the official notifications of their cardinalatial elevations could be read in traditional ceremony. Bill Callahan of the *Boston Globe* tells us that the outpouring of congratulations was endless. "As dusk fell, black limousines drove slowly through the streets of Rome, bearing the long-time members of the College of Cardinals to their new colleagues, to welcome and congratulate them."

It was at the North American College that Cushing had donated an organ, and this was duly acknowledged. At the College which he wanted to attend, but could not because of World War I, he was the star of the show. Yet he could not respond fully to this acclaim because of a pall of sadness which had been thrown over his spirit. For he was well aware that his unmarried sister Elizabeth had passed away on Saturday. Members of his family, his nephew, Father William Francis, and his two sisters, Mrs. Anne Francis and Mrs. Mary Pierce, had returned to attend the South Boston funeral while the Cardinal's brother John remained at his side.

Father Francis celebrated the requiem Mass at the old family church of St. Brigid's in Southie on the 16th and a requiem Mass was sung by Bishop Jeremiah Minihan, in the Cardinal's presence, at his titular church of Santa Susanna the next day.

The ceremony of the presentation of notifications has been portrayed for millions in Otto Preminger's movie, *The Cardinal*. A prototype of Tom Tyron stood in Rome in 1958, tall, lean, nostalgic, deeply moved, and certainly stormed by reminiscent memories as Auxiliary Bishop Minihan read the notification in Italian. Monsignor Robert Sennott, Chancellor of the Archdiocese, served as the Cardinal's chamberlain and the English translation was read by Bishop Wright, then of Worcester. Serving as chaplain to the Cardinal at the ceremony was Rev. George A. Schlichte, then vice-rector of the North American College and now, home and a Monsignor, tapped by Cushing as rector of the burgeoning Pope John Seminary for belated vocations in Weston, Massachusetts.

Cameras were snapping, priests, nuns and laity were standing on chairs—six hundred of them from Boston—and Archbishop Cicognonani, speaking for all three designates, ignited a burst of applause when he said: "We renew our dedication and expression of gratitude to Pope John. All of America offers its heartfelt thanks."

Thirteen hundred years of tradition were packed into that announcement which stormed Cushing's ears, mind and heart: "For the glory of Almighty God and the honor of the Holy Apostolic See, receive the Red Hat, the special insignia of the cardinalatial dignity . . ."

For his sister Elizabeth, seven other requiem masses were said simultaneously at the altars of Santa Susanna, the next day, while Bishop Minihan celebrated the principal mass. The Bishop was at the main altar, Bishop Smith of Lebanon was at the crypt altar, and at six side altars were Monsignori Murray, Dowd, McNamara, Sexton and Twiss, of Boston, and Msgr. Johnson of Portland, Maine.

The then Mayor John Hynes of Boston who wrote an observant and witty diary for the Boston *Globe* during the Roman journey, tells us about Santa Susanna during the multiple requiems: "High over the nave of the Old Church, the wall was covered with resplendent paintings of scenes from the Old and New Testament . . . four great prophets: Isaias, Jeremias, Ezekiel and Daniel looked down in amazement . . ."

And indeed they might, at the overwhelming spectacle of the Holy Catholic Irish Church of Boston taking over old Santa Susanna's on every side.

That afternoon there was a semi-public Consistory in the

Vatican Palace at which the new Cardinals received their cape-like mozettas and the well-known red birettas. There, Cardinal Cushing got a good look at Pope John for the first time. A private audience came later.

On the 18th, in the sweeping basilica of St. Peter, where it is reported that over 30,000 people witnessed the ceremony, the great Consistory took place. Here while 10,000 candles burned and actually illuminated the Basilica, here amid the flower-banked main altar and the pews red and purple with prelates of the Church, here before the enthroned Pope, Cardinal Cushing took his place in line to receive the flat, low-brimmed galero or traditional Red Hat.

John XXIII was to make twenty new Cardinals in thirty-five minutes. When Cushing reached the top of the altar and knelt before the Pope, two ceremonial officials suspended the flat-crowned red hat over his head while Pope John recited in Latin: "In praise of the Almighty God and as an ornament to the Holy Apostolic See, receive the red hat, singular distinction of the cardinalatial dignity, which signifies that you must show yourself intrepid, even unto shedding your blood for the exaltation of holy faith, for the peace and tranquility of the Christian people, for the increase and honor of the Roman Church."

Then the red biretta was held by the Pope over each head, symbolically, and he leaned over and whispered to each new Cardinal: "Brother." While the Pope held the biretta over Cushing's head and whispered the loving, elevatial word, tears were to be seen filling the eyes of Boston's greatest living Irishman and he was observed swallowing hard several times. The American "Hurrah" the Italian "Viva," echoed from the soaring marble columns of the Basilica, and Boston had a Cardinal once again.

The next ceremony, closed to the public, was the Secret Consistory held in the 100 foot long Consistory Hall in the Vatican Palace. Here, Pope John presented Cushing and the others with a topaz ring, admitted them to the privilege

202

of counseling him and speaking at Consistories. Said John: "We open your minds so that you may give your opinion in consistories, congregations and other cardinals' functions."

That night the Cardinal tossed a festive dinner for his Boston pilgrims and friends at the Grand Hotel, Rome. He would accompany about fifty-five of them to a special audience with the Holy Father on Saturday, the 19th.

There was considerable effort to hold the Boston Party together, at least until the dinner and the private audience had taken place. It is curious that the prosperous young Boston-Irish in the party turned their thoughts to other things now that the Cardinal had been officially elevated. Some were in a hurry to leave ancient Rome to watch a televised football game back in the U.S.A. Mayor Hynes tells us in his newspaper column: "Most of the young people are anxious to get back so that they can see the Giants-Browns professional football play-off game for the Eastern Division Championship."

Hynes also reported on the dinner. He said that the Cardinal seemed remarkably refreshed after the strain of the long day of ritual and ceremonies. Cushing talked that evening of the Universal Church. "Likes Rome . . . Likes Italian people and their faculty of arriving at inner peace . . . Thanks all on tour . . . Says they are representatives of all in Archdiocese . . . Reiterates that honor to him is pleasing only because it is honor to all Archdiocese. Happy mood. Relieved that strain is over. His days have been full." It was duly noted that Cardinal Spellman attended the dinner: "Jovial, courteous, happy for Boston that Boston boy now a Cardinal."

The journalists were talking and writing of how quickly Cushing had caught on as a celebrated and recognizable world figure. It was said that the demonstrative Romans would yell: "Cardinal!" whenever they saw him entering or alighting from his car. He was mobbed several times in public, and there was little question that he was *the* American Cardinal of stature and significance in the minds of the people.

On the 19th, the Cardinal took possession of his titular Church of Santa Susanna, staffed by American Paulists. It was then that Father James Cunningham compared him with St. Paul, finally getting to Rome, triumphantly, gloriously.

The devil has seemed to make mischief with fire and smoke more than once when Cushing is in the midst of an enormously important event. At the Presidential inauguration of John Kennedy the microphone caught fire while the Cardinal was speaking. Here, at Santa Susanna's such diabolical trickery might have ended in human tragedy. During the ceremony of possession, the cassock of an Italian Monsignor accidentally touched a lighted candle and burst into flames. The garment was literally torn from his back by those around him and his life was saved.

Later that Saturday it was a private audience and a chat with Pope John that was probably the supreme delight of Cardinal Cushing's trip.

"There's nothing put on," the Cardinal remembered about his first great meeting with his special "Beloved Shepherd." "Ah," Pope John said, "Cushing of Boston!"

The kind, democratic manner Cushing had heard about was a fact. There were 350 in an audience that had started out to be a small one, mostly Americans. The Pope talked directly to the Americans, in Italian, and was promptly translated.

He said that America is blessed with riches and many gifts of nature which he hoped each would use in such a manner that they wouldn't interfere with his chances of going to heaven.

"Serve God and neighbor," he told the pilgrims, then reacting to their great hand-shaking cordiality, he said: "Your American enthusiasm will tear off my arm, but I love it."

In a more private audience later Pope John said to Cushing: "We hope to meet again in Paradise and there we will speak in English."

It was time to go home. The Cardinal left with the good feeling that he might be back soon, back to see his friend Pope John.

At Ciampino Airport Cushing repeated his theme of gratitude to the faithful of "the New England area." He said the Universal Church is a buffer to, yes, Communism. He let fly at his favorite whipping boy, Communism, sensing he had an international sounding board of journalists right there at the airport. "The faithful of Boston are cognizant of the evils of the ideology of Communism, which is intrinsically evil, not only from a religious viewpoint but from the economic and social viewpoint."

Back at Logan Airport, after a stopover at Shannon in Ireland, he confessed to the press that he had fallen asleep while over Erin's shore. He talked to the press with enthusiasm and affection about Pope John. "The Pope is a very kindly and humble man. I hope I'm not being irreverent but he is somewhat my type. He likes people. He likes to be of service to people."

Cushing said that it was he who had characterized the Pontiff as "Good Pope John" and he expressed the hope that the phrase would catch on. And it did.

There at the airport he said Mass for fifty of his group in the chapel of Our Lady of the Airways. Before going on home he ruminated some more for the press as so often before:

"I'm happy to be home."

"I was the happiest priest in the world before this ecclesiastical honor was conferred upon me."

"The higher you go, the more difficult it becomes and the heavier the crosses you have to carry."

One of those future crosses, which he would carry out of loyalty and perhaps gratitude was waiting right there to escort him home, in the person of Boston Police Commissioner Leo Sullivan. Sullivan would resign his post under fire in about a year and the Cardinal would find himself in a frying pan with regard to his position on the Key Shop bookie scandal.

It was almost 1959. In little more than a year, Jack Kennedy would be in the thick of a campaign for the presidency of the United States.

The new Cardinal had said it at Logan International Airport, once and for all: "The higher you go . . . the heavier the crosses you have to carry."

CHAPTER XIX

Cushing and J. F. K.

"They told me, Heraclitus,
    They told me you were dead,
    They brought me bitter words to hear,
    And bitter tears to shed."

As the reader may surmise, "the Kennedy chapter" is the most difficult chapter to write in such a book as this. So much has been said about this staunch and affectionate relationship between Cushing and his "best friend," the late and still sorely lamented President of the United States. So very much has been said and written about the relationship by Cushing himself, the feature writers, commentators, reporters, that one despairs of approaching it well. Yet for a native Boston writer who has watched both Cushing and Kennedy out of the corner of his eye for twenty years, there is probably the obligation to add his few observations and insights, however limited.

The public record is familiar: the Kennedy Memorial Hospital for retarded children in honor of Joe, Jr., concerning which the Cardinal gave Joe, Sr., public credit for a million and a half dollars, but grumbled privately that he only received about $600,000 and that the maintenance, salary, development, and research expenses were dropped directly in his lap. There was the growing relationship with Jack, who gave Cushing some good, fat checks and items like the royalties from *Why England Slept*. Again, Cushing officiated at the nuptials of Jack and Jacqueline in Newport. He introduced the young Jack, then a second-term Senator, at a Catholic Telephone Guild Communion breakfast in 1959 as "the next President of the United States"—quite a bold statement for an American Cardinal and one which was printed in the daily press. Cushing gave, of course, the impassioned and long-winded invocation at the Inaugural. At Bobby Kennedy's request, he raised a million dollars to help ransom the Bay of Pigs prisoners and get them home for Christmas in 1962. And then he had a lachrymose, yet nobly restrained role in the heart-rending pomp and panoply, the Graeco-Roman splendor, of the Kennedy funeral. Most of this the public saw with its own eyes, but somehow we sense there is more to it than the conventional ballet in which the public shared.

It would seem that Cushing's interest in the Kennedy family is authentic and long-standing. A former Harvard Square newsboy, Alec Milley, tells us that both Joe, Jr., and Jack were steady customers of his for the then staunchly Republican *Boston Herald* in the morning and the *Traveler* in the afternoon. Milley says that, in the late thirties, Joe, Jr., apparently taking graduate studies, lived in the Bay State Apartments on Massachusetts Avenue, Cambridge. Milley also used to see Joe's brother the young Jack Kennedy, a student living at Dunster House; and more than once, to that apartment there came an ecclesiastical visitor, the new auxiliary bishop named Richard James Cushing.

Were these friendly visits, at parental suggestion, also calculated to cast a keen, clerical eye at how the two handsome, scholarly, fun-loving young bachelors were getting along?

The role of the watchdog was never so much Cushing's, in any event, as it was that of the present Boston Municipal Court Judge Francis Morrissey, who was for many years a high-class legman for Big Joe Kennedy. Morrissey, for many years, both as law student and as lawyer, was the devoted and dedicated servant of Big Joe. One of his assignments was to keep an eye on the "boys" and, it is believed, report their deportment to the master of Hyannisport, Washington, D.C., Chicago, Miami, Hollywood, or wherever Joe, Sr., was holding forth in one of his many fabulous caps as financier, high government bureaucrat or Hollywood tycoon. It is believed also that Morrissey was a little unpopular with the boys, because of his onerous but required duties as beadle, tattle-tale, or what you will.

When Jack became President there was a big push on, backed by Big Joe, to award a vacant Federal Judgeship in the Boston area to Morrissey. Morrissey is a devout son of the Church and father of a large and attractive family. The former Senator John Kennedy had earlier prevailed on the then Governor Foster Furcolo to make him a Boston Municipal Court Judge. But in 1960-61 a report by the Bar Association on Morrissey's legal qualifications for a Federal judgeship left something to be desired, and this seemed to give President Kennedy the "out" he might have been looking for. Morrissey did not get the White House plum.

Cardinal Cushing told us that Big Joe Kennedy felt bad about this and wanted to make it up to Morrissey. The Cardinal said that while he was out on a Hyannisport boat trip with Joe Sr., the latter asked him to talk to Judge Morrissey on the way home to Boston, and ask him if he'd accept a trust fund for the Morrissey children, in the vicinity of $75,000. On the automobile ride back to Boston with Morrissey, the Cardinal did so. Cushing told us that Morrissey in an admirable stand of integrity and independence would have nothing to do with the proposal. The Cardinal used all his powers of persuasion, and even said he thought he could get Joe Sr. to double the original offer. Morrissey would have none of it, according to Cushing.

Cushing's informal observations about the Kennedys help us find the range of his true relationship, which is deeper and more sincere than the popular pablum of press, radio, TV. He told us once with rasping irritation that he deeply resented any innuendo which implied that the Kennedys had "made him." "They never made *me*," he could growl despite his avowed affection for Jack and Jacqueline and his long-standing cordial relationship with Joe, Rose, Bobby, Teddy and the girls. The whole testimony of this book, indicates that Cushing was "made" by other factors than the Kennedys—the chief factor being himself. It is true, however, that Jack's accession to the Presidency and Cushing's elevation to the College of Cardinals, which were close enough in time to be considered almost simultaneous, gave Cushing an ocean swell of prestige, nationally and internationally.

Cushing says almost paradoxical things like: "I was never close to the Kennedys; Jack, yes . . ." He was also close to Jacqueline, especially in the period of mourning. But the paradox of closeness and distance must be true, because it comes out of a deep place in his feelings.

And the truth one repeatedly senses is that Cushing is not close to any one. He is really, starkly, so alone, God's lonely man, it would appear, in the solo money-raising dynamism of his life, in the do-it-yourself compassion of his days. Cushing is often his own secretary, his own parish and institutional visitor, his own press agent, and despite occasional ghost-writing help, his own sermonizer and statement maker—alone, a towering example of one of God's lonely men.

Next to Jack Kennedy's horrible and tragic death, the political campaign and election were probably Cushing's greatest trials in the early 'sixties. Cushing wanted to get into the campaign and help where he could, yet he knew any outward show could hurt the candidate, so he had to continually brake himself and lean over backwards to stay out of the fight.

He tells us that he did have a telephone conversation with Governor David Lawrence, of Pennsylvania, a devout Catholic, at a crucial point just before the Democratic National Convention in the summer of 1960. He thinks he may have had something to do with influencing the Governor, who warmed up to Jack Kennedy very slowly, and who controlled the big, key Pennsylvania delegation. The Cardinal said something about "holding the purse strings for old Joe," which we couldn't quite understand. But he made it clear that in the first ballot at the Convention, the Pennsylvania vote was crucial. And: "It was the first ballot—or else!"

We sensed the surge of political blood and sporadic political savvy, for an instant, in this thoroughly South Boston man, who can also reach such heights as a holy priest and as the foremost man of compassion and aid in the Universal Church. Cushing's complexity and enigma as an individual always and inevitably remain.

Cushing said he was not particularly sure that the late President Kennedy's election was any sign of growing tolerance among the people. "I was never certain that Al Smith was defeated primarily on the religious question. There were so many other issues. My personal opinion was that I didn't care who was elected President as long as someone was elected like a Jew or a Catholic, in order that we might break through this iron curtain of intolerance." But this typical *non-sequitur* probably means that Cushing truly *does* believe Al Smith was defeated because of religious intolerance.

"As for the martyred President Kennedy personally, I liked the way he got ahead of it all. He gave his honest opinion: *'Here I am. This is what I believe, and I am a Democrat who is a Catholic. I am not a Catholic running for office. I am the nominee of the Democratic Party. I happen to be a Catholic. I am responsible for my conduct in that religion, but as President of the United States I am obligated to the Constitution.'* He had courage, he had confidence; his election has clarified a lot of false thinking."

The Cardinal, while seemingly admitting to a little chicanery around Democratic Convention time, which politicking was pretty much within the Irish-Catholic family, insists that he played no part in the actual Presidential campaign. Nor would Jack Kennedy allow him to do so.

"He really didn't need me. But I did want to silence a

211

whispering campaign among the Catholics themselves that Kennedy was not a practicing Catholic. I drew up a statement denying this, and submitted it to the candidate and his father. To their undying credit, they said: 'Don't publish it.'

"Then, at the request of a leading national magazine, I prepared an article on a Catholic for President, and at the last minute submitted a rough draft to Kennedy. The pay I was to receive for the benefit of one of my favorite charities was extraordinary. After a day and a half Kennedy telephoned me and said that the piece was the best of the kind he had read so far, 'But I don't want to get you involved. So forget the whole thing.'

"I withdrew the article. All that Kennedy asked of me was: 'Say a prayer for me and leave the rest to the Lord.' Thereafter, I remained still."

The Cardinal implied something that everybody in the Archdiocese knows: it was very hard for him to keep quiet. He said he longed to answer charges made by Catholics and non-Catholics alike. But Kennedy would only repeat: "I don't want you to involve the Catholic Church in this campaign in any way whatsoever."

"I think this was a great tribute to him. I admire him. Granted that he made some failures. He was able to take the responsibility for them."

Then Cushing reminisced further about the man he had called eulogistically "my dearest and nearest friend."

"I think I have seen him at very close range. I looked upon him as a Presidential possibility even before his first election to Congress, and during his first early campaign I used to introduce him at various charity and social functions. I saw him as a man of ability, very objective, an acute politician. However, over and above that, his greatest earthly ambition was to be of service to his country.

"I don't think the late President would want me to say that he was a very religious man. As a matter of fact, I wouldn't want anybody to say that *I* was a very religious man, because I was sort of a natural type. President Kennedy, when he became President, became a prayerful man. Since he assumed the office, he had many sleepless nights, and during those periods of sleepless hours, he would get up out of his bed and kneel down and pray.

"How do I know this? His own father told me!

"So we had a President with courage. I think we had a President with one hand in the hand of God; but for some reason God permitted him to be taken from us."

Yes, but before the Lord took him from us, he gave him to us. And there is no other consolation for the enduring sorrow of Kennedy's tragic death than to banish the choking bitterness and repeat with the Psalmist: "The Lord giveth and the Lord taketh away; blessed be the name of the Lord!"

Never in our lifetime, and perhaps not in that of our children, did many of us believe that a Catholic could become President of the United States. But there he was, handsome Jack, winner by a nose in a photo-finish; there he was in the White House, the man whom the late Massachusetts Governor, Paul A. Dever, had called "The first of the Irish Brahmins." Warm pride burned in the heart of Richard Cardinal Cushing, and in that of many others besides. And the Cardinal of Boston would himself travel to Washington for the Inaugural.

The paralyzing blizzard which struck Washington, D.C. and its environs, long and relentless, on the evening of January 19th, 1961, and into the wee hours of J. F. K.'s glorious Inauguration Day, will long and starkly be remembered by all who fought through it toward the Capital by air, rail or automobile.

This writer was in a station wagon with three officers of the Massachusetts Legislature, inching, it seemed, toward Washington through the heavy, relentless swirling storm when the announcement came over the radio that our Cardinal-Archbishop and his companion, Monsignor George

Kerr, were high up above us in an airliner hopelessly circling Washington and preparing to fly back to New York. We wondered, Would he make it? Would he be there, standing beside the President in the fulfillment of the long belief in America, its idea and Constitution—that surely a Catholic, a Jew, a Negro, could one day be President?

We were on our own. No fancy invitations, no reservations, no special "in," but on the other hand, we were to experience a hearty cordiality and feeling of welcome which was to be fulfilled all over Washington, because we were fellow Boston-Irish; we had seen the President-Elect growing up in our town, had seen him walk our narrow, cow-path streets which for him were to broaden now into Pennsylvania Avenue, Fifth Avenue, the Rue De La Paix, the Autobahn, and finally, tragically, the wide and bloody thoroughfare directly in front of the Texas Book Depository at Dallas.

The Cardinal, meanwhile, had to endure an interminably cold and dreary train-ride from Pennsylvania Station, but he made it. He sat on the platform with the Apollo-like young President-Elect in the blinding sunshine that had, almost as irritatingly, replaced the blinding snow.

Everybody knows the Cardinal talked too long and the nation, not yet familiar with his raspy and at times braying eloquence was perhaps a bit uncomfortable and unreceptive. The lectern almost caught on fire, the smoke was rising and the Cardinal told us that someone behind him quipped: "The devil is asking for equal time."

We asked the Cardinal, in 1964, about the original composition of his too-lengthy remarks of Invocation. He said he had received some help from a layman, Professor Walsh of Newton College of the Sacred Heart. Walsh was the father of a very large family of a dozen children or more, and had written a humorous book about Catholic family life. The Cardinal learned of Prof. Walsh and, showing his partiality to laymen, especially those with the burden of a family, he commissioned him to do editorial work here and there. But Professor Walsh was a bit of a character. Even at hours when he was supposed to be teaching at that very proper college of the Madames, he and his wife used to take off and go to movie houses in Boston. A Newton banker who held the Walsh mortgage told us that, one day, Professor Walsh bought a second-hand school bus, packed in it his substantial tribe and all their impedimenta, and disappeared from Boston. Thus, over the horizon, the author of an Inaugural Invocation. (We later asked Monsignor Lally if he had had an editorial "shot" at the manuscript. He said he had, and that he did some work on it but perhaps had not shortened it as much as he would have liked.)

Like many another Washington visitor, fearful of the "cauld blast" of Inauguration Day, we watched and listened to the Cardinal and the President in the cozy warmth of our bedroom in Washington's Hotel Statler. Later, we did get out into the cold to view the Inaugural Parade in a box just under the Huntley-Brinkley aerie, and just across the street from the President's reviewing stand. We had hoped to see the Cardinal there also, but we wangled our way into that choice, if open and unsheltered lower box, by patiently, step-by-step, showing our badges and credentials from the Massachusetts Legislature. They seemed to work the necessary magic with the Federal and city guards. President Jack waved at us, while he rubbed his gloved hands together cheerily and stomped his feet against the relentless cold.

But the Cardinal was not there. He was too smart for that, and shrewdly considerate of the President and his family. He had given away his ticket to the post-inaugural luncheon, and had already begun to make his way home to Boston. The Cardinal did not want to create a national image of a President's Cardinal-Archbishop, lurking Richelieu-like against maroon curtains. There would be no ecclesiastical tunnel to the White House from 2101 Commonwealth, nor were Pope John's Swiss Guards digging an

215

especially large-doored underground passage from the Vatican to Jack Kennedy's desk.

Such images were all a lot of baloney, even in Al Smith's time, and many American citizens were to find that out, perhaps with some twinges of remorse, as Jack Kennedy's administration got well under way. The American Catholic hierarchy, the clergy and the religious, despite the glowing pride of many of them concerning the late President (and the antipathy of others) remained low-key and unobtrusive while he was in the White House. Even the great difference of opinion concerning Federal Aid to private schools, especially on the primary and secondary school levels, was conducted with remarkable composure and, indeed, with a sense of mutual respect for J. F. K.'s position as President of all the people.

The pattern of the Cardinal's relations with the President and his family, meanwhile, had always been touched by great joys and great sorrows. There was the Cardinal's concern for Joe Kennedy when he was stricken with a cerebral hemorrhage in December of 1961. The Cardinal flew out to see him when the fabled architect of a great American family regained his alertness and told him he would be well again. There was the Cardinal's mustering of a million dollars toward the ransom of the Bay of Pigs prisoners, at Bobby Kennedy's telephoned request in December of 1962. "I'll call you back in an hour," the Cardinal had rasped. He did, and the money was put on the line. Using the sources of his annual million-dollar contributions, to the Latin-American St. James Society, the Cardinal put the amount together, revealing that the largest single donation was $1000.

Although Jacqueline got to see Pope John, the Cardinal sometimes expresses regret that his two favorite "Johns," so much in admiration of each other, actually never got to meet in person.

The Cardinal tells us that Kennedy was particularly taken with John's great encyclical "Pacem In Terris" in which the Holy Father called for the settlement of international tensions in the Kennedy style of meetings and negotiations. John had also exhorted the nations to overcome racial and national barriers and called for general disarmament, all of which suited J. F. K. excellently well. The Cardinal remembers that J. F. K. had said about "Pacem In Terris": "This encyclical of Pope John makes me proud to be a Catholic."

Cushing wrote in his biography of Angelo Roncalli, entitled: *Call Me John:* "Before John died, he bequeathed to the late President an autographed copy of that encyclical with some other personal tokens of esteem. His Holiness had hoped to present these mementos to the President of the United States when he visited Rome. But when that visit took place Pope John had been called to his reward. I had the privilege of presenting to my dear friend these gifts when President Kennedy came to the Eternal City shortly after the election of Pope Paul VI."

The Cardinal greeted J. F. K. on that occasion, in the summer of 1963 at the North American College, throwing him a mock haymaker to the chest, much to the delight of the press and photographers. Sadly, also, in that summer of Pope John's death, infant Patrick Kennedy was to die shortly after birth. The Cardinal officiated at the funeral mass of the Holy Angels and on through the burial. He noted at the service that J. F. K. would not take his hand off the little white coffin, just as Jacqueline, the noble woman of sorrow, kept her hand so often on the bronze casket of her martyred husband in that coming dark November.

Jack Kennedy continued to be the Cardinal's financial benefactor, assigning to him the television royalties of his best-selling Pulitzer Prize book, *Profiles In Courage.* Who knows what wonderful things, not just financial, he might have done for the Cardinal, had he lived on through at least five more years of the Presidency and on into the golden autumn of the young-elder statesman and scholar? Such, sadly, is just one aspect of what still seems the appalling waste of such a useful, golden life.

The Cardinal was apprehensive that Kennedy would not have been re-elected in 1964, because he believed that J. F. K. in honoring his campaign promises and his own growing convictions, had pushed Civil Rights action and legislation too far, too fast. Cushing expressed this view as late as the eve of President Kennedy's funeral, in a twenty minute informal conversation with several state and federal employees who happened to be on the plane with him as he flew from Boston to Washington on that sad duty. He took the view that the South was lost to Kennedy and that continued Civil Rights legislation and enforcement would cost too many votes in the North.

It is typical of Cardinal Cushing, both in his conservative view of the pace of the Negro ascendancy and in his extreme, unpredictable candor, under any circumstances, that he would say these things enroute to the Kennedy funeral. It is also typical of him to revert to the puritanical Irish priest when he commented informally on the speculation about an earlier secret marriage of J. F. K. He expressed a certain bitterness about the story to a wealthy Boston friend, even though the story later died. He is always his own man when it comes to faith or morals—and often in political, social and economic areas also—he speaks for himself and by himself on the abiding beliefs and traditions of the Church and he is never deterred by close friendship when it comes to expressing an honest opinion that may drive the shiv in and twist where it hurts.

Newspapermen, intellectuals, publicists, teachers, writers, continually ask: What's behind these sporadic wild and droll vocal outbursts of Cushing's which comes out both formally and informally? Does he drink? Is he getting senile?

One editor for a major weekly magazine asked us in 1964: "Does he drink?"

218

The honest reaction to that question is: "Of course he does. Do you know a good Irishman that doesn't?" But there's a lot more to it than that. People who know Cushing say he used to take a few when he was younger. His favorite, then, was brandy and maybe a highball or two. Perhaps he would drink a bottle or two of beer while acting as host or while visiting friends—out on the waters of the Cape on contractor Louis Perini's cabin cruiser, for example. His lusty episcopal voice was once heard around the second floor dining hall of the Ritz Carleton in the evening but is seldom, if ever, heard there now.

Perhaps the Cardinal's favorite place of relaxation is "across the lawn . . ." For almost on the grounds of the Residence and Seminary is the home of the Cardinal's chauffeur. There he finds a congenial downstairs rumpus room, maintained by Mrs. Alfred Wasilauskas, the devoted widow of his long-time chauffeur and assistant who died in 1958. Genevieve Wasilauskas has served as the Cardinal's faithful stenographer for years. One of her sons is Cushing's chauffeur now, succeeding his father in that post. There in the re-finished cellar of Mrs. Wasilauskas, with old classmates, friends, trusted monsignori, Cushing might have one or two brandies even now. Maybe some good records are played, somebody sings an old Irish song, his old friends call him "Dick" again. In such a wholesome, informal place, right near the Residence, the big guy can ease a little of the pressure of raising $35,000 a day and the endless grind of ceremonies around the Archdiocese not to mention the rigors of Rome, Lourdes, South America, Washington, Civil Rights, the haunts of the John Birch Society, the Boston Pols, the ecumenical movement.

But the Cardinal seems to drink very little in these recent years. He suffers constantly from asthma and migraine headaches and constantly takes oxygen, particularly at night. He told us that one night in the winter of 1964, the asthma and the migraine almost drove him insane. "I went down and knocked on Father Joe Maguire's door, woke

219

him up and asked him if he had a bottle in his room. He gave me a couple of good shots of rye, but it didn't do me much good." That doesn't sound like the routine of a man who drinks. If Cushing wanted the stuff, he wouldn't need his secretary's "medicinal bottle." He could have cases of rye up in his room if he wanted them, and at no charge. No, Cushing's ideosyncratic pronouncements don't come out of anything like alcohol. The razor-edge of some of his off-the-cuff rhetoric may be honed by extreme physical discomfort, at times, but its base is invariably his unconventional personal convictions: the same pill as ever, but sometimes without the sugar coating.

Is he getting senile? This "senility whisper" recurs, especially among those temporarily bewildered by Cushing's shifts and contradictions on public issues like the John Birch Society, and Robert Welch.

The John Birch Society had absurdly stigmatized John F. Kennedy as a Communist and yet the Cardinal has recently and partially repudiated that group because of a hoax about one particular smear, in April 1964. Cardinal Cushing's seemingly contradictory position on the John Birch Society is not so bewildering or inexplicable as it at first seems, however. It is important to remember about the Cardinal that he is swayed more by people than by ideas. He is always basically the priest, in this regard, and is ultimately more concerned with the dignity and sanctity of the person as an individual. Whether that person is a liberal or a John Bircher, really doesn't matter to him.

On April 21, 1964, in a live Boston radio broadcast, the Cardinal said:

I would prefer imprisonment and death under a slave state than membership in an organization which has branded a martyred President of the United States as a Communist.

If it is true that two members of this society called my nearest and dearest friend, the late John F. Kennedy, a Communist, they and their associates owe the people of all nations who loved him and who will never forget his tragic death a profound apology.

If it is also true that these two members of the Birch Society

220

identified me with such an incredible remark, I cannot dignify them with an answer save to say—shame, shame, shame for attempting to blight the character and mar the memory and distort the image of a martyr for his country to that of a traitor.

This is pure Cushing rhetoric, by the way; there seems to be no editorial advisor involved in this statement. Such eloquent and impassioned rhetoric pours right out of his Celtic heart and soul.

Cushing's indignation was based primarily on the sustained irritant of one of those letters he'd probably like to have back again, which under the double stimulus of his fierce anti-Communism and his quite friendly relationship with Cambridge, Mass., candy-maker Robert Welch—John Birch Society Founder—he had written in 1960. He wrote then in answer to C. M. Crawford of Los Angeles, who had inquired as to the Cardinal's view of the Society:

I beg to advise you that I do not know of any more dedicated anti-Communist in the country than Robert Welch. I unhesitatingly recommend him to you and endorse his John Birch Society. Under separate cover I am sending you some literature that may be of interest to you.

The literature enclosure probably consisted of some of the reprinted addresses against and analyses of Communism which the Cardinal has published over the years.

However, since the accession of John F. Kennedy to the Presidency in 1960, and Kennedy's somewhat liberalizing influence and that of the ecumenical movement the Cardinal has been increasingly irritated by the John Birch Society. He has been especially piqued by the Los Angeles chapter's use of his letter as a shield, in their political controversies out on the coast and probably elsewhere. So when a mythical correspondent named Gretchen Van Heusen, who said she was a correspondent for Swiss and Italian Newspapers, wired him on Sunday, April 19, 1964, that two editors of *American Opinion*, the Birch Society's organ, appeared on Long John Nebel's radio program in New York City, and had quoted the Cardinal's letter and then, by juxtaposition, smeared John Kennedy and Franklin Roosevelt as Communists, the Cardinal went right into holy and irrepressible indignation.

By Friday of that week it was proven to his satisfaction that editors Scott Stanley, Jr. and Tom Davis of *American Opinion* had not made the statement about Kennedy. It was also evident after considerable checking that there was no Gretchen Van Huesen and that the telegram was a cruel hoax.

The Cardinal then became exercised about his error and possibly uncharitable remarks toward Stanley, Davis, Welch, the Society. Typically, without cozy regard for his own image, he wrote another letter and made another public statement which was headlined in the *Boston Herald* and the national press.

The second letter, which conceivably the John Birch Society could start using all over again, wherever and whenever an excerpt will help, is better than the first.

Developments since my statements on the Heywood Vincent program (in Boston) have convinced me that I was misinformed as to what had been said on your own broadcast. Also, my memory was at fault concerning my letter of April 28, 1960 to Mr. Crawford. Since I did not specifically state in that letter, that it was not to be published, permission certainly could have been implied.

My statements were made with an if, and were conditional on the accuracy of the information I had received. Under the circumstances, I now feel that many of them were unjustified. Because of my own dedication to the fight against the atheistic Communist conspiracy, I certainly do not want to do any harm to fellow battlers in the same cause. While I think the Crawford letter is now too out of date for continued use, therefore I should be glad to have Mr. Welch print this letter in the Bulletin of the John Birch Society if he wishes to do so.

And with my regret at the temporary worry caused many good people by the hoax perpetrated on me, I send you and your associates all good wishes and kind regards.

Note Cushing's phrases about his own "dedication to the fight against atheistic communism" and the more significant sentence: "I certainly do not want to do any harm to fellow battlers in the same cause." On the previous Monday, however, the Cardinal had said that he considered Welch to be a "dedicated anti-Communist" and also that he disapproved of the Society's methods. So why this lavish reversal on Friday?

The key points for any understanding of Cushing's position are his implacable opposition to Communism, his considerateness of individuals whom he may have inadvertently wronged and, apparently, his continued good feeling toward Robert Welch. The fact that the "Van Huesen" telegram was a ruthless hoax, taking cynical advantage of the Cardinal's open-heartedness and prevailing naivete, redounded to the advantage of the Birchers, in this instance, because it brought them renewed sympathy from the Cardinal. The hoaxer hurt his own cause—if he had one, or was not himself a Bircher. The result was a total loss all around—for the Cardinal and the Kennedy position. The John Birchers seem to have run off with the marbles.

But why this continued good feeling or even cordiality for Robert Welch? It appears that the Cardinal simply likes the guy, possibly on the personal level, and certainly because Welch is "a good Baptist" and a sincere, if misdirected, anti-Communist. The Cardinal admits that he met Welch during a promotion to expand the circulation of the Birch publication *American Opinion*. He says he has not seen him since then. Cushing, in fact, made an effort to promote *American Opinion* in the 1959-1960 period. Paradoxically enough, this was the time when his dear friend John F. Kennedy, who advocated every cause which the Birchers despise, was a major contender for nomination and election as Democratic President of the United States.

By some arrangement, undoubtedly through the largesse of Robert Welch, free yearly subscriptions to *American Opinion* were available to Cushing. We know of at least one Dean of a local Boston Catholic College who received a copy of *American Opinion,* a free yearly subscription, and a letter commending the magazine, over the Cardinal's signature. Presumably this package must have been sent to other Catholic educators and moulders of public opinion in Catholic ranks. Thus Cushing's anti-Communist obsession and his susceptibility to individuals, seem to have trapped him into supporting people whom, as a group, he privately calls "nuts."

The Cardinal is not now, never was, or ever will be ungrateful to people of good will who have helped him finance his monumental social, educational and religious projects. If some of them have eventually gotten into hot water in one way or another, he is not one to spit in their faces or ignore them. It is possible that in the early days, Welch was a great help to the Cardinal; but no proof of such an early relationship is known.

Undoubtedly, in his enduring sadness about John F. Kennedy's death, this great Prince of the Church regrets that he had gotten himself so innocently and naively associated with one of the major groups responsible for the emotional climate which existed in Dallas at the time of J. F. K.'s assassination.

In November of 1961, President Kennedy continued his program of entertaining American newspaper publishers at the White House and had as his guests the press executives of the Lone Star State. Among these was a contumacious violator of hospitality known as Edward Musgrove Dealey, 69-year-old publisher of the Dallas *Morning News*. In the presence of his gracious host, Dealey read an offensive statement reflecting the militant sentiment of some in his tortured community:

> We need a man on horseback to lead this nation and many people in Texas and the Southwest think that you are riding Caroline's tricycle. The American people are aroused and rightly so. They are, as a body, way ahead of Washington. If you don't believe this, read the letters from readers' columns in most United States newspapers. The general opinion of the grass-roots thinking in this country is that you and your Administration are weak sisters.

It is to the enduring dignity and stature of President Kennedy, a hot-headed, two-fisted Boston-Irishman, when he wanted to be, that in reaction he contained himself masterfully and commented: "I don't subscribe to that paper. I'm tired of reading its editorials."

The Birchers go for such warlike, impassioned prose; they look for men on white horses. The hatred and accusation and Communist-baiting which flooded the Dallas newspapers before and during the President's assassination gives us their image of what constitutes Americanism, patriotism, anti-Communism; and if you listen carefully you can hear the ominous cadence of the brown-shirts marching in the background.

This tragic event could have taken place in any city, any town in America, it is true, for nuts can create nutsville wherever they go. But it is reported that in one Dallas classroom children applauded when the news of Kennedy's death was announced. Such an atmosphere, in Dallas, Los Angeles or any place, can not warrant a Cardinal's approval.

In an address intended for the Dallas Citizens Council, but obviated by the assassin's bullets on the day of his death, President Kennedy would have said:

There will always be dissident voices heard in the land, expressing opposition without alternatives, finding fault but never favor, perceiving gloom on every side and seeking influence without responsibility. Those voices are inevitable.

But today other voices are heard in the land—voices preaching doctrines wholly unrelated to reality, wholly unsuited to the sixties, doctrines which apparently assume that words will suffice without weapons, that vituperation is as good as victory and that peace is a sign of weakness. At a time when the national debt is steadily being reduced in terms of its burden on our economy, they see that debt as the greatest single threat to our security. At a time when we are steadily reducing the number of Federal employees serving every thousand citizens, they fear those supposed hordes of civil servants far more than the actual hordes of opposing armies.

We cannot expect that everyone, to use the phrase of a decade ago, will "talk sense to the American people." But we can hope that fewer people will listen to nonsense. And the notion that this nation is headed for defeat through deficit, or that strength is but a matter of slogans, is nothing but just plain nonsense.

This was, in effect, J. F. K.'s "letter to the Birchers in Dallas."

We know how Cardinal Cushing prayed and wept in his private chapel after the news of Kennedy's assassination electrified the world. He gave an informal eulogy before the television cameras in his garden, swallowing the lump in his throat over and over again, looking up to the sky above him, finding the words there, somehow.

He later formalized those words in a published eulogy which will be an anthology piece for many years to come; the occasion of its delivery was a Requiem Mass broadcast by the Archdiocesan TV Studio, WHIS, November 24, 1963, and some of the phrases should be included here:

For me it is proper to recall him during these days of mourning, as husband and father, surrounded by his young and beloved family. Although the demands of his exalted position carried him often on long journeys and filled even his days at home with endless labors, how often he would make time to share with his little son and sweet daughter whatever time would be his own . . .

. . . charming Caroline "stealing" the publicity; jovial "John John" on all fours ascending the stairs of an airplane to greet his "daddy," and the loving mother, like all mothers, joyfully watching the two children of her flesh and blood, mindful always of three others in the nurseries of heaven . . .

We will miss him; he only waits for us in another place. He speaks to us from there in the words of Timothy: *As for me, my blood already flows in sacrifice . . . I have fought the good fight; I have finished the race; I have redeemed the pledge; I look forward to the prize that awaits me, the prize I have earned. The Lord, whose award never goes amiss, will grant it to me; to me, yes, and to all those who have learned to welcome his coming."*

. . . As for myself, I have lost my dearest and nearest friend. History will never record how close we were in life. I assure his loved ones that I shall never forget him and them whenever I pray at an altar or elsewhere.

We saw the great, gaunt Apostle of the Poor at St. Matthew's Cathedral, quiet, unobtrusive, wiping his eyes, as with helpless compassion he watched Jacqueline and the children descend the steps.

And then the ultimate prayer, at graveside that "the martyrs of all time will lead him into Heaven."

At Christmastide the Cardinal took up the theme of mourning again, in his Christmas message called "The President of Peace." It is significant that Cushing emphasized the one facet of Kennedy's presidential career that might rank him among truly great Presidents: The turning of the tide toward peace. There is no question but that President Kennedy would have been a great Chief Executive if he had lived. But he simply was not in the seat of power long enough to establish his great programs on both the national and international levels.

Cardinal Cushing seems to sense this in his Christmas Message of 1963 when he examines the Test Ban Treaty and its great possible significance in the lives of President Kennedy and all mankind. The Cardinal took as his text the Old Testament theme, from the Book of Isaiah, "The people that walked in darkness, have seen a great light. To them that dwelt in the region of the shadow of death, light is risen."

We can certainly advance the educated guess that so very much of the domestic and moral instability which plagues our families, our school decorum, our religious practice, has been due to the terror and fear implanted in the human spirit by the constant threat of holocaustal atomic war.

J. F. K. knew, in the words of Isaiah, that all too many members of the human family walked in darkness and "in the shadow of death" because of the dread of the H-Bomb.

Beset by sore domestic problems though he was: Civil Rights, the unfinished business of Abraham Lincoln; Aid to Education in which the common interest aligned him against many of his co-religionists; the liberals versus the conservatives, with life-long friends arrayed on both sides; always, he knew that world peace in a climate of dignity and justice was the mightiest challenge of his high calling.

This is the thoughtful, wise, much-experienced Cardinal, in the peak of his princely, sophisticated grace, speaking of his beloved J. F. K. in terms of the sound values J. F. K. understood. Cushing can always rise to this level; he will do so again and again. He is not himself narrow, bitter, or extremist. He is himself more in the mold of his beloved Pope John, more in the mold of all that he loved about John F. Kennedy, his "nearest and dearest friend."

CHAPTER XX

Latin America—and Boston Bookies and Pols

"I am not condemning gambling as such, but the abuses. The latter must be controlled by enforcement of the law. The so-called 'bookies' must be taken out of circulation. Countless people in our times have as the first order of business every day the placing of bets."—Richard Cardinal Cushing, December 6, 1958.

1959 was a difficult and draining year for the great new Cardinal from Boston. Early in that first full year as a Prince of the Church he got his St. James missionary band off to Peru. In the spring, at the lucrative annual Communion Breakfast of the Catholic Telephone Guild, he publicly introduced guest speaker, Senator John F. Kennedy, as the "next President of the United States."

A former official of the local telephone company, reportedly now retired, was the strong right arm of the Cardinal in the Telephone Guild. He was probably as close to Cushing as any layman gets, and the principal reason for this was his determined and unfailing ability in coming up with large sums of money to ease the Archbishop's pressing needs. He ran the fund-raising operation, with the Catholic Telephone Guild and the annual Communion Breakfast as vehicle, like a disciplined Army captain.

Several thousand members of the Guild, many of them Irish-Catholics, made monthly or weekly pledges to the Cushing Charity Fund of a dollar and up. The official and his lieutenants, most of them in key management posts, did the collecting with a check-list, and the money flowed in. As this official had most of the say on who got promoted and who got raises in the Greater Boston area, it was much more comfortable for employees to be on that check-list, and to be checked off regularly. Most of the Catholics wanted to give to Cushing, in any case, but the pressure was there, if needed. And to Cushing it was worth a bona-fide check for between fifty and sixty thousand dollars annually, usually presented to him at the Guild's Communion Breakfast. Since the official retired, it is reported that the money doesn't come in to the Cardinal as munificently from the telephone group. A strong, dedicated personality can supervise and coordinate the collection of charity money, otherwise people simply won't get it up in any kind of volume. This is true of the archdiocese, too. No successor of Cushing is going to be able to raise money like Cushing. But then, on the other hand, his successor probably won't need as much because he probably won't spend as much. He'll be a little more than busy, however, figuring out just precisely how much he owes, who he owes and how he may proceed to pay it all off.

Similar Cushing Fund employee groups have functioned informally in Boston firms, utility and city worker groups for years, especially where Irish-Catholics have been and are still prominent. There has always been good money for the Archbishop and will continue to be on a reasonably organized basis in organizations like the Boston Gas Company, the Boston Edison Company, the Boston Fire Department, Police Department, Boston City Employees, Gillette Razor Blade Company. Irish-Catholics are still strong in these organizations and give through them over and above what they give at the local parish.

1959 was a difficult year for the Cardinal because he was to feel an agonizing backlash of physical distress. The strain of his travels, the Consistory, his sister's death, the Latin American fund-raising and the new arrangements for his St. James Society priests, contributed to the excruciating asthma attacks, the piercing migraine headaches,

230

and the new affliction of shingles which forced him into St. Elizabeth's Hospital in June.

Speaking at a youth conference in Kansas City, in November, Cushing experienced a fainting spell, came out of it, collapsed completely, revived, and not only went on to deliver his vigorous address but continued his cross-country itinerary.

Then the Boston mayoralty election of 1959 turned out to be a close and bitter struggle for that most powerful and influential post. The favorite was the diminutive, hard-bitten, wily, and resourceful State Senator, John Powers and the underdog, the polio-stricken former City Councilor and State Senator, John F. Collins, who campaigned with skill, drive and tenacity from a wheel chair. Senator Powers' lifetime ambition was to become Mayor of his beloved native city. Twice previously he had run strongly against the retired incumbent Mayor John Hynes, and, now with the former popular and affable Mayor out of the running, Powers seemed, at long-last, to have the prize within his grasp.

The Mayor of Boston, under the existing charter, has almost supreme powers, is little limited by the City Council, and is in some ways more powerful and influential than the Governor of Massachusetts. Johnny Powers, a South Boston man, like Cushing, was a self-made man, in both politics and education. He had struggled mightily out of poverty and a mediocre background and had developed himself as an astute and discerning legislator and Democratic party leader. Almost everybody with influence and money in Boston, including his good friends, Archbishop Cushing and the then U.S. Senator John F. Kennedy, were openly and enthusiastically in support of his candidacy for Mayor.

His opponent, John Collins, an able lawyer and successful state and city office-holder from the more fertile vote-

231

producing expanses of Jamaica Plain and Dorchester, had valiantly overcome a devastating attack of polio, which had confined him to bed for many months and left both his legs incapacitated. With the aid of his indefatigable and dedicated wife, Mary, and a handful of heroically loyal friends like Legislative Assistant Paul Burns and Park Commissioner William J. Devine, he had conducted a campaign for the Boston City Council from his sick room and managed to win a seat on that body. Roosevelt-like, he was courageous enough and shrewd enough to sense his opportunity in an open Mayoralty fight. He wheeled his chair right into the middle of that municipal fray in which his opponent, Johnny Powers, seemed to have all the big-shots and all the campaign money. He sensed, rightly, that Powers had everything going for him *but the people* and it was to the people, on radio, TV, on the platform, and in every conceivable way, that Collins took his campaign.

The victory dinner for Johnny Powers at the Hotel Stat-ler, prior to the election, was certainly one of the most grandiose and impressive in Boston's political history. Such was the tumult and the jam of people and automobiles, such the excitement and festivity, that one would have thought the President himself was being honored. Indeed, a future President, without hesitancy, had indicated clearly in the Boston papers that Powers would make a fine Mayor. And it should be remembered that the endorsement of John F. Kennedy, then and later, was feverishly sought by Massachusetts politicians and not frequently bestowed.

Cardinal Cushing was at the head table that night at the Statler, ostensibly to give the prayer of invocation. He was proud of his friend Johnny Powers from South Boston and he was "right on the line for him," as they say. The ban-quet that night, lest we forget, meant more than acclaim and mammoth publicity, it meant money for Powers' cam-paign chest. And there were many other well-heeled sources from which the campaign money flowed in. Both as Senate minority leader, and ultimately as President of

232

the State Senate Powers had done countless favors for people, and these were appreciated. Undoubtedly, he had opened many a legal and legislative door in loyal compliance with the Cardinal's needs and wishes. The Cardinal is complex but never ungrateful.

In the face of all this, Collins, also a loyal if somewhat chagrined son of the Church, continued his appeals directly to the voters and used the effective slogan, "Power-Politics." Coyly, almost boyishly, from that wheel chair Collins convinced the come-day, go-day people of Boston that Powers had all the big-shots and the money with him, and that he, John Collins, would appreciate the support of those out there in the neighborhoods and the wards, "the little people."

Close to election day there was considerable newspaper publicity given to a bookie raid on a bar-room in East Boston which sported a large Powers campaign sign on its roof. It was in this same establishment that a rally for "Johnny" had been held some days previously, at which a well-known Monsignor had been in attendance. The prelate had been photographed with the notables at the head table. His beaming countenance was later deleted from the photo when it was run in the newspapers in connection with the bookie raid. The implication of the political dinner at East Boston, whether true or false, was that the book-making brethren were present to back Powers with their contributions. It was, therefore, no place for a Monsignor, allegedly close to the Cardinal. The prelate was an older man, by the way, and not one of "the young Turks" presently bulwarking His Eminence.

The whole business of the raid and the publicity surrounding it was unfair to Candidate Powers. Why the newspapers played up the Powers sign on the bar-room roof has never been made quite clear, since the papers were not officially endorsing Collins. In any case, John Collins and his followers deny to this day having had anything to do with the bookie raid or the attendant publicity,

233

and they are probably telling the truth. The biggest argument that the Collins people were innocent in this unfortunate juxtaposition of Candidate Powers and the bookmakers is that the raid and publicity had little effect on the final result. For the votes were practically in, by then; the money and the influence were with Powers, the people were with John Collins. Collins won that election by some 30,000 votes and has turned out to be a highly regarded Mayor, now permanently identified with urban renewal, redevelopment, and what is monotonously but validly called "The New Boston."

Powers himself would have made a fine mayor, let no one ever doubt that. But destiny, not Cardinal Cushing or John F. Kennedy, chose John Collins, and in his phenomenal and brilliant development as a municipal executive and Democratic party leader he seems destined to play an even greater role in the public life of Massachusetts and possibly the nation. There is something almost mystical about soldiers and about the physically afflicted who are successful in public life. There seems to be no political horizon which is not attainable to them, once they have tasted major political success. Ulysses Grant, Teddy Roosevelt, Ike Eisenhower, achieved the White House after military fame; Franklin Roosevelt and John F. Kennedy won the Presidency as they emerged from major physical affliction. The Collins wheel chair will bear watching.

It would seem that Cardinal Cushing was truly disappointed about the pathetic defeat of his loyal and generous friend Johnny Powers. There now ensued a certain coolness between the new city administration and the spiritual leader of predominantly Catholic Boston. Mayor John Hynes had been most cordial and cooperative with the Archbishop as Collins himself was soon to be. With Cushing's approval, Hynes had appointed Monsignor Francis Lally to the controversial Boston Redevelopment Authority. Lally retains the post under Collins.

At one of his many impromptu "ecumenical councils,"

however, addressing 300 Protestants at the Old South Church on May 11, 1964, the Cardinal said: "I cannot understand why the Boston Redevelopment Authority insists on demolishing homes before new homes are readied for the displaced families. The authority should encourage owners of salvageable homes to fix them up." The Cardinal was told by Rt. Rev. John M. Burgess, Suffragan Bishop of the Episcopal Diocese of Massachusetts that the BRA's philosophy is to tear down homes "beyond redemption." Whereupon, as the *Boston Herald* reported on May 12, Cardinal Cushing rejoined: "This is information even Monsignor Lally hasn't given me."

The BRA, be it noted, explained their position to the Cardinal promptly, through urbane master planner and BRA director, Edward Logue. The upshot of his position was that the BRA actually was successfully renewing and redeveloping certain home and apartment blocks in the South End. He implied that the authority had great respect for the architectural value of churches and that the pace of the whole program was necessarily and judiciously slow.

The Cardinal made one other fetching remark about Boston's massive urban renewal program. He said he agreed with Bishop Burgess that Christian Churches should not be overawed by the millions of dollars being spent in Boston for new buildings. "It is the church's responsibility to be concerned with the people," the Cardinal said. For whatever reasons, none of this dialogue was reported in the usually ecumenically sensitive pages of *The Pilot*.

Betimes, during the brief "cool war" between upper Commonwealth Avenue and City Hall, the new Mayor Collins saw the advantage of retaining and cultivating Monsignor Lally on the Redevelopment Board. The latter was made Chairman.

It was Cushing's prevailing interest in the well-being of patients at the Boston City Hospital and the astuteness of

Hospital Board Chairman William H. Ellis, a Collins appointee and close supporter, which finally completed the thaw between Cardinal and Mayor and gave added impetus to an era of good feeling between town and red gown. Ellis, an East Boston dock builder and a devout Catholic layman whose Dartmouth background has brought his interest in the Church into sharper focus, had succeeded a hospital trustee friendly to the Cardinal and one who perhaps had especially looked after the prelate's spiritual and charitable interests at the Hub's vast and teeming public hospital.

The new Board Chairman habitually goes to Mass and Communion at the Jesuit church of St. Ignatius, across the street from the Cardinal's residence. Ellis was bothered by the Cardinal's seeming aloofness and pique regarding the reshuffled City Hospital Board. He is a man clean and open of heart and he decided to go directly and see the man. So after Mass one morning at St. Ignatius, Ellis did the best thing that anyone who wants to see the Cardinal can do. He walked right up to the Residence and rang the doorbell. His Eminence answered the door himself, as he sometimes does, and he wasn't in a very good mood. Ellis introduced himself, both as a businessman and as Chairman of the Hospital Board. He said he had come there to ask the Cardinal's "blessing."

At first, the gaunt, gruff prelate hardly let him inside the door, searing him in the anteroom with: "What do you know about hospitals?"

Ellis said something to the effect that he didn't know too much but he was learning. He then repeated that he had come for the Cardinal's blessing.

The Cardinal seemed a bit nonplussed.

"With my Welsh name and my non-Irish appearance," Ellis revealed, "I think the Cardinal thought I was a 'Prot.' By 'blessing' he must have thought I meant some kind of courtesy call. Of course, my predecessor's name was Con-don and he was friendly with the Cardinal. I was in kind of a tight spot."

The Cardinal remained glum and unfriendly, almost implying that Ellis should leave. The new trustee was determined, however, to get his blessing. He said: "Your Eminence, you don't seem to understand. I've just come from Holy Communion right across the street here at St. Ignatius. I'm asking your blessing on my new work at the Hospital."

The Cardinal finally saw the light and melted completely, as he is prone to do after he has been rather harsh with a person. He gave Ellis his blessing, raised him up, put his arm around his shoulders and brought him into his private office for a long and cordial chat.

Perhaps, however, Ellis *was* there for more than a blessing. There was a vacancy coming up on the Hospital board of trustees and he thought Mayor Collins might do well to fill that vacancy with the Cardinal—if the prelate was interested. He reminded Cushing that, with all his long and generous interest in Catholic hospitals that the Boston City was now, and always has been, the refuge of the poor. He invited the Cardinal to tour the wards with him. Cushing eagerly accepted.

The idea of appointing Cushing to the board appealed strongly to the Mayor and it was done. The Cardinal, as a full-fledged trustee toured the hospital, cheering people up, clowning, spooning food into the mouths of old folks and infants, and wisecracking his way into the hearts of all.

In the summer of 1960, Pope John sent Cushing to Lima, Peru, as Papal Legate to the Eucharistic Congress. The arrival of Cushing sparked manifestations of overwhelming, sheer love and enthusiasm from the Peruvians to whom, of course, he had already sent his own Boston priests, not to mention goods, services and facilities.

The original recruitment of the St. James Society had

sent fifteen priests, ten from Boston, to Peru in February of 1959. There are now 110 priests and ten brothers laboring below the Rio Grande. And the St. James Missionary work has expanded from Peru into Ecuador and Bolivia.

"No one serves America so wonderfully as you do and in no one does patriotism inspire so magnificent a sacrifice," Cushing told a group of young Maryknoll foreign missionaries on July 21, 1946; "yet in no one must love for one's own people be so strictly disciplined and personal patriotism be so subordinated to other love and loyalties."

Yet over and above Cushing's apostolic zeal and his inexhaustible generosity toward the poor, the sick, the socially deprived, Cushing's Latin American program is also a manifestation of his iron dedication to thwarting by constructive means the growth and spread of Communism. His fight against Communism in Europe, America and China has sometimes ended up as a lot of brilliant words, badly thought out associations, maddening frustrations, and painful memory of associations with Stepinac, Wyzanski, Mindszenty and especially the Hungarian freedom fighters. In the U. S., the Communist problem seems well under control, after all the dubious hysteria of the fifties; China and Hungary are *fait accompli*—Cushing still meets cordially with a group of Hungarians each year. But it is in Latin America, where the fight against Communism and atheism is still in the balance, that Cushing's prevailing passion against Red materialism seems to find practical expression and may even achieve its greatest fulfillment.

When Cushing has talked, since the fifties, of Latin America, he constantly speaks of the Communist take-over, the Marxist threat to masses of people who are traditionally Christian and must continue to be so. "The larger part of my concern and extra money," he said, in a rambling but significant tape-recorded reminiscence he gave us, "is dedicated to the continent of Latin America, now sinking beneath a rising tide of totalitarianism."

He speaks of his institutional hopes for the tri-country St.

James mission area, much of which has already been achieved. His hopes in 1960 included a five-hundred-thousand-dollar university in Bolivia, three seminaries in Peru, and a seminary in the United States for "students who desire to be incardinated in the dioceses of Latin America where they are most needed."

He has, by now, financed a major seminary in Trujillo, Peru and a minor seminary in Lima, along with new parish churches, clinics and social centers.

The Cardinal ruminates and philosophizes about Latin America: "When I went to Peru as a Papal Delegate for Pope John, I saw what was happening. You can't have spiritual paupers in Latin America while we have spiritual millionaires in the U. S. A. That's why I sent the priests in there among the poorest of the poor, as fast as I could.

"I am the one who got Ted Kennedy to visit Latin America. I said, 'Look here, Ted, please go! The on-the-spot impressions you gain will be of great value.'

"Down there, some of them said I was a socialist, but they call a lot of people communist down there, because they advocate the very things I was advocating. But you cannot compete with the enemies of Christianity in the 20th century with methods of the 18th century.

"We are missing (still) a wonderful opportunity down there. The tragic situation is the herculean task of fighting communism while you try to get across the meaning of democracy or a just social order."

In complimenting President Kennedy's South American "Alliance For Progress" the Cardinal, in an excellent magazine article for *Extension* Magazine in the Spring of 1964, candidly made a grave admission: "Despite the enormity of these problems and our heavy responsibility, the people of the United States have been asked to sacrifice relatively little in support of the Alliance. Less than one percent of our Federal budget is allocated to assist half a hemisphere." Cushing credits the program originally sponsored by "our beloved friend Jack Kennedy" with very great significance,

239

saying flatly: "It represents the greatest task undertaken in our history."

On the necessity of major U.S. backing for the social and educational projects of the Alliance For Progress, the Cardinal astutely reminds us:

Some have claimed that the "Alliance For Progress" has not accomplished all that was expected. But they have not come forth with a substitute that will be more successful. Great patience, great confidence and, indeed, great faith are required to reach the maximum good anticipated by this bountiful ten-year project of the United States. More than a decade, however, will be necessary to realize its goals. It should not be abandoned nor should the money to finance it be reduced. Added to that program will be the "know how" which the Peace Corps and others can give with more and more personnel in the future.

Sometime, somehow, those who control the wealth of Latin American countries and those who govern them will see the necessity of giving maximum cooperation to the Alliance For Progress. If they fail to do so, and if they do not produce a better program for changing a social order that has brought fortunes to the elect and misery, starvation and premature death to forgotten millions, then they are hastening the day of reckoning when, urged on by evil forces, the multitudes will arise and more Cubas will be the result. The handwriting of this prophecy is visible to all who refuse to close their eyes to the facts.

That is the way Cushing is talking now, after President Kennedy's death, because he believes so implicitly, and even desperately, in a vast "Point Four" program for Latin America. In his informal and unpublished ruminations on Latin America and Communism the Cardinal continues:

The Communists are on the march. They spend billions to tell the Latin Americans how good Communism is for Latin Americans. All over the world you see magazines, pamphlets and books, the like of which we have never produced. Nor have we trained men and women in psychological warfare, effective people, power personalities. That's what the cold war is essentially all about, a thirst for the minds and souls of mankind.

The Literature in Latin America emanating from Communistic sources is all over the place. Hundreds of missionary agencies in

Latin America are looking for literature in English and Spanish and Indian to counteract the avalanche.

What do we publicize down there? Our motion pictures, our autos, our gadgets! But the peasantry of Latin America, the people living under sub-human conditions don't even know what we are talking about. They want to see from the darkness of their lives stars of hope shining through the Western world, the star of God representing the dignity of man, represented by our love for one another, and so forth. They are looking for ideals. No matter what their religion is, they are all worthy of our love. They are our best friends, but if they think we are letting them down . . .

Why, in Heaven's name have we never organized a powerful team? Why have we no trained workers for psychological warfare who know the Spanish language idiomatically? Why have we no effective speakers who know what Communism is all about and meet the evil head-on?

We could counteract and pulverize every argument that the Communists have. With a hundred men like St. Francis we could lead those people anywhere.

I've done what I could in the propaganda area. I sent one hundred thousand copies of a booklet *Questions And Answers On Communism* into South America. When no one would pay the bill, I paid it myself. I was afraid that the Communist dockworkers would toss them into the ocean so I sent them down by priests. When I learned some more about the literacy problems of Latin America, I made up a primer on the third or fourth grade level. (All of this material is in Spanish.)

Only ideas, I am convinced, can thwart ideas. I do not go along with the thinking that the way to stop Communism is by the physical destruction of its international organization. It cannot be conquered with bombs. Putting down a specific Communist system might not end the idea. I define Communism as applied atheism. Atheism is born of materialism. If Communism ceased to exist, this country would still be up against the problem of materialism and materialism is the root of Communism.

In fifty years of my lifetime, I have seen Communism absorb one third of the human race. The best way to conquer it or prevent its growth, as of the present, is to train dedicated men and women in psychological warfare.

Everyone who believes in God should put up a united front and reach the people behind the Iron Curtain and the Bamboo Curtain who also believe in God. Those people south of the U.S.A., the

241

poorest of the poor, are wonderful people and they would never go for Communism if we would help them and give them what they want, and they don't all want money.

Then the Cardinal, in typical fashion, came out with some extremely strong observations:

The fact of the matter is that those poor people never see the money we send. It never gets to the poorer people. I by no means minimize the economic aspects of the struggle. But I am appalled at the lack of social consciousness on the part of the fabulously wealthy. Why, some of them think they are wealthy by the will of God and that those poor masses are poor by the will of God.

If the Catholic Church is anywhere identified with an unjust social order, the Church should clean her own house and follow the principles and precepts of the Gospel of the Divine Founder. The Catholic Church must get rid of all its land holdings in Latin America. We are not in business.* This is a new day. Read Pope John's Encyclical on the social order. If we don't practice the principles therein, how can we expect that others shall practice them? I see Church landholding as a hangover from feudal times. *My idea is that the states should buy up the lands at minimal costs, give them conditionally to the peasants, along with farm tools from American aid, and give them five years to produce.*

It was perhaps for this very practical and courageous thinking that Cushing was labeled a "socialist" by certain powerful and reactionary echelons of thought in Latin America.

The Cardinal has high hopes that the need for priests and well-trained lay apostles in Latin America will be recognized and fulfilled by the Vatican Council. He supports, along with the South American bishops, the revival of the order of the Diaconate "so that married or unmarried deacons, as a part of the structure of the Church, could substitute for priests in all phases of pastoral work save those pertaining to purely sacerdotal functions." "The civilization of Latin America was born in the bosom of the

---

* The Cardinal is fond of saying: "We are in business to go out of business." He means he expects the development of a native clergy to take over the St. James work.

Church," the Cardinal says. "The dialogue between the Church and the modern world, which the Second Vatican Council seeks to establish, reveals to the people and leaders of Latin America the horizons suited for the solution of its problems."

After his second trip to Latin America as Pope John's Legate to the Eucharistic Congress at Santa Cruz, Bolivia, in the summer of 1961 it seemed that the Cardinal was almost totally obsessed with the challenges and needs of the Church and its people in that colorful and complex land. He tells us that he actually asked John if he could resign his Boston Archbishopric to spend the rest of his life toiling with his own priests in the vineyards of the St. James Society.

The Pope wouldn't allow it and yet the Cardinal was utterly sincere. The Archdiocese is a marvelously "going concern," in some ways a working model of the Universal Church, largely because of Cushing. He would be intensely missed in Boston. Yet he sometimes thinks that most of his life's work is already done in the Archdiocese, while his labors and those of the Universal Church, in the modern era, are just getting underway in Latin America. The challenge is down there, now, and that's where he wants to be.

He talks of Bishops distributing the land belonging to their dioceses and he tells us specifically about one Bishop he knows who has "given his episcopal palace to working families and taken a small house for his own residence."

In the late summer of 1964, exhausted and sick as he almost always is, Cushing undertook another long, rigorous journey to his Latin American missions to visit with, minister to, and bolster with blessings, money, and encouragement the priests, brothers, and the people of the tri-nation St. James Missionary Society area. Covering hard, exacting, arid and mountainous terrain by buffeting air and by bumpy motor car, he set out to visit his 110 priests, 10 brothers, their lay assistants, and above all, the faceless

Indians, peasants, half-starved urchins, all of whom have a shining identity to him because they are the "poorest of the poor."

"Believe me, I don't want to go," he said to the *Boston Herald*, on the eve of his departure, August 1, 1964, "but I feel it is my mission, just as St. Paul 'stung his flesh' and just as President Kennedy 'stung his flesh,' I must sting my flesh to fight the enemies of decency and morality." He accentuated his long-held convictions: "These countries are the most critical in our fight. One third of the world's baptized Catholics live in Latin America. We are losing them at the rate of a million a year. That is why I say our fight against Communism centers on Peru, Bolivia, and Ecuador."

Meanwhile, in the winter of 1961-62, a famous CBS television film exposed the now famous Massachusetts Avenue Key Shop bookie parlor in the South End of Boston. The old Massachusetts Crime Commission, a blue-ribbon panel with lots of investigative information but no punitive powers, was moribund. Democratic leaders, constantly under pressure, were not keen on shooting a scatter-gun among the sporting set who were always good for political contributions, whether they were connected with illegal gambling or not. The Democrats had not been in a hurry to summon a legislative doctor as the Crime Commission lay dying.

After the surprising Massachusetts gubernatorial victory of Republican John A. Volpe in the presidential year election of 1960, there was much agitation among the executive people of the old Commission and among citizens' groups to revive and put teeth in the body. Volpe, a successful Italo-American contractor, a former Commissioner of Public Works under Governor Christian Herter, and a devout son of the Church, was in an uncomfortable position. He was, like all politicians, against crime, of course, but his "Vote The Man" campaign, somewhat cynically disassociated from the Republican ticket, had won him the votes of thousands of working people, most of them Democrats, who liked to gamble a little themselves.

The Cardinal, too, while against the unsavory aspects of gambling, saw sheer hypocrisy in making it respectable to gamble behind a pari-mutuel fence, but a crime outside that fence. He said publicly that he was unequivocally against a State Lottery and an increase in racing dates. But he also said he was not interested in a crusade against gambling.

Meanwhile, soon to be caught in the net of the bookie publicity were his beloved Boston police and his close friend, the Police Commissioner, a clever and resourceful former state and county elected official named Leo Sullivan. Now, of course, journalists know that in any big city, many policemen and their wives, like other little people, like to gamble. This writer for example, once did a picture story about a Boston police hero, and when we showed up at the officer's house to ride with him around his downtown beat, his wife was on the phone calling in some daily doubles to a bookie. If she had time, she could have taken the subway train to Suffolk Downs for twenty cents, and made the identical wagers there, with thousands of others who are considered utterly respectable. But the law is the law, and the bookie profits go into crime syndicate coffers instead of the state treasury, as they would not do if off-track betting was legalized.

In any case, the residual Crime Commission group, interested in being reborn legally, with punitive authority, gave CBS all the leads and cooperated with them in photographing a rich harvest of citizen, police and bookie action at the Key Shop on Mass. Avenue. The production was televised nationally in December of 1961, though Boston was blacked out for legal reasons, under the title: "Biography of a Bookie Joint." The furore was on.

Lenses had been trained on the location for weeks from an apartment across the street and Jay McMullen of CBS, acting like a "player" walked in and out of the shop gathering snippets of unrehearsed dialogue with a hidden microphone. It appeared that the place had been operating under heavy local police protection. The shop was later raided by the State Police. Charges and counter-charges ensued.

After the telecast and the raid, Governor Volpe demanded the resignation of Police Commissioner Sullivan, which he eventually received. Sullivan had become pretty much of a loner politically. Under the state law at the time, he was appointed by the Governor and was not answerable to the Mayor for the police department budget. He had been appointed by former Democratic Governor Furcolo; he was not the favorite "baby" of either Governor Volpe or Mayor John Collins. Collins wanted the appointive authority of the Police Commissioner back in City Hall where he would have some say about Police Department budgets. Volpe wanted to appoint his own man.

In the middle: Cardinal Cushing.

Commissioner Leo Sullivan, his top aides, especially Superintendent Hennessey, and the entire Boston Police Department had been devoted to their Archbishop in every conceivable way. In many personal services, escorts, security, protection, fund-raising, donations, in endless courtesies toward his priests, his nuns, brothers, parishes, schools, the Boston Police, then and now, stand solidly with the Cardinal-Archbishop.

The Cardinal was on the spot. Along with his own personal indignation at what he believed to be the almost ruthless national indictment and exploitation of the Boston Police Department by CBS, his friend Commissioner Leo Sullivan was deep in hot water, most of it of his own heating. Cushing's part-time chauffeur was a Boston cop and a high officer in the Police association. The wives of the Boston police were relentlessly on the telephone to get him to say something vigorous in defense of the honesty and integrity of their husbands. The annual Policemen's Ball at the Boston Garden in December gave him his opportunity to speak out.

Amid great enthusiasm, the golden blaze of the Department band and thunderclaps of local pride, the Cardinal stood on the platform and ringingly defended the Boston Police. "In my theology, gambling itself is not a sin any more than to take a glass of beer or of hard liquor is a sin." He said he had not seen the TV show, nor was he interested in seeing it. But he strongly maintained that whoever was behind it owed an apology to the City of Boston which had been "betrayed."

His sheer Boston-Irish loyalty to the police department and the city itself aroused the high-minded ire of Marya Mannes in *The Reporter*. *The New York Times* and, locally, the *Harvard Crimson* and *Christian Science Monitor* also commented.

In a pungent and sensible letter to the editors of *The Crimson*, Michael Novak, prominent young American Catholic journalist, probably reasoned out as good an analysis as any. In his letter, published in *The Crimson*, Novak wrote:

The first reports were word-of-mouth, and then in the papers. They left me wishing Gilbert and Sullivan belonged to our generation. The sight of the police band spontaneously breaking into "For Boston! For Boston!" so that the Cardinal could not immediately complete his written statement; the sound of the rifle butts of the honor guard pounding on the floor in enthusiasm; the sense of renewal, loyalty, pride and closing of ranks, should not be allowed to die unsung.

But the text of Cardinal Cushing's remarks had a wisdom, at once commendable and too-limited, which opened the way to events for our more subtle amusement. His remarks were commendable in that they restored dramatically the spirit of a police force low in morale, bitter because of what it took to be still one more instance of political opportunism at its expense, humiliated by sweeping allegations against their professional honor: integrity in the law. The cruelest allegation, until proved, against a professor is sophistry; against a fighter, cowardice; against a policeman, crime.

Cardinal Cushing's wisdom lay in restoring honor to the force, without which the force has no professional use. The limitation of his wisdom lay in the short-term, immediate nature of his aid and the unsolved problems it does not address.

Novak properly spoke of the traditional difference in the human drama between the colder, more rigid Protestant ethic and the warmer, more tolerant Catholic understanding: "The Protestant and the liberal joined in the moral lines, upholding the written law. The Catholic pointed out the hypocrisies in the present confused system of federal, state and civic gambling laws, and held up a case not simple but complex. In his theology, he said, men are free to gamble if they choose; and he may have been hinting that he failed to see why his conscience should be bound by other people's moral requirements, and that perhaps the issue of gambling laws should be reopened *au fond.*"

Novak then summed up Cardinal Cushing's position, in a paragraph that supports the central theme of this book. "Cardinal Cushing perhaps erred in judgment in speaking only of the immediate morale of the force, and not also of the larger question of political corruption in Boston; some of his words like 'betrayal' may have smacked too much to non-Boston-Irish of local pride; *but he showed his genuine humanity.*"

Later in 1962, a gubernatorial election year, Governor Volpe got his Crime Commission "with teeth in it," ex-Commissioner Leo Sullivan passed away, perhaps with a broken heart, and Cardinal Cushing was moving from Boston concerns to international ones.

Governor Volpe, who was always proud of his personal friendship with the Cardinal, might now have been wondering at the extent of his cordial relations at 2101 Commonwealth Avenue. A pathetic incident occurred at Leo Sullivan's public wake which the Governor attended, for whatever reasons he felt advisable. It is said that the Governor's spiritual bouquet was handed back to him personally by an immediate member of Sullivan's family in a most agonizing display of bitterness.

In November of 1962, in a photo-finish, Volpe was defeated at the polls by Democrat Endicott Peabody. The whole Key Shop and Crime Commission uproar may have had something to do with Volpe's ultimate defeat—if the solid Boston-Irish vote for Peabody, a former Republican and a Harvard-Episcopalian-Yankee, is any indication.

The Cardinal told us in the Spring of '64, in his bluff, scoffing manner, that Volpe, again a successful candidate for Governor, had visited him after Volpe returned from an audience with Pope Paul in Rome.

"He said that Pope Paul had asked him to run again for Governor!" the Cardinal chortled.

It is easy to understand how such an implication could be made, or an inference drawn, there in the Vatican chamber. There were two sons of Italy, one a Pope, one a former Governor of Massachusetts, both conversing in Italian.

"What do you do?" Pope Paul could have asked Volpe.

"I'm the former Governor of Massachusetts." Volpe could have answered.

"Oh!" the Pope could have exclaimed in a perfectly natural outburst of cordiality. "And you are going to run again?"

So here, as the decade of the 'sixties opens, is the portrait of the compassionate, loyal shepherd of the Boston-Irish, quick to protect his own, regardless of bookies, scandals, and the cold, high-minded, righteousness of the *New York Times* and the *Christian Science Monitor;* here also is, towering over it all, the great and monumental Cardinal of the Universal Church, implacable foe of International Communism, loving servant and patron of the Latin American poor.

249

BOOK FIVE

The Cardinal Today

CHAPTER XXI

Cushing and Civil Rights,
The One-Man Vatican Council

"Earth shall be fair and all her people one,
   Nor till that hour shall God's whole will be done.
   Now, even now, once more from earth to sky
   Peals forth in joy, man's old undaunted cry:
   'Earth shall be fair and all her folk be one.'"
                                        —Holst

One felt guiltily secure to be working on the final sections of this book at the same time that the indomitable but exhausted Cardinal Cushing took off from Logan Airport, Boston, and winged his way across the Andes on his fourth apostolic trip to South America.

He ostensibly had gone there to visit, console, bolster with love and financial generosity, his St. James Society priests, associated brothers and laymen; he would linger affectionately with the peasantry, the Indians, the miserable masses of slum-dwellers on the edges of prosperous communities, those whom he calls, over and over again, "the poorest of the poor."

The thought went through one's mind that this might well have been his last trip to Latin America. Although he did not do so, it was possible that he could have resigned his Archbishopric de facto, to stay there, work there, die there, in the field, among the kind of people he loves: the despised, the bereft, the off-scourings of a cruel, ruthless, selfish, no-room-at-the-top society. Thus, might he have chosen to spend the rest of his days, far from the vast, mod-

253

ern Boston Archdiocese, of which he has been the visioned and munificent architect, happy, contemplative, working amid the sheer, fundamental dynamics of the Universal Church.

He could well have died there, because of the rigors of one of those long and arduous auto, jeep or donkey trips into and through the jagged mountain trails of his tri-state mission areas. As it turned out, he had to curtail some of his scheduled visits because of illness and exhaustion.

He came home to Boston again, without his usual light, wise-cracking touch at the airport. He was highly incensed about the *Time* cover story which had appeared on August 21, shortly before he returned to Boston from Latin America. And he said so to the Boston press, on his arrival in the Hub.

The strong and majestic, rough-hewn painting of the Cardinal by Robert Vickrey adorned the cover. But the story was really in two parts: one, concerning *Catholicism in the U.S.A.*, two, a profile of Cushing flowing from and somewhat integral to the central topic.

Time's lady correspondent for New England had accompanied the Cardinal to South America. She had been in charge of the collection of fact and opinion, in the Boston area. All this had been relayed to her New York office for the final processing of the story, which traditionally at *Time* is not without the ingredients of both charm and strychnine.

We happened to be one of the many Boston journalistic devotees of Cardinal Cushing interviewed by *Time*'s Boston Bureau Chief, Ruth Mehrtens. We found her to be warm, sympathetic and constructively bent regarding the Cardinal; and never did we see any signs of the asp beneath the flower.

If the folksy information about the Cardinal which she got from us is similar to what she received from other Boston sources, then she couldn't have had much influence upon the final product: little or none of our particular interview made the final, printed pages.

The Pilot editorial, Saturday, August 29, reflected the Cardinal's pique about the *Time* piece with considerable good reasoning. "Time Ran Out!" was the subject of the editorial:

". . . only the merest caricature of the churchman survived the famed *Time* process of collection, selection and interpretation. Combining a long look at the changing American church with a close look at the Boston Cardinal proved too much for both subjects; the church and the prelate ended up badly out of focus."

The Pilot may have made a telling point about the *Time* two-headed portrait when it said: "It is hard not to believe that the pattern of the article was set first and the facts made to fit it later."

Time accurately sensed lay American Catholic unrest and even legitimate rebellion against clerical authoritarianism. American Catholic laymen are finally alert to the truth that "the Church exists for the Faithful and not the Faithful for the Church." But the "surge of renewal" does not include "dissent with the Pope," birth control against the laws of the Church, lay election of Bishops; nor would Cardinal Cushing, identified by *Time* with much of the surge of lay rebellion, ever go along with any of these extremes in opinion or action.

In a letter written to this reporter, concerning the *Time* article, and dated August 26, 1964, Cardinal Cushing wrote: "*Time Magazine* certainly failed to present me for what I am, 'a slave of Christ.' I gave the representatives of that magazine more cooperation, more time, more knowledge than they received from any one whom they interviewed. Their Boston representative (Miss Mehrtens) was welcomed by me wherever I went with every possible service and comfort. What was the result? The editors simply used me for one of the worst forms of journalism that I have ever experienced, namely, false and disgraceful reporting of facts. I am not a member of the Birch Society and would never join the society. Nevertheless the article tried to tie me in with that cause, with birth control, with the idea that the Hierarchy of the Catholic Church was divided on religious issues. All of this is absolutely untrue. But why continue. As far as I am concerned *Time Magazine* is for the waste basket in the future."

This writer does not believe that the *Time* article was as damaging to the Cardinal's image as he himself thinks it was. In an answer to the letter, above quoted, we wrote the following to the Cardinal on August 31, 1964:

"Your disturbance at the *Time* article which you conveyed to me personally, and which has been reflected both in the daily and the diocesan press is quite understandable. (Do you realize, for example, that some lovely, human things about yourself which were given to Miss Mehrtens by myself and others, were never printed simply because much of what she sends down there never sees the light of day?)

"I can tell you, however, that most of the people I talk to who have read the piece feel that the positive things of the article exceed the more negative things; it is my view that many thousands of people who have wanted to know you better, across the land, are not disappointed by the article."

In our view, the major, unfinished business of the Cardinal's entire magnificent career would be the positive resolution and firming-up of his see-sawing, somewhat generic stand on the Negro question—especially in Boston.

There is not now, nor has there ever been any question of the Cardinal's religious or moral position on interracial justice. He has written and spoken extensively on the subject over the years. By contrast or comparison with Cardinal McIntyre of Los Angeles, for example, on the Negro issue, Cushing is the liberal of liberals.

256

"Let it not be said of us that the voice of our brother's blood crieth to Thee from the earth. Open our hands and our hearts to all the oppressed and afflicted. Let us bury hate that hope may be reborn. Before we offer gifts to others let us be mindful of our debts to them; before we speak of charity, let us answer the demands of justice."

These are the words of Richard Cushing, uttered years ago as Archbishop in a leaflet called "A Prayer For Brotherhood." On the face of the leaflet, typically, is a photo of the Cardinal leaning over affectionately as a fetching, white-garbed little Negro girl, newly-come from First Communion, kisses his ring. Many have been charmed also by candid pictures of the Cardinal with colored folk— like the one in which he sits by a hospital bed and spoons food into a baby Negro girl's mouth, with the caption: "Many a heart has been broken by those great, big, beautiful eyes . . ."

"Here in our own country," he continues in that early brotherhood prayer, "as everywhere in the world, let us not set the value of man in terms of race or color or social position, but teach us to see deeper into the riches of each human soul that is destined for eternal life with Thee. By our actions let us inspire others to break down the barriers history has cruelly built between brothers, and, make us, O Lord, leaders who seek to exalt the universal dignity of man."

Cushing was finding the range on his expressed interracial philosophy and tenets when he wrote, articulated and disseminated that noble and hard-fibered prayer.

In his pamphlet called "Inter-Racial Justice" issued by the Daughters of St. Paul in 1963, and based on an Archdiocesan letter, published in *The Pilot*, he gave us a most profound, concrete, and comprehensive manifesto of Christian principles and philosophy to Boston, America and the world.

All of his statements, since, however eloquent, are paled

by this one. And no other blueprint or repetition of his promulgated views on race is necessary if these could be implemented in the practical order.

It is no great secret that Cushing, particularly as Cardinal and during the recent months and years of the intensified American Negro Revolution has been somewhat at odds with the Negro community of Boston, with a number of his priests, and even with active and prominent members of his own Archdiocesan Catholic Interracial Council.

For a prelate of his stature, great-heartedness, genuine sanctity, to be even partially involved in a serious, if unpublicized, family squabble over this issue seems almost as absurd as it is lamentable.

In fairness to him, any confusion and disagreement about interracial programs and policies, lie in the area of ends and means. He is in total agreement with the ends but seems to have some reservations about the means.

There is, too, the very real problem of the Boston-Irish, his beloved people, his almost idolatrous benefactors. The Italian-American block is a problem, here, also, as witness the near-riot of summer, 1964 in heavily Italo-American East Boston when a Negro family moved into a "Noddle Island" public housing project. It would appear to be curious and regrettable that the Italo-American block in its rapid social ascent from the docks and tenement back-streets of immigrant ghettoes, have learned well the cruel snobbery and disdain of their former Yankee masters toward alleged social inferiors.

Although he may not admit it, all this has been a pressure upon the Cardinal. The Irish, Italians, and others, new-come to status in Boston—as perhaps comparably elsewhere in the major industrial American cities—have been and are resisting the inexorable rise of the Negroes to social, political and economic equality under the law of the land.

The Irish, the Italian, the other varied white blocks of Catholics in high and low middle-class status are largely the ones who pay the freight for all the parishes, the institutions and most of the social, educational and religious projects of the Archdiocese. They influence the Cardinal perhaps more in his private thinking and slowness in positive action, than in his public statements. It seems evident to this observer, at least, that white middle-class Catholic attitudes in Greater Boston are, in the main, coldly neutral, if not outrightly unfriendly toward Negroes and their legitimate claims to a rightful share of American abundance, dignity and freedom.

We can see the Cardinal's cautionary and individual approach to a practical expression of his fine Catholic philosophy in a review of his stand on student boycotts of de facto segregated Boston schools, in his relations with the Catholic Interracial Council, in his private tendency to advocate gradualism in Civil Rights, in his temporary disapproval of priests and religious extremely outspoken and active on the race question.

Yet no one could have been more outspoken than he has been in his magnificent letter of former years called "Inter-Racial Justice," and in quite recent public statements which we shall cite.

Perhaps some inter-paragraph comment as we quote the pamphlet would serve as commentary upon the philosophical and the actual in the Boston world of the Negro revolution, where the Cardinal-Archbishop may be concerned.

In his introduction, the Cardinal speaks of the emotional climate of interracial justice which is, of course, strained, highly-charged, one of those topics which so-called "nice people" seek to avoid. Right off the bat, the Cardinal indicates his honest, gradualistic approach when he writes: "The problem in any field of human relationship is to keep emotions under control and to bring them into proper integration with the other human forces which function in the development of the society in which God has destined us to work out our eternal destiny."

Both the majority and the minority have these emotions, but, in Boston, as elsewhere, the majority can express these emotions in terms of what is considered legitimate self-interest, by containing Negroes, however subtly and indirectly in neighborhoods, schools, jobs, which do not threaten white security or supremacy.

There are many, many wavering whites, of good conscience, who tend to go along with those, Catholic and otherwise, that maintain the status quo. These "waverers" can be swayed and turned into the camp of Christian social thinking and action, but the instrument must be the aggressive Christian leadership of figures of the stature of Cardinal Cushing. The emotion will always be there. The Civil War emotions of the Old Confederacy seem as intense and vindicative in the North as they are in the South. When, for example, does a major Southern city have a major race riot? Very seldom.

And what of the reasoned plea from both northern and southern whites for a general policy of gradualism? What is so gradualistic about whites who say, or imply, or act: "We don't want Negroes in certain places, in certain jobs, in certain schools, in certain neighborhoods!" The white answer is usually: *"No! Out! Stick to your own kind!"*

Is there anything gradualistic or emotionally controlled about that predominant white viewpoint?

The Cardinal continues in the letter and brilliantly demolishes the sophistries and stupid prejudices about Negroes being biologically inferior, anatomically inferior, psychologically inferior:

"Nor is there any valid scientific evidence for the claim that skin color, or any pattern of bodily constitution has a positive correlation with either intelligence or personality . . . We are thus forced to the conclusion that *it is the prevailing attitude toward racial differences*, rather than the biological makeup of so-called races that is fundamental to the inter-racial problem. Whatever superiority one group may have over another is completely the result

260

of environmental factors, or of hereditary factors which have no relation whatever with racial differences. *The superiority of one group over another must therefore be regarded as temporary, and as subject to change as environment brings about changes in socio-economic status."*

Witness the Boston Brahmins' former superiority over the Boston-Irish; the Boston-Irish' former superiority over the Italo-Americans; and now both the Boston-Irish and Italo-Americans—two jumps out of steerage—flouting their socio-political-economic superiority over the Boston Negroes!

"So, all right now," the Cardinal seems to say, "a racial problem does exist in the field of social and personal relationships." He speaks realistically of "an incompatibility of emotion and temperament . . ." a problem which, in the gradualistic view, the passage of time admittedly should solve." Thus, "we all look forward to the day when human friendships and personal relationships will tend more positively toward the broader and firmer basis of intellectual interests and devotion to the ideals of virtue.

"All who are born," he continues, in the gradualistic view, "have the right to continue to live and to enter freely into personal relationships and contractual agreements which can be peacefully and profitably maintained."

Now comes the heartland of "gradualism," the gray area of statement where one heads into legitimate disputation about the "means" while still in full agreement about the "ends." Here, perhaps, is the basis of Cushing's somewhat stubborn stand against the Boston Negro community's successful one-day boycott of the Hub's "de facto" segregated schools:

"We must be careful to avoid the tempting methods of violent reform when the harmful, immediate effects will be out of proportion with the long-range improvements for which our ideals move us to agitate."

On January 25, 1964, Cardinal Cushing in a local TV news interview said that the proposed boycott of local

261

schools "is a very, very dangerous thing . . . I am all for human rights—for every living, breathing human soul. But I think there is a better way of attaining those rights than by violating laws of society and by endangering the community by sending a number of children, emotionally upset, through the streets of the city."

The Pilot somewhat uncomfortably supported his position and took its stand against one of its own regular and highly popular columnists—an old friend and school mate of the Cardinal—Monsignor George Casey. Also vigorously arrayed against the Cardinal's view were three local Jesuits: one, the prominent, journalistically articulate Dean of the Boston College Law School, Father Robert Drinan; the second, Father William Kenneally, former B.C. Law School Dean, and one of the most eloquent and courageous pleaders for Negro justice in America; the third, Catholic Interracial Council zealot, Father Richard L. Twomey of the Department of Theology, Boston College.

The Pilot acknowledged that Boston education of Negroes left much to be desired but warned that: "School programs must be intelligently planned to be effective; the 'crash' program often ends in not much more than just that —a crash."

The Pilot, in its commendable tradition of freedom of the press, printed just about everything the opposition wanted printed, including a stinging, perhaps justifiably bitter note from Father Twomey; statements about the legal aspects of "truancy" in the area of human rights, by Father Drinan, and various communications from Negroes and whites, pro and con the boycott.

Oddly enough, the Cardinal has a paragraph in his Inter-Racial Justice pamphlet which seems at variance with the general gradualistic view and with his rigid stand against the boycott: "True Christians must support all efforts at legislation which writes into law the claims of justice for our citizens; *they must not even shrink from the difficult course of demonstration, denunciation, witness and testi-*

262

mony, when these are required of them . . . Those who give lip service and no more are the hypocrites condemned by the Lord, and their actions expose them before angels and men."

"Does he read his own writing?" Negroes friendly to, or members of the Catholic Interracial Council were saying bitterly and privately, about the Cardinal.

"Talk, talk, talk, all we get is talk!" one active and articulate Negro Catholic lady said, in connection with the boycott and its aftermath.

"Does he read his own writing?" one priest formerly associated with Council leadership is reported to have echoed quite devastatingly.

This is, of course, an unfair exaggeration, but it reflects the tragic flaw in the established and accepted use of ghostwriters on the part of prominent people in our society. There is no question but that the Cardinal critically reads his own writing and that of any ghost he may have had or has. His ideas and guiding hand are invariably in on any ghost-writing assistance he receives, like any other responsible principal who receives "editorial" help.

As far back as Leo XIII, we had Cardinal Manning who, by all historical admissions, did a major job of indirect ghost-writing on one of the most famous social documents of all time, *Rerum Novarum,* for which Leo gets all the credit, prestige and glory. Henry Edward Cardinal Manning originally published his observations on a Christian doctrine for labor in the form of a pastoral letter to the Catholic faithful of London. Pope Leo XIII, his friend, was literally influenced by Manning's thoughts and words; the similarities of phrasing and ideas in both the pastoral letter and the encyclical are obvious.

Cushing is no Manning intellectually; Cushing is not a scholar, an intellectual, a writer of natural talent. But he has great perceptions. He is, in our judgment, the inspired recipient of what Jacques Maritain, in speaking of Leon Bloy, called "flashes from the depths."

263

As earlier indicated, who will ever forget the great, gaunt Cardinal eulogizing, off the cuff, our slain, beloved young President; what television viewer will ever experience again the heart-breaking beauty of the old Cardinal, his eyes brimming with tears, his throat swallowing a lump, looking up at the sky above his Residence garden, finding the words there, which so eloquently memorialized the American Galahad so wantonly slain. What ghost-writer was around Cushing then? Only the ghost of J. F. K. wreaking out of the Cardinal's sundered heart the love and the poetry of *memento mori!*

In cold objectivity one can assert that it is completely justifiable, in the furtherance of the work of the Universal Church, for a Bishop or any other religious leader to accept "editorial assistance," particularly in an era of mass communications.

Say it over and over again in a thousand different eloquences: Christ is God; the Church is One, Holy, Apostolic; Seek Ye First the Kingdom of Heaven and all things shall be added unto you; say it with or without ghost-writers, on radio, on TV, in the newspapers, but say it in answer to the flood of ghost-writing from the forces of materialism, and anti-Christ and anti-Man. This Cushing has done and will continue to do, with or without editorial help.

The tragic flaw of ghost-writing may well be that it does not impel the signatory to "actions which speak louder than words"; it is perhaps obvious that the words growing out of the deepest self would be more integral to the osmosis of words and action. With the possible exception of the gap between his words and actions in the area of interracial justice—a fast-narrowing gap one must admit—the Cardinal does not seem to have suffered from the "occlusions" of ghost-writing.

Here's how he handled the temporary disillusionment of agitator-nightclub entertainer Dick Gregory, for example.

Gregory had come up to Boston in February of 1964 to

participate in the school boycott. He had expressed his keen disappointment with Cardinal Cushing's opposition to the school-emptying demonstration. He implied that Cushing was the ultimate person in the whole world whom the Negroes could trust completely and to whom they could unfailingly go for help.

We were sitting with the Cardinal when he was deliberating an answer to Dick Gregory. He was primarily interested in reassuring Gregory and the Negro community that he was still, and always would be, their friend. He said he was more concerned about neighborhood and home conditions of the Negro children, by comparison with existing educational inadequacies. Home study, under decent, dignified conditions, was at least 50% of the problem, Cushing believed. He agreed with a statement of James Baldwin that the finest educational facilities in the nation wouldn't help Negro children sufficiently if they continued to be ill-fed, ill-housed, and retarded by unsavory, congested neighborhoods. Within his press statement, inculcating the foregoing ideas, the Cardinal addressed a little love-letter to Gregory and the Negroes offering to open up Catholic schools for afternoon and evening study, with the additional proffering of hot evening meals where needed.

Boston Negroes say he has been slow to act on these matters. Yet he recently gave some indication of coming to terms with the Catholic Interracial Council with whom he has been somewhat at odds. It was reported that he had agreed to help finance a Montessori method school program for Negro children of working mothers to be taught by a skilled Negro lay teacher, in coordination with the Council. The program is to be centered at a Catholic mission in the South End, a facility of Blessed Sacrament Parish. New reports indicate the money is in their hands.

A pilot program, involving twenty to thirty youngsters is, in fact, already under way. It is a day-care center for Negro children whose parents are working. It is partially supported by Federal grants of foodstuffs. Volunteer white

Catholic ladies cook hot meals for the children and the whole atmosphere of the place is filled with the warmth and friendliness of Christian brotherhood.

It appeared to this writer that the Interracial Council suffered from the backlash of the Cardinal's displeasure, if not anger, toward the priests who differed with him so strongly and so publicly on the school boycot issue. His Eminence expressed particular bitterness to us concerning some Jesuits from Boston College who were arrayed against him in the controversy. He has been an enormous benefactor of his Alma Mater and he was raw-sensitive about the open opposition coming from a current and former Dean of the Law School, and a theology professor, all Jesuit priests. Be it remembered that he has helped Boston College grow with the help of about four million dollars in direct and indirect fund-raising.

The Cardinal told us that Boston College President and fellow South-Bostonite, Father Michael Walsh, had called on him and personally apologized for the aggressive and outspoken activities of at least three of his Jesuit faculty members.

When we mentioned that one of the Jesuits was a classmate of ours at B. C. and a very sincere and dedicated person—as we also assume the other Jesuits to be—the Cardinal dismissed the observation gruffly with: "You can have him!" He then expressed the droll possibility that he might buy a couple of houses across the street from the B. C. Law School and put two Negro families in them.

"Let's see how they'd like that!" he snorted.

The Boston College Chestnut Hill neighborhood is not only hoity-toity but is almost completely lily-white.

The Interracial Council's chief problem seems to have been to get a qualified, dedicated, permanent priest-chaplain who is acceptable to both the Cardinal and the membership. This problem has apparently been solved.

The Cardinal was also miffed by what he believed to be

266

certain "insulting" letters received from Council members impatient with his gradualistic position. Yet under the responsible leadership of Boston Negro attorney, David Nelson, President of the Catholic Interracial Council; and people like Mary Hogan, Vice-President and also Registrar of the Boston College School of Social Work; Mary Geaney, sister of a Catholic priest and herself, a City of Boston social worker; under such leadership, typical of the quality and dedication of the membership, there is bound to be a warm rapprochement. Predictably, the Cardinal will resolve residual tensions and misunderstandings with one great, loving burst of generosity which will send the Council board members out of the Residence talking to themselves.

As for the Boston school boycott, it seems to have been a huge success. A blue ribbon panel, headed up by the Massachusetts State Commissioner of Education, and including the President of Boston College, Father Walsh, has generally agreed with the Negro community's indictment of de facto segregation in the schools and has made constructive recommendations to the reactionary unsympathetic Boston School Committee.

The Cardinal himself is reported to be regretful of his stand on the boycott and since has issued strong public statements on interracial problems. The first is a Pentecostal Letter, May 17, 1964, in which he talks "cold turkey" to employers, landlords, educators, and pastors about the need for action as well as charity and understanding: "To every believer I say, love all men and especially love Negroes because they have suffered so much from lack of love. Make yourself truly color blind and, if you think of color at all, let it be to love the more."

The outbreak of major big-city race riots in the long, hot summer of 1964 prompted a benevolent broadside from the Cardinal just before he departed on his Latin American voyage. Fathers Drinan, Kenneally, Twomey, Casey, et al., seem not to have toiled in vain if we read aright the warming trend of the Cardinal's more flexible Negro position:

"As one in spiritual authority, I summon before all others those who share with me the care of souls. *I commend and encourage the clergy who have involved themselves in the toils of the Negro and have made witness of their Christian faith.* To those who have held back, I issue again a call to action. Let no pulpit be silent, no wrong left uncondemned; let every altar be a place before which we dedicate ourselves anew to that brotherhood of redemption in which we were all born in the blood of Christ. In this hour, if the men of God are silent, the very stones will cry out."

The Cardinal was bound to heal any rift between him and the Catholic interracial actionists. Fundamentally he always believed as they did, but they perhaps moved a little too fast for him. They were perilously close to telling him off and telling him where to head in. But you don't do that to a Cardinal. After all, if you're a Roman Catholic in Boston, he's the boss and that's that!

Many would be happy if he would move more and more into concrete action on the Negro question. He could, for example, as has been suggested to him by this writer, strike a real blow for Negro faith and security in his sincerity by coming out for an Archdiocesan policy like "Selective Purchasing." He could simply announce that from such and such a date the Archdiocese, which purchases millions of dollars in goods, services and supplies from various vendors would no longer buy from any vendor who discriminates against Negroes, employment-wise or in any manner.

This, or a similar concrete move, would overcome any lingering fears amid the Negro community that he is more a man of words than action when it comes to the interracial question. Will he? Won't he? The chances are he will!

The man whom one journalist called "the all-time freestyle champion of Catholic liberalism" positively cannot miss on the interracial issue. He has his quirks, his prudent hesitancy, his South-Boston-Irish residuals of stubbornness, but you can fit this paraphrase to the familiar spiritual chant of Negro hope and consolation:

"HE SHALL OVERCOME . . ."

Even as he went from mild to strong in his posture on the race question, so did he go from a certain detachment and bewilderment to a stance of outright statesmanship regarding his participation in the Vatican Councils.

As a participant in two successive sessions of the Vatican Council, the Boston Strongboy of the American Hierarchy was thrown off his usual Seven-League-Boots stride by a lack of language communication and the starchy rigors of cardinalitial protocol.

Extended commentary about Cushing and the Vatican Council are not needed here. It certainly appears that he helped line up the American bishops for Pope John. Angelo Roncalli had said: "I'm in a box." and his devoted protege from a bizarre land called South Boston had proceeded to help him out of that box. We know that Cushing didn't fully understand the Latin speeches; he was restless and he didn't stay around too long at either session. His beloved Pope John died in June of 1963 and the once rustic and rough-hewn Cushing, now a famed, sophisticated figure in Rome, was back again in the Eternal City for his first Papal Election.

In the electrifying third session of the Vatican Council, in the fall of 1964, Cushing was to emerge as the towering figure of the conclave. In lusty Latin phrases, which *The Pilot* kindly described as "clear and somewhat oratorical in style," Cardinal Cushing, as predicted, made two liberal exhortations at two separate meetings of the world-wide bishops, priests and laymen who awesomely represent a stunning synthesis of the brains and power of the Holy Roman Church.

In his first ringing statement Cushing called on the Council to take a stand on religious liberty, using the classic phrase from the Declaration of Independence in advocating: "a decent respect for the opinions of mankind." He swung his eloquence through the aula of St. Peter's Basilica like an old Boston Elevated Railway sledge hammer, demolishing the conservative opposition and invoking astutely the memory of Pope John who had originally demanded a declaration on religious liberty. Protocol was further shattered, all the press reports tell us, in the mighty explosion of applause that saluted the great, gaunt Cardinal when he finished his clarion call for a society which "seeks to guarantee its members a life according to truth, justice, love, and freedom."

We learned, too, that Lord Acton said something else besides "Power corrupts, absolute power corrupts absolutely." For Cardinal Cushing cited Acton's magnificent phrase, "freedom is the highest political end" in his religious liberty exhortation on Sept. 23.

Six days later, on Sept. 29, he took up the Latin cudgels again, this time in behalf of the exoneration of the Jews. Out the window went the classic crutch of anti-Semites concerning the culpability of the Jews for the death of Christ. The following excerpt sums up Cushing's position succinctly:

"We cannot judge the leaders of Ancient Israel. God alone is their judge and most certainly we cannot dare to attribute to later generations of Jews the guilt of the Crucifixion of the Lord Jesus or the death of the Savior of the World, except in the sense of the universal guilt in which all of us men share."

How binding and how formal the ultimate decrees of the Council will be on both of Cushing's exhortations, in companionate support with Cardinals Bea, Suenens and all the other liberal cardinals and bishops, remains to be seen.

This writer is still haunted by a remark of Cushing's which he made to us privately, after he had returned home from the second session of the Council and there were encouraging pyrotechnical displays being projected in the Vatican chamber by the irrepressible liberals.

270

The Cardinal calmed my burst of ebullience with the slowly drawled phrase: "Nothing's gonna happen!"

He was right. Nothing very much happened, with the liberal bishops maneuvering for position and the conservatives led by the wily and redoubtable Cardinal Ottaviani, holding the line. But that was the second session. Cardinal Cushing and the liberals have made major moves of liberality in the third session, as we have seen. The Church still makes haste slowly, regardless of the revolutionary speeches and proposals. Maybe, just maybe: "Something's gonna happen!"

Our especial interest in this book, however, must be concerned with the Cardinal Cushing whom we may call "The One-Man Ecumenical Council." He is again phenomenal in that he has been pretty much of a one-man ecumenical movement throughout his entire priestly and episcopal career.

Concerning mixed marriages, for example, he has long been a progressive. He told us: "I remember when I was ordained a priest, mixed marriages were so frowned upon that the 'erring' couples could only be wed in a five-minute ceremony in the rectory. As soon as I became Archbishop I said to myself, 'I won't stand for that kind of thing; in the future, they will be married in church.'

"My own sister married a Jew and I never knew a finer lad nor a happier couple. When a group of Jewish leaders called upon me to ask my advice on what was to be Brandeis University, I answered: 'This university is tremendously needed, and you should not hesitate about starting the project.' Later, I lent my strength and services to Brandeis when the Jesuit president of St. Louis got permission for Brandeis to be the only institution in the United States to reproduce the micro-films of Judaic manuscripts now in the Pope Pius Library in St. Louis.

"I went right out and raised the $20,000 needed to pay for the job." Then Cushing, typically, gives a nod to the source of those funds. "I got it from the people like the people I come from—working people, who'd give me five dollars, ten dollars, fifteen dollars, the grass-roots people who prayed me into office."

In his Lenten notes, published in the spring of 1964, in the *Boston Traveler*, Cushing said some very conclusive words about brotherhood with the Jews—a position which is a definite harbinger of his strong posture against Catholic anti-Semitism at the third session of the Vatican Council. Wrote Cushing, then: "The spiritual ancestry of Christians is Jewish. We are the sons of Abraham, Isaac and Jacob, even as they. The Cross is a point of separation in our spiritual traditions, but we must all be keenly aware of the essential Christian doctrine: Christ died for the sins of all men, those prior to His time, His contemporaries, those who came after Him. Anti-Semitism is a profoundly unchristian attitude."

Father Joseph McInnis, a former Jesuit, now a member of the diocesan clergy and occasionally on special assignment as a feature writer for the *Boston Traveler*, handles items like the Lenten Notes for the Cardinal. Writing as "Joe Mack," Father McInnis brings a lively insight into Catholic news of the Archdiocese to the *Traveler's* P.M. pages. With his unbounded energy, wry wit, and shrewd Irish ways of getting news beats—sometimes ahead of the official coverage of *The Pilot*—he was occasionally referred to as "The Grey Eminence" of the *Boston Traveler*.

The printing and press specialists from sunny Italy, a religious community known as The Daughters of St. Paul —whom the Cardinal brought into the Archdiocese and who also seem to function as his private printers—have collected the Lenten Notes and sold them quite successfully as a spiritual trade book. Father Mack, who did the editing on the volume in the Cardinal's interest, said that one of the nuns made a "slip" and exulted about how well the book was selling. This she did in the presence of Father McInnis and her Mother Superior.

"Don't tell him that," Mother Superior said. "He'll expect something."

The Daughters of St. Paul who run a modern, non-union printing plant in Jamaica Plain, Mass., recently brought off a self-proclaimed "scoop" of the publishing world with a vanity-type, luxuriously-made biography of the Cardinal which was allegedly written "in secret" over a seven-year period. With the Cardinal's approval, the Daughters hustle this and other volumes much as the Father Feeney cult used to sell its books, pressing them on the predominantly Catholic office help of Greater Boston.

The Cardinal says they print up just about everything he releases to *The Pilot* in the form of sermons and letters. They do most of this in quite attractive pamphlet and book formats and get good prices for most items. They travel about the city briskly in a station wagon, somewhat in gypsy fashion, constantly invoking the name of the Cardinal in their aggressive selling technique.

"They never give me a dime," Cushing said to us once, concerning them.

Yet they are extremely useful to him as a kind of unofficial press; witness, for example, Cushing's handsome biographies of St. Martin de Porres, Pius XII, and Pope John. The "Daughters" also publish many things of his which both he and his well-wishers would rather consign to Limbo.

The year 1964, then, showed Cushing at the height of his liberal and articulate powers on the floor of the Vatican Council itself and more typically as "The One-Man Ecumenical Council" in the Archdiocese of Boston itself.

Let us relish the more folksy and informal Boston preludes to his Vatican statements as they emerged spontaneously from earlier appearances before various Boston religious groups.

To several hundred Congregationalists in Wellesley,

Mass., on March 3, 1964, Cushing said: "Organic unity of the faiths is not possible in the foreseeable future but the ecumenical movement can achieve the unity of love. In the past we have been living in our ghettoes. We have hardly talked with one another, and sometimes we were fighting."

At Christ Church Episcopal, Harvard Square, Cambridge, on March 19, 1964—a session attended by President Pusey of Harvard—Cushing again called for "the Unity of Love." He got in a few manifestations of his patented lusty humor also when he dwelt on his lifelong lack of fluency in Latin:

"Even the Russian observers at the Council were better off than I was. At least they had interpreters. When the bishops addressed the Council in Latin, for once in my life, I kept my mouth shut."

He predicted accurately his high hopes for the fall, 1964, session of the Council:

"The biggest contribution that the United States bishops can make to the Council is their strong emphasis on a demand for freedom of conscience for all faiths and a call for firmer belief in the separation of church and state."

Cushing expressed the hope that the Council would clarify Catholic doctrine in simple, understandable language. He described still another goal of the modern Church fathers in the upcoming Council as the updating of the pastoral life "to keep up with the times." That part of the Mass which can now be celebrated in English is an example of this updating as is the current hearing of Confessions with the language of the priests' sacramental prayers and pronouncements now in English.

"The Church always needs reform." Cushing told the Christ Church assemblage. He went on to talk about biblical scholars and theologians of various faiths who have long been establishing valid dialogue with each other. We are told he gave out with one of his wide, impish grins. "The ecumenical spirit will fall flat on its face if we're going to leave it to the scholars. It must be one of grass roots fervor," said the traditional lover and mocker of intellectuals.

Cushing talked then of the rise of the layman in American Catholicism: "For many years the Catholic layman was all right to take up a collection and run beano games when they were legal and sell chances on the pastor's hat, but they had no part in the structure of the Church."

Speaking at a Baptist Church in Framingham, Mass., on April 7, 1964, Cushing gave out with some personal reminiscence whose echoes will seem familiar to readers of this book:

"My only claim to glory is that when I became a priest 43 years ago in May, I didn't have a nickel and I don't have any money today. I have made millions for causes throughout the world, I know how to make money with money and I hate money. I give it away as I get it.

"When I became a priest, I made a promise never to take any money for myself and that is one promise I have kept.

"I don't know a fourth of the Cardinals even though I sat with them at the Council, but I know all the poor missionaries with long beards and many poor people."

He then made some fresher observations on the threat of Communism than have been usually forthcoming from American Catholic prelates of his high rank:

"Communists don't care for old people. They know they are going to die. They have outsmarted us. They take children at the age of three and four and control their absolute knowledge of education and formulate their own ideas within them that they may become the Communists of the future."

The audience was made up of more than Baptists, including guests from all the local churches as well as 20 Grey Nuns.

In the spring and early summer of 1964, Cardinal Cushing entertained three great European Cardinals: Koenig, Suenens and Bea. The former two were presented at public lectures sponsored by the Paulist Fathers in downtown hotels. The latter, the outstanding Jesuit liberal, Cardinal Bea, came to Boston on a quick visit to receive an honorary Harvard degree.

There were two distinct meetings with Koenig and Suenens for Archdiocesan priests at which, it is reported, Cushing talked quite as extensively, if not more so, than his Cardinalitial guests.

At the Suenens public lecture, Cushing chimed in on the Belgian Cardinal's exhortations to nuns, regarding the desirability of their more aggressive participation in secular affairs, making this observation: "The constitutions of many of our congregations were drawn 100, 200 or 300 years ago, and have been in the deep freeze ever since."

Around this time, the Cardinal announced that he would deliver one of the principal addresses at the fall session of the Vatican Council. He was not referring to his eventual addresses on Religious Liberty or the Exoneration of the Jews. Although the event never took place during his September sojourn at the Council, he revealed his interest in the advocacy of the Canonization of his beloved patron, Pope John XXIII. It is inevitable that he will do so. One cannot help but recall that Cushing, as a young Archbishop, was an advocate of the Canonization of Pius X, on his very first visit to Rome. Interestingly enough, Pius X was one of Angelo Roncalli's patrons, much as John was to Richard of South Boston.

It is not far-fetched to predict that in our lifetime, some prelate like Bishop Wright, or perhaps fittingly a prominent Catholic layman, may stand before some future Consistory or Council and propose that the name of a Boston boy, Richard James Cushing, be enshrined on the altars and in the calendars of Holy Mother Church.

Who Will Succeed Him?

Now some final observations and reflections amid the inevitable nostalgia one knows as a book like this draws to a close. How marvelous is life, how very good to be alive, that one may observe in Cardinal Cushing such a towering thrust of traditional virtue emerging from a deep rocket silo of such infinite complexity.

So well did Pope John say, in his very first words to Cardinal-Designate Cushing, as if slaking a long, dry thirst of the modern, Universal Church for such a priest, such a prelate, such an omnibus man:

"AH! CUSHING OF BOSTON!"

Out of all that simple, immigrant lowliness of life in the South Boston tenements, out of the vulgarity, the stridence and chicanery of Boston pols, out of the rustic, rote, strait-laced Jesuit and St. John's Seminary education; out of the deadly, daily dunning for money, money, money; out of the uneasy, yet implicitly admiring mucker poses amid scholars, intellectuals and those with riches or to the manor born; out of this dross, this swamping mediocrity, such human quality, compassion, cardinalitial grace!

Over all this, we know, in the noble words of Dylan Thomas: "Death shall have no dominion."

Gratefully, it has no dominion now. And we recall, as a guest at a private Sunday Mass in his residence chapel, how richly the cardinalite has bestowed grace upon him.

Kneeling there, close to his altar, with his household nuns gathered humbly in the pews behind us, we felt this deeply. How devout a priest up there saying Mass, with burning fervor and yet with a certain majesty, as on the throne at Holy Cross Cathedral, or on an improvised altar before 60,000 people in Fenway Park.

When he swung his great cardinalitial yardarm across us in the final blessing of the Mass, it seemed that seven times seven howling devils leaped out of our flesh and went swirling in smoke up the Residence chimney.

We watched him, later, leaning over his files in his office, and saw the princely grace so much a part of this former Boston-Irish bumpkin, the ease, urbanity, the aplomb of presidents and kings, now so deservedly his.

Still later, he took us in the ominous-sounding, slow-climbing elevator, up to his room to loan us a manuscript which was in his desk. It was the same commodious bedroom where Cardinal O'Connell had rested his princely bulk and awaited the Particular Judgment which would weigh his scholarly and apostolic achievements against his agility and astuteness in the world of stocks and bonds.

Here, now, was a successor preoccupied with the world of finance more intensely and more successfully, but only in terms of manipulating and yielding it for the sick, the poor and the social religious and educational uses of the Universal Church.

"What do yuh think of a room like this?" demanded the Prince, shifting, as he invariably can, into the lower gears of the earthy Boston Irishman. "I got no closets. I got no place to put my pants on!"

He opened the drawer of an unpretentious, old mahogany desk and took out the late President's dogtags which Jacqueline had given him. After offering us a look at them, he dug out some notes about his life and views which he said we could use.

Jacqueline. He strives to pronounce her name with the French touch, to please her, and comes out with a rather droll: *"Jock-ell-lane!"*

We had been thinking of Princess Radziwill, sister of

Jacqueline, and her successful annulment which had been recently in the news. We wondered if he had helped in the process, because of his high regard for the President's widow, but did not ask. He told us he had received a phone call—he did not say from whom—regarding a possible annulment for former J. F. K. alter ego, Theodore Sorenson, who was eventually to be in process of divorce. The Cardinal seemed highly irritated about that phone call and wanted nothing to do with any such proceeding.

The two oxygen tanks were standing upright there: one by his bed, the other beside his stuffed leather chair. In the interminable nights of asthma, migraine headaches, and who knows what other forms of physical distress, he sits in that chair, or paces the floor.

It is in the "morning after" such a night that one would be lucky not to have a personal appointment with him at the Residence. In such a situation one might encounter what may be called "the cardinalitial buzz-saw" that would seem to cut right through a California redwood tree with swift dispatch, and which is so markedly at contrast with the more familiar embodiment of what we call "the benevolent Irish uncle."

It was an outstanding lay friend and benefactor of the Cardinal who told us to be wary of calling upon him in his "buzz-saw" mood:

"I learned this the hard way," this gentleman told us. "He must have been sitting up in his chair the night before —with about two hours, sleep—when he gave me the 'business' one morning.

"After that I arranged to wait for a phone call from one of his secretaries when I wanted to see him about some important matter.

"She'd call me and say: 'You'd better not come today.'

"Or again: 'It would be a lovely day to see the Cardinal.' "

It would have been valuable to have had this forewarning one Saturday morning when we dropped by to deliver

279

some editorial work. He dished it out pretty good that morning to two little nuns who had tiptoed meekly in without an appointment. He obviously had had a miserable night when he raked the little nuns over the coals.

Luckily, we were standing in an anteroom near the doorway listening, and well out of the line of fire. His angry yet dignified formality with the nuns seemed a little hilarious from the anteroom distance.

Obviously, they had been reading several of his habitual public litanies about the religious buildings he builds and the fabulous sums of money he bestows on nuns, priests, brothers. These members of religious orders who constantly need construction funds periodically hear him, or see him quoted as saying, characteristically:

"I gave a million for a university on Formosa, a million to the Medical Missionaries of Mary in Ireland, etcetera . . ."

The order which these two nuns represented perhaps needed a new dormitory, chapel, school, or refectory. Up in Boston was a munificent holy man of God, who by his own admission was handing out buildings worth a quarter of a million dollars and more like a fairy godmother.

One can well imagine a meek, little German nun saying to meek little Mother Superior: "If Catherine of Siena could go to the Pope, you can go to Cardinal Cushing! He will help us with our new building."

So off they went, on holy pilgrimage, and there they were, confronting, without an appointment, the man who conceivably had walked the floor for half the night, racked with migraine, or asthma, or both.

"You have to have an appointment!" I could hear him saying.

"Forgive us, Your Eminence," meek little Mother Superior said. "How do we get an appointment?"

"Write to my secretary!" he said.

"How long will it take?" persistent Mother Superior asked.

"Two or three weeks!" the Cardinal thundered, inserting one of his fetching and unpredictable non sequiturs. "And even then I may not be able to see you. I'm going to South America!"

Mostly gentle, though, is he with nuns, as we observed one quiet evening when he and Monsignor Joe Maguire were chatting with the household sisters about the routine of the Residence. An important household rearrangement had been discussed, as he later told us, and now there was the bantering and gaiety between the Cardinal, the Monsignor and the nuns which spoke volumes for a very happy Residence.

One of the nuns was urging him to buy some clothes, protesting that only so much sewing and patching could be done on his clothing.

"For God's sake buy some clothes!" she said.

The Cardinal later told us that he was going to move his business and financial offices from the spacious first floor to the more sequestered second floor, for security reasons, on the strong recommendations of the F. B. I. and the Boston Police Department.

The belief was that the counting of money on the first floor, and the easily available person of the Cardinal himself were too accessible to sheer nuts and possible bandits.

He seemed reluctant to move things upstairs. As we have shown, he likes to answer the door himself and be around where people can see him.

Ruminating upon him, in this afterword, we continually see him as a "sign of contradiction" which, indeed, the Galilean Himself was called. If Cushing, in the Boston *Record-American*, could denounce the American Civil Liberties Union as Communist-dominated, and then perhaps modify that position, he could also at the epistolary request of Dorothy Day, the so-called "Catholic Communist" of *The Catholic Worker Movement*, seek out the dying playwright, Eugene O'Neill, in the hope of offering him some spiritual consolation at the end.

281

It is fairly well-known that, as a budding young drama-
tist, Gene O'Neill was the lover of the then Bohemian, but
now austere and saintly Dorothy Day.

In a moving act of purest love, near the end of O'Neill's
life, she had written to the Cardinal, asking him to call on
America's greatest playwright. He sought O'Neill out at the
Ritz in Boston where he had been staying. It was too late.
O'Neill's wife had transferred him elsewhere. He was to die
beyond the ritualistic reach of his childhood religion.

How vividly many hundreds remember Cardinal Cushing in June of 1964 as guest speaker at the Centennial ob-
servance and graduation of Boston College High School.
Our own son, Gregory, was a member of that Centennial
Class, and along with his classmates, received his diploma
from the most distinguished graduate of that venerable old
Jesuit school.

It will be recalled that the Cardinal's motto *Ut Cog-
noscent Te,* "That They May Know Thee," is identical with
that of Boston College High.

Certainly, at that ceremony, on that sea-breezy open
campus, bordering South Boston Harbor, the Cardinal
talked too long. But there was a zest, a fascination about
his checkered, droll, at times profound and eloquent remarks, which was endearing of him and which held most of
his audience in awe and interest.

He did the autobiographical bit for his tender fellow
alumni, striking well that familiar mucker pose, telling
them he had never *earned* a college degree in his life, but
had enough honorary degrees to "paper the walls of this
institution."

For those, apparently, who would not go on to college,
he continued the debunking line, saying that he personally thought college board exams were a lot of nonsense.
He also said: "Geniuses are a nuisance!"

His remarks were constantly and raucously interrupted
by thunderous jet planes taking off from Logan Airport,

across the harbor, and up-angling directly over the Commencement area.

During several interruptions he paused, resuming his address when the plane was gone. Finally, in sheer exasperation, he crossed himself impishly, turned to old and venerable Father Hewitt, a former Jesuit provincial, who shared the platform with him and brayed out: "Father Hewitt, I told you years ago, *not* to buy this land!"

For those who intended to go on to college he blueprinted the space and financial difficulties of higher education, particularly in Massachusetts. Only 22% of higher education, he pointed out, is financed by the state, with 78% being underwritten by private institutions. He called eloquently for increased state aid and announced his public backing of a bill which would carry the burden private institutions can no longer bear.

He said Cardinal Bea was in Boston and the press was anxious to know the purpose of his visit. The Jesuit Cardinal was in the Hub to receive a Harvard University degree, news of which is customarily kept secret until Commencement Day. Indicating his mastery over himself in this instance, Cushing announced: "If I could keep my mouth shut, I wouldn't be getting in trouble."

To the contrary, how fortunate it has been for many of us, and indeed for a goodly cross-section of the poor, the sick, the needy among all mankind that he has exercised his goodly vocal chords over the years. His eloquent pleas for money, his tirades against social, political and economic injustice, his deeply spiritual sermons, meditations, letters, all have been the product of an open mouth and an open heart, without which mankind would be the poorer.

And when we think, in these last reflections, about his possible successor, there is both the sense of rich inheritance and the fear of inadequacy.

Who will succeed him? We can speculate journalistically on this matter, but with the hope that Cardinal Cushing will reign in honor and well-being for many years to come.

As earlier mentioned, the popular choice and heir-apparent may well be Boston-born, Pittsburgh-reigning, Bishop John Wright. Surprisingly enough, to this writer at least, it has been reported that Cushing himself said that he hoped Wright would succeed him. This happened in a deleted portion of a WBZ-TV interview given to Arch McDonald of that station on the occasion of Cushing's 25th Episcopal Anniversary in June, 1964.

We have earlier reported the Cardinal's somewhat jaundiced remarks about Wright, even while trying to keep that most capable prelate in his proper high perspective. But, in the final analysis, as in his racial views, in the liturgy, in political involvements, and vis-a-vis the John Birch Society, Cardinal Cushing always seems to arrive at the statesmanlike standpoint. Thus does the compelling grandeur of his life invariably rise above all his quirks, inconsistencies and residual prejudices.

Thus has "Cushing of Boston" become "Cushing of the World."

Our candidate as his successor, if we must have one, would sentimentally be Bishop Wright whom we have known and admired since boyhood. But we have had enough experience as an observer of the American hierarchy to know that things don't always work out as predicted.

Boston, after Cushing, may be both a major attraction and repellent to the eligible American bishops and archbishops. Cushing has certainly made his Archdiocese "the Rome of America," perhaps outdistancing formidable Chicago and New York as a center of world-focus and in the very dynamics of the Universal Church.

For Cushing, the financial conduct and manipulation of the Archdiocesan debits and credits is a grand organ console of which he is master virtuoso. This could not be said for a newcomer, nor would a successor approach this complex instrument without fear or trembling.

Cardinals Francis Spellman, Joseph E. Ritter of St. Louis, James F. McIntyre of Los Angeles, Lawrence J. Shehan of Baltimore and some other older Archbishops are permanently settled. They will not look longingly toward Lake Street at Commonwealth Avenue.

Closer to Wright in Vatican prestige, perhaps greater, and thus a strong possibility for Boston, would be Bishop Ernest John Primeau, of Manchester, New Hampshire, now more than fifty years old. Bishop Primeau, a Chicago-born, Chicago-educated, Chicago-ordained priest, was reported to have been sent to New Hampshire in 1959 at the wish of Pope John himself, who looked with favor upon him as a possible Coadjutor or successor to his ailing friend Cushing. Primeau has superb educational and administrative background as former Rector of St. Mary of the Lake Seminary in Chicago, and as a Vatican official and member of the Sacred Congregation of the Holy Office.

He is, according to Barret McGurn, "the man who organized a program of updating lectures for the American Catholic bishops at the second sessions of the Ecumenical Councils. A long-time resident of Rome, he organized in effect a school in which to educate the American churchmen in modern discoveries of biblical science and in the new theology which is more open to an understanding with Protestantism."

We are further informed by McGurn, whom this writer knew as a former fellow contributor to *Yank* magazine in World War II, that it was Bishop Primeau who was called upon to answer charges of disloyalty made by the Italian bishops against American churchmen who were said to have bolted to the position of internationalist liberals. Chicago, Bishop Primeau's original area, will have a new Archbishop, now that Cardinal Meyer has passed away.

It is entirely possible, however, that Bishop Primeau may return to his well-known archdiocesan area of Chicago, now that Cardinal Meyer has so tragically passed away.

Other able administrators, also ecumenically active and

285

aware who could well home in on a hierarchical beam to a possible vacant Boston, would have to include: Archbishops John F. Dearden, age 57, of Detroit, Paul J. Hallinan, 54, of Atlanta, and Bishop John King Mussio, 62, of Steubenville, Ohio.

All of the above are scholarly and statesmanlike stalwarts in the ecumenical movement, and any one of them would bring prestige, integrity and ability to any eventual vacancy in the Boston Archdiocese. They are worthy peers of Bishop Wright and would lend both honor and grace, as Wright would, to the Archdiocese, if and when Cushing should go along.

Any of the local Auxiliaries, Bishops Minihan, McKenzie, Riley, would bring vision and experience to the Boston Ordinary's post. Among the younger Monsignori, it would appear that Monsignori Lally and Kerr stand out as potential episcopal timber.

Following another phenomenal recovery from a serious intestinal operation in the spring of 1965, Cushing again showed his cautionary approach to street demonstrations, this time applying a bit of a damper to Archdiocesan nuns who may have caught the "Selma fever" and wanted to get right out there to whoop it up with the placards and the folksy chants.

On Sunday, May 2, 1965, he dedicated a giant bronze statue of Mother Julie Billiart, founder of the Sisters of Notre Dame de Namur, at the latter order's new Novitiate in Ipswich, Massachusetts.

Hundreds of cheering and applauding nuns lined the convent road to meet their renowned spiritual leader who, seemingly against all signs and predictions, had once more shown evidence of his inexhaustible "psychic force" or "determined will" which could propel him away from death's door.

He reminded these long-established nuns of the Archdiocese—and thus, all his nuns—that they were teachers, "not marchers." He told them bluntly that the nuns belong in the classrom and that they wouldn't have found Mother Julie Billiart out on the highways and by-ways.

All hail, then, to the Stentor, Apostle of the Poor, New Testament Saint! He who has given so many rich and vigorous Apostolic years to Boston Catholics and to the peoples of all the world! He, of whom the ultra-liberal columnist, Murray Kempton could write in *The New Republic*, at the funeral mass of John Fitzgerald Kennedy, as the Cardinal descended the staircase of St. Matthew's Cathedral:

"Cardinal Cushing came down the steps, under his mitre, looking, to his credit, a trifle irritated with God; we could be grateful for the Catholics and grateful to them for providing one Cardinal who looked like a Prince of the Church."

287

CARMELITE MONAS
Beckle
B
DATE BORROW